The Springfield Reformation

THE SPRINGFIELD REFORMATION

The Simpsons™, Christianity, and American Culture

Jamey Heit

continuum

NEW YORK • LONDON

2008

The Continuum International Publishing Group Inc
80 Maiden Lane, New York, NY 10038

The Continuum International Publishing Group Ltd
The Tower Building, 11 York Road, London SE1 7NX

www.continuumbooks.com

Printed in the United States of America

9780826428967

Library of Congress Cataloging-in-Publication Data

Heit, Jamey.
The Springfield reformation : the Simpsons, Christianity, and
American culture / Jamey Heit.
       p. cm.
   Includes bibliographical references.
   ISBN-13: 978-0-8264-2895-0 (hardcover : alk. paper)
   ISBN-10: 0-8264-2895-9 (hardcover : alk. paper)
   ISBN-13: 978-0-8264-2896-7 (pbk. : alk. paper)
   ISBN-10: 0-8264-2896-7 (pbk. : alk. paper) 1. Simpsons (Television
program) 2. Television broadcasting--Religious aspects--Christianity.
I. Title.

PN1992.77.S58H45 2008
791.45'72--dc22
                              2007043014

For my beautiful wife, Amy

Contents

ACKNOWLEDGMENTS

This project has been developing for about eighteen years. I can still remember watching my first episode of *The Simpsons* when I was ten years old, getting my first Bart Simpson T-shirt soon thereafter, and spending a lot of Sunday evenings with my siblings in front of the television. I owe a debt of gratitude to my parents for allowing my siblings and me to watch *The Simpsons* from the outset. Their permission to do so ran against the grain of a lot of prevailing cultural common sense, a decision that reveals but a skin-deep layer of the intellectual encouragement and freedom they instilled in me from a young age. Likewise, I need to thank my brothers and sister for spending those hours with me and helping me memorize an inanely large amount of quotations when I probably should have been focusing on my homework.

In my sophomore year of college, I proposed to write my final paper on how *The Simpsons* treated Edgar Allan Poe. Dr. Annie Ingram gave me the green light for the project, which allowed me to justify spending my final exam study time watching *The Simpsons* in the Davidson College library. For that academic freedom, I am truly grateful.

My hall mates at Princeton Seminary probably deserve credit for providing what was perhaps my most influential theological education. Erik Daly, Keeva Kase, and Blake Couey were kind enough to host nightly viewing sessions of the show. Moreover, Blake and Jim Mladic deserve a specific measure of thanks for watching even more reruns and making sure that we kept those memorized lines ready to recall at a moment's notice.

I want to thank David Barker for his immediate and sustained enthusiasm for this project. His willingness to sign on no doubt led to a significantly better book. Likewise, the wonderful people at Continuum deserve more measures of thanks than I can capture in words. They have been a pleasure to work for and with.

Finally, I want to thank my wife, Amy, for her support (and patience!) during this project. When I learned that I would be writing a book on *The Simpsons*, she bought me the first season on DVD, and then did not object when I proceeded to buy seasons two through ten. She did not mind, at least not too much, that our apartment was in a constant state of disarray throughout the project. Thank you, my dear. This book is dedicated to you.

Introduction

Taking Stock of Christianity in *The Simpsons*

"You prayed for this. Now your prayers have been answered. I'm no theologian; I don't know who or what God is exactly, all I know is he's a force more powerful than Mom and Dad put together, and you owe him big."

—Lisa Simpson[1]

"Whatever you ask for in prayer with faith, you will receive."

—Matthew 21:22[2]

"I've created Lutherans!"[3]

Though Martin Luther could have said these words, Lisa Simpson makes the claim in "Treehouse of Horror VII." In doing so, Lisa provides a rich introduction to the way in which *The Simpsons* portrays Christianity. For her science project, Lisa sets out to study the ruinous effects of soft drinks on teeth. She places one of her teeth in a dish full of Buzz Cola to watch it decay. The experiment takes on a different meaning when, after Bart zaps her with static electricity, Lisa decides to do the same to her tooth and the experiment ceases to be wholly scientific. In a moment that recalls Michelangelo's painting on the Sistine Chapel ceiling, Lisa's finger does not touch the tooth, but it does send a jolt of electricity. She thinks little of what she has done until the next day, when, after looking more closely at what appears to be mold, Lisa discovers several mini-cavemen gathered around a fire. "Oh my God!" she exclaims. "I've created life!"

In this mini-episode, entitled "The Genesis Tub," one cannot mistake the thematic layers that the writers employ. Lisa plays a godlike role, which allows her to create a world. This act clearly recalls the Genesis account wherein God creates the world ex nihilo.[4] Lisa is proud of her accomplishment, but she soon loses interest in what has happened when her mom calls her to breakfast. After returning, Lisa checks on the world she has created. To her surprise, the tooth world is in the midst of a Renaissance. The defining moment she observes is not, however, something that recalls artistic elements associated with this era in European history. Lisa does not see a Florentine master painting, a Medici exchanging money, or any other secular humanist activity.[5] Rather, she sees one of her created citizens nailing a set of theses to the church door. The defining moment for Lisa's new world, then, is religious. Given the clear allusion to Michelangelo at the episode's beginning, the fact that the writers chose to represent the Renaissance with the Protestant Reformation's most famous act is telling. Though in a Halloween episode,[6] the one definitive representation of Western culture during the development of Lisa's world is also a defining moment for Christianity. By nailing his theses to the church door in Wittenberg, Martin Luther fundamentally altered the course of Christian history. This new direction ultimately produced the Protestant denominations that would enable and affect the founding and developing of American culture.

The extent to which *The Simpsons* incorporates religion into its narrative fabric is a point discussed at length elsewhere.[7] Even the casual viewer can recognize that, at the very least, the Simpson family participates to some degree in Christianity. The intent of this book is to explore more deeply the extent to which Christianity influences the lives of Springfield's residents. The goal in identifying how Christian beliefs and practices unfold in a town that reflects contemporary American culture is to examine in depth how *The Simpsons* understands a fundamental social institution that affects Springfield. The results formulate a critique of Christianity that recalls Martin Luther's need to confront the church's increasingly secularized character. Likewise, *The Simpsons* portrays how Christianity has lost, or actively given away, its integrity as a socially relevant institution in contemporary American culture. In Springfield, as in America, Christianity's traditional doctrines often shift to fit individuals' desires. As Mike Scully, the show's executive producer, explains, "We try to represent peoples' honest opinions about religion."[8] The idea of faith in *The Simpsons*, then, is very real, but what faith means and why different characters cultivate their faith in different ways is a project that often fails to generate significant theological reflection.

Too often, the show draws attention for a supposed lack of values. Perhaps the most famous example occurred in 1992 when President George H.W. Bush called for more families like the Waltons and fewer families like the Simpsons.[9] Rather than receive praise for its incisive social critiques, *The Simpsons* is often accused of undercutting traditional American values. Another common point that ignites discussion of religion in *The Simpsons* is the Catholic question. More than other Christian groups, the Catholic Church often criticizes the show for how it portrays Catholicism.[10] Approaching the show from these kinds of angles pigeonholes the show as excessively negative or flippant in its treatment of religion. While the writers of the show are clearly not out to produce a systematic theology, the ways in which they explore the role of Christianity in America are genuinely complex. The show's writers and producers thus deserve acknowledgment for undertaking a serious study of how Christianity functions in contemporary American society. There is more going on than the occasional potshot at a particular component of Christianity in American culture. Rather than dismissing the show's treatment of Christianity as excessive or unfair, this project seeks to understand Christianity's portrayal on *The Simpsons* as responsible criticism. The point is not to devalue Christianity's role in society. Rather, *The Simpsons* seeks in its treatment of Christianity to identify the ways in which Christianity fails to live up to its traditionally valuable social role and to point out the risks that breakdown produces; the show also suggests that, despite its shortcomings, Christianity can still positively affect contemporary American culture.

To understand how *The Simpsons* characterizes Christianity as a part of life in Springfield, one must not forget the obvious. Springfield is not just an abstract secular or amoral town but a town with distinct historical ties to a tradition that has influenced a good portion of American culture. Hollis Hurlbut, who works at Springfield's Historical Society, recalls clearly Springfield's past: "According to spotty historical records, half of the pioneers—led by Jebediah Springfield—were searching for a place where they could freely pray [and] justly govern."[11] In the show's particular context, and thus in American culture, Christianity is not a throwaway element of the town's identity. Rather, the town's Christian roots, be they residual or active, reflect a tradition that may have been obscured by the secularized, postmodern culture that is contemporary America. However, this cultural trajectory does not erase the past. Those who settled America often came in search of religious freedom. Even outside of the show itself, the writers are careful to construct a past that reflects much of America's own history. Thus, the qualities of

Christianity in Springfield, as they emerge in the show's individual and institutional representations, should remain a focal point in studying what *The Simpsons* says about contemporary American culture.

To say that *The Simpsons* merely incorporates religion into its narrative structure as part of a broader, and thus more important, social critique is to fall into a trap. To understand why faith appears so prominently in the show, one must resist the temptation to reduce religion in *The Simpsons* to a punch line or to regard religion's presence in the show "merely as a satirical element."[12] As William Irwin and J. R. Lombardo note, "The allusions in *The Simpsons* are very 'American' in one rather unflattering way, pointing to America as a fast-food society in which the masses don't like to 'think too much.'"[13] The risk, which manifests itself often in academic studies of *The Simpsons*, is to understand the show in abstract terms rather than treat it as an authentic representation of everyday American life. That is, religion in the show tends to attract attention only in general terms.[14] For example, Paul Cantor recognizes that "even when it seems to be ridiculing religion, [*The Simpsons*] recognizes, as few other television shows do, the genuine role that religion plays in American life."[15] Rather than elaborate, however, Cantor groups this distinctly religious element with Springfield's (and thus America's) broader cultural identity. "It is here that the treatment of the family in *The Simpsons* links up with its treatment of politics. Although the show focuses on the nuclear family, it relates the family to larger institutions in American life, like the church, the school, and even political institutions themselves."[16] Cantor provides a helpful jumping-off point for this project, but he fails to explore more deeply how the relationship between Christianity and other social institutions affects life in Springfield. Rather than consider religion as a minor signpost on a broader cultural map, this project treats Christianity as central to Springfield's, and thus America's, cultural identity. Christianity receives a theologically astute treatment in *The Simpsons*. As a society with deeply Christian roots, America is religious at its core. To discuss religion in *The Simpsons* in generalized terms is to dilute or ignore altogether a fundamental component of life in Springfield.

"Brother from Another Series" offers a good example of how the religious element can quickly recede in the broader context of an episode. Early in the episode, Sideshow Bob acts in a way that suggests he has repented of his earlier crimes.[17] He belts out "Amazing Grace" in the prison's chapel as Reverend Lovejoy smiles approvingly. Even the other prisoners seem to enjoy the hymn. However, one cannot help but find the prison bars over the chapel windows distracting. In a brief visual image, *The Simpsons* calls into question Christianity's role in the context of the American prison system. In this scene, there is little doubt as to which institution is, culturally speaking, more important. The chapel is not a sacred space. Rather, it is a place that permits worship only within the parameters that the prison allows. Just as the justice system asserts its authority over the prison chapel, so too does law enforcement, as an extension of that justice system, determine whether Sideshow Bob's conversion is legitimate. Thus, at the conclusion of "Brother from Another Series," the point emerges again when Chief Wiggum ignores the fact that Sideshow Bob's conversion at the episode's outset seems to be genuine. Even when Sideshow Bob saves Bart's life, Chief Wiggum insists that he must be guilty of another crime. Faith can be a positive thing in Springfield, so long as that faith does not threaten other secular institutions that exert authority.[18] Wiggum's refusal to acknowledge Sideshow Bob's reformed behavior makes clear that Springfield's justice system is blind, at least when it comes to recognizing the legitimacy of spiritual development. In the end, Christianity fades into the background, while Wiggum ensures that Springfield's secularized power structure stays in place.

The risk here is to follow Cantor's lead and understand the social critique as something that primarily targets the justice system. Granted, justice in Springfield takes its knocks in this episode, but the religious element frames this critique. The problem is not so much that the prison insists on placing bars over the chapel windows but rather that Sideshow Bob's sincere conversation in the context of the episode counts for nothing. Christianity provides the narrative foundation for the entire episode, but it lacks any substantive influence outside of the prison's walls and thus in how the episode concludes. Whereas the Christian tradition clearly calls on its followers to embrace people from all walks of life, the Christian tradition in American society has sacrificed its integrity by hemming in precisely those who should be received by forgiving, open arms. Moreover, Christianity is complicit in allowing other social institutions to exert control over it at its own expense. The fact that Reverend Lovejoy does not seem to mind the presence of bars over the chapel windows is telling. Reverend Lovejoy watches Sideshow Bob insist that he has changed his ways.[19] When Sideshow Bob leaves prison, Reverend Lovejoy walks out with him, alongside Mayor Quimby and Chief Wiggum. Here, the spiritual authority that Reverend Lovejoy represents, which affirms that Sideshow Bob truly has changed, seems to stand equally alongside the town's political and law enforcement representatives. However, in the end, Reverend Lovejoy is nowhere to be seen; the church's authority has once again yielded to other forms of social authority. Despite the legitimacy of Sideshow Bob's conversion, Springfield's power structure as embodied in law enforcement rejects the notion that Christianity can truly alter an individual's character. Thus, by the end of the episode it becomes clear once again that Christianity constitutes little more than a minor social influence. Sideshow Bob finds himself back in jail, no doubt to sing another set of hymns in the shadow of prison bars. Rather than viewing Christianity as relevant vis-à-vis a criminal's repentance, one sees only a faith tradition that stands silently by as political and judicial figures determine whether or not Sideshow Bob has repented.

An understated but still explicit lack of authority defines Christianity in *The Simpsons*. This nuanced social identity, which appears consistently throughout the show, is often understood as a secondary point of concern in the show's broader satirical targets. One should not, however, ignore the fact that in Springfield, Christianity's significance often serves as a vanguard in the show's clear intent to expose authority in American culture as impotent. Despite the obvious intention to explore and expose how morality functions in American culture, Christianity's historical role as moral guide is often absent in Springfield. More specifically, *The Simpsons* caricatures social institutions as divorced from their imperative to act in a way that benefits American citizens.[20] As a result, the common person comes to distrust or reject the authority in question, a quality that runs against the grain of an inclusiveness that defines Christianity in the first place. With respect to Christianity in particular, this divorce proves to be doubly problematic, as the decay that results from the other corrupt institutions should not infect the Christian tradition that defines America's moral identity. The result is a distinctly postmodern turn inward; when the Christian Church cannot provide leadership, morality becomes a question of personal effort.[21] More importantly, this dynamic dissolves any authority that Christianity might have in contemporary American culture.

The breakdown of Christianity's authority in secular culture was a significant impetus for the reformers during the Protestant Reformation. As Alister McGrath explains, a secularized, economized notion of Christianity characterized the religious climate in Luther's Germany: "By Luther's time, misrepresentation and misunderstanding has set in. People seemed to believe that indulgences were a quick and convenient way of buying forgiveness of sins. . . . The idea of forgiveness by grace had become corrupted into that of the purchase of God's favor."[22] Christianity, then, had ceased to be a faith that required sincere commitments from individuals and from churches. One's spiritual identity became a matter of social concerns, especially one's ability to pay. The central tenet of Christianity, namely that God had forgiven the fallen world through the sacrifice of Jesus Christ, had been diluted into practices that served other, secular interests. Such a lack of institutional integrity, coupled with a breakdown of ecclesial leaders in their personal commitment to their faith drove much of the reforms during the Reformation.[23] Life in Christian culture had lost direction. John Calvin, who initiated the Reformed Tradition, sought to instill a biblically based, morally stringent, and ecclesiastically oriented notion of Christian faith.[24] The overall trajectory of the Protestant Reformation points away from the secularized culture that had lost a sense of what its religious heritage demanded in both personal and corporate life.

The Simpsons often echoes this traditional moment of crisis in how it characterizes contemporary American Christianity. The show thus suggests implicitly that American Christianity finds itself at a similarly significant historical crossroads. Much is at stake in the current state of American Christianity. In the following chapters, I will explore the causes that have generated this crisis, the contemporary effects those problems produced, as well as a troublesome trajectory that awaits if Christian leaders and laypeople fail to recognize what is at risk in the breakdown of their faith tradition. Consequently, I will argue that *The Simpsons* is a rich, theologically astute (if subtle) commentary on Christianity in American culture, a quality that emerges readily through a close analysis of how the show portrays Christianity in Springfield.

I will address several salient characteristics from traditional Christian theology in the wake of the Protestant Reformation to argue that the show echoes a time of crisis in Christianity's history in order to critique similar failures of faith in contemporary American culture. After some introductory remarks concerning the show's postmodern approach to critiquing American culture, but before discussing broad theological topics, I will take Springfield's spiritual pulse. By surveying quickly several salient features of Christianity in Springfield, I will capture the town's broad relationship to its Christian roots. I will then explore how Springfield, and by extension American culture, understands religion in terms of convenience and a diluted sense of the sacred. Using this analysis as my critical basis, I will then evaluate how Christianity interacts with broad trends in contemporary American culture. From here, I will discuss how specific points that concerned the reformers with respect to traditional Christian doctrine have been recast in a contemporary American culture. The consequent spiritual footprint on the lives of Springfield's Christians presents telling conclusions about the state of American Christianity, which are already leading to troublesome developments between Christianity and other social institutions, especially American politics.

More specifically, I will discuss how *The Simpsons* portrays God and how this understanding mirrors many of Luther's and Calvin's concerns. Much of the problem stems from how Christians understand the biblical tradition, a fact that is very much present in *The Simpsons*. A lukewarm knowledge of the Bible perpetuates much of the crisis that faces Christianity in Springfield. From here, I will analyze how these fundamental shortcomings translate into the kinds of spiritual concerns that warrant critical attention on *The Simpsons*. These theological qualities affect significantly how religion unfolds in everyday life for Springfield's Christians. They often understand faith in economic terms, which, as Luther so strongly pointed out, makes Christian faith a question of economic expediency rather than a substantive spiritual commitment. Ultimately, understanding the Christian faith in economic terms distorts how faith ought to affect the Christian's day-to-day life.

I will discuss such results in Springfield's two most prominent representations of Christian faith: Reverend Lovejoy and Ned Flanders. Finally, I will argue that the way in which *The Simpsons* portrays faith in economic terms points back to the agnostic or even atheistic humanism that preceded the Protestant Reformation. This tendency to dismiss Christianity in the face of America's secularized trust in scientific thought spreads an antisectarian residue over questions of whether Christianity is even relevant in contemporary American culture. To conclude, I will suggest how these elements of Christianity, as characterized in Springfield, point toward a moral and spiritual crisis in how America understands and relates to its Christian heritage.

Chapter One

A Televised Sunday Evening Service: Postmodernism and *The Simpsons*

"Wow. Wow. God does so much for me and he doesn't ask anything in return."

—Homer Simpson[1]

"All things are wearisome; more than one can express; the eye is not satisfied with seeing, or the ear filled with hearing. What has been is what will be, and what has been done is what will be done; there is nothing new under the sun."

— Ecclesiastes 1:8–9

Exploring *The Simpsons* from an academic angle presents immediate challenges. To suggest that the show is rich in theological insight, or to argue that the show echoes in its social criticism problems within Christianity that ignited the Protestant Reformation is to place the burden of proof squarely on the following project. Oftentimes, those who claim such intellectual depth in *The Simpsons* face a cool response. After all, some say, *The Simpsons* is just a cartoon; perhaps academics are reading too much into the show. However, two broad counterarguments meet this objection: the show's postmodern approach to critiquing American culture and the fact that humor provides the vehicle through which such criticism takes place.

Anything, so the saying goes, is possible in America because America is the land of opportunity. This "dream," according to Kevin J. H. Dettmar, often fails to reflect the reality of many peoples' lives.[2] The disconnect between the idea of a limitless horizon that America romantically nurtures and the difficult everyday experiences of many Americans' lives suggests that something does not match up between what Americans envision their faith to be and the practical ways in which that same faith plays out in their daily lives. This disjointed cultural reality demands critical exploration and *The Simpsons* happily obliges. The show is forcefully self-critical in its writing; few topics remain off-limits. Broadly speaking, *The Simpsons* exhibits a consistent goal: to critique various offices of authority in American culture.

More specifically, Christianity is a significant institution, with a measure of cultural authority, in America.[3] As a substantive element of America's identity, Christianity plays implicitly and explicitly a role in the fractured dream that so often is treated as intact. Supposed cultural leadership often turns out to be vacuous, a fact evident, for example, in Reverend Lovejoy's ineffectual spiritual leadership. It is this cultural void that *The Simpsons* wants to expose in order to critique the cultural realities that produce such problematic results in American lives. Rather than appeal to broad social ideals, the show wants to recognize that, in particular contexts, the concept of "the American dream" lacks credibility. The willingness to embrace this inward-looking analysis of American culture reflects the way in which postmodern thought wants to ground questions of social identity in localized contexts. The goal is to address the ways in which the social structure of contemporary American culture fails by exposing the weaknesses in the very things that should enable success.[4] As a fundamental part of this culture, Christianity thus invites critical analysis as it affects everyday life in Springfield.

In critiquing the generalized notion of the American dream, *The Simpsons* is able to represent through various stereotypes in Springfield how different individuals interact with American institutions. This dynamic defines much of Christianity's presence on *The Simpsons*. For example, Homer understands church not as something that will enrich his life, but rather as a chore.[5] He can understand what Christianity is supposed to bring to his life, but his actual experience provides reason to doubt the truth of such claims. In "Homer the Heretic," Homer explains to God in a dream why church fails to enrich his life:

God: Thou hast forsaken my church!

Homer: Uh, kind-of . . . b-but . . .

God: But what?!

Homer: I'm not a bad guy! I work hard, and I love my kids. So why should I spend half my Sunday hearing about how I'm going to hell?

God: [after pausing for a moment]: Hmm. You've got a point there.

God agrees with Homer. Based on the evidence Homer cites, God grants that, for Homer, church is not all it is cracked up to be. In his individual experience, Homer fails to find value, and this is the starting point for the show's postmodern critique of religion. Christianity should not blanket people with abstract ideas. Rather, for faith to be relevant the individual must understand his/her faith as relevant to his/her own context. What *The Simpsons* accomplishes, then, is to focus its criticism on the discord between what Christianity claims to accomplish for its adherents and what actually happens in those people's lives.

The goal in specifically sketching how actual life experiences fail to resonate with Christian ideals is to provide a resource for the viewer to relate to when exploring his/her own identity within American culture. *The Simpsons* is obviously not about real people, but that fact does not prevent the show from providing reference points through caricatured examples to help real-life viewers understand how Christianity affects their own lives. Brian L. Ott recognizes this quality as fundamental to the show's postmodern identity: "[*The Simpsons*] furnishes [viewers] with the symbolic resources—the actual cultural bricks—with which to (re) construct identity. Viewers continuously construct and deconstruct their identities from those bricks."[6] The individual must do his/her best to makes sense of the void that results from the dissonance between an institutional ideal and actual experience. Homer recognizes that he does his best to uphold the demands that Christianity places on him, but in return he only hears about his failures. Thus, he must deconstruct his identity as a faithful person with good intentions in order to understand himself as somehow flawed. For Homer, this fluidity creates enough confusion that he simply does not want to revisit the authoritative voice that generates doubt in the first place.

Such spiritual uncertainty represents the broad cultural problem that *The Simpsons* addresses through its postmodern approach. Individuals desire stability as they interact with their surroundings, but too often culturally authoritative elements destabilize efforts to shore up the basis for personal identity. Ott understands this lack of stability in an individual's self-perception as the necessary result of cultural institutions: "Having no base to return to, Homer models a radically decentered subject who appears to be simply another product of culture industries. . . . In essence, Homer models an anti-identity; his being critiques the modernist idea of a unified, coherent subject."[7] In Ott's example, rather than enriching Homer's experience, Christianity only problematizes his self-understanding. Whereas Christianity should provide stability vis-à-vis its theological claims, Homer's experiences suggest otherwise. In place of spiritual peace, Homer feels unsettled. The Simpsons thus creates an easily identifiable and understandable example of issues that viewers likely encounter in their own lives. The show provides stable resources for viewers to shore up their own identities by capturing the spiritual dissonance that individuals recognize in their own experiences within American culture. The result is a picture of Christianity in Springfield that characterizes accurately and critically the spiritual lives of characters on The Simpsons, which in turn pinpoints similar cultural realities in contemporary American society.

As a postmodern show, The Simpsons relies in part on its viewers to generate meaning. The Simpsons recognizes the viewer's role as important, a move that constitutes a fundamentally postmodern approach to social criticism. The Simpsons is thus like a mirror wherein viewers can watch, safely, a topically clear and theologically consequential portrait of how Americans often reject an important component of their cultural identity. In turn, viewers watch the show actively, which necessarily produces a bond between the show and its audience. The Simpsons asks its viewers to recognize for themselves the cultural elements that are in play, but it does so without forcing the point. For example, Christian components are clearly present in Springfield's cultural makeup, but the show does not call undue attention to them. Rather, Christianity is an organic, authentic presence in the life of Springfield's residents. Viewers thus must be able to recognize and subsequently lift out from their own responses the ways in which this authentic Christian element proves to be problematic. By viewing their culture as represented on the show, the audience thus becomes an important component in how The Simpsons unveils its critique. William Irwin and J. R. Lombardo note that "audience members . . . enjoy recognizing, understanding, and appreciating allusions in a rather special way. . . . Audiences enjoy being involved in the creative process; they enjoy filling in the blanks for themselves rather than being told what to do."[8] The distinctly postmodern approach in The Simpsons invites the audience to dig more deeply into the show's narrative structure in order to identify how Christianity falters in Springfield. To present obvious, heavy-handed critiques about how Christianity interacts with the rest of American culture would likely alienate the audience.

Viewers must be able to recognize vis-à-vis their own experiences what they see on the show. The ability to layer the world of Springfield over the viewer's own experience creates space to understand the show's cultural criticism. Often, those who do not engage the show in this way will dismiss it, but this is precisely the point, or they will simply focus on the overt physical comedy.[9] Meaning must grow out of *The Simpsons* interacting with, not dictating to, its audience.

This strategy produces a way for the viewer to approach how Christianity functions in his or her own life with a measure of safety. When looking in a mirror, one can always look away if one does not like what one sees. Such control allows one to take ownership of one's experience with the text, or, as in the case of *The Simpsons*, with the episode. This sense of ownership allows the viewer to transform Springfield in his or her own mind into an accurate analog of his or her own personal experience. According to Arnold Bennett, one can then see "[the]very street as a mirror, an illustration, an exposition, an explanation, of the human beings who live in it. Nothing in it is neglected. Everything in it is valuable, if the perspective is maintained."[10] Kurt M. Koenigsberger adds: "Bennett's formulation suggests that without strict attention to 'the street,' any representation of a 'domestic organism' must appear as a free-floating ego and will ultimately prove inadequate and narrow due to the loss of perspective."[11] The show's success rests on the ability to transform Springfield's streets into recognizable elements that parallel actual experiences of Christianity in American culture. Viewers can thus understand what is happening in the show because in the show's characters viewers can see an accurate analog of their friends, families, fellow churchgoers, ministers, and themselves.

As viewers peel back the layers of *The Simpsons*, the analogy of a street that mirrors their own experiences generates several critical points about Christianity's role in American culture. The result is a postmodern web that inevitably snags the viewer. Consequently, the viewer begins to explore more deeply the precisely built cultural texture that makes Springfield a viable representation of Anytown, USA. Koenigsberger emphasizes, however, that the individual's ability to use *The Simpsons* as a personal touchstone first must be maintained. He writes, "There can be no single street that can serve as 'a mirror, an illustration, an exposition, an explanation' of the individual. Rather, there must be multiple mirrors, local illustrations, and a plastic play of multifarious contexts that situate and motive the individual subject."[12] So long as *The Simpsons* represents life in Springfield as authentically American, the mirror provides a helpful metaphor for how *The Simpsons* functions as a critical voice. Because the mirror allows viewers to approach critical issues from multiple angles, interactions between the show and its audience will produce viable resources for understanding oneself as an American individual.[13]

The characters on *The Simpsons* thus provide stereotypes that are broad enough to incorporate a multitude of individual experiences, attitudes, and beliefs about cultural institutions, such as Christianity. In "Homer the Heretic," a complex portrait of an individual's struggles with personal faith unfolds within a larger familial and corporate context. The details of the episode narrative are specific to Homer's character, but in Homer viewers can recognize either their own tendencies or, at the very least, the tendencies of someone they know. Homer responds to Lisa's question about what he will do if his decision to reject Christianity is wrong by saying, "If I'm wrong, then I'll recant on my deathbed." Homer's strategy puts into words a reaction that is common to those who dismiss Christianity as morally prohibitive. In fact, Homer answers Lisa's objection with a logically sound point. If God's forgiveness is as Christianity describes it, then Homer could repent at the last moment and still receive God's forgiveness. Still, Homer defines the issue in self-interested terms, which represents a pervasive spiritual attitude in contemporary American culture. As Homer illustrates, Christianity can be altered to produce a spiritual praxis that is convenient rather than transformative. Homer thus provides a crisp example of what often results when individuals eschew a rigorous commitment to their Christian beliefs.

Homer is a complex metaphor for "the average American Christian," and though every part of his personality may not resonate with every viewer, he does speak in familiar terms, which in turn allows the viewer to grasp the critical point that the show makes. Consequently, viewers can recognize how Homer's faith unfolds in a particular situation's strategy and thus understand what happens when their own spirituality follows a similar trajectory. By understanding what is at stake in this particular example, viewers can, if need be, apply a similar critical apparatus to their own experiences with and within Christianity. Lisa's objection draws out Homer's response in order to point out that he is not only gambling spiritually, but he is doing so in a way that assumes a particular interpretation of what Christianity says about God's forgiveness. Suffice to say, Homer is far from theologically astute, so his response actually serves as a warning against naïvely invoking this kind of argument.

The critical point, then, is to capture how such responses run against the grain of a reasonable and responsible Christian faith. In her article "The Function of Fiction: The Heuristic Value of Homer," Jennifer L. McMahon offers a helpful reading of Martha Nussbaum, which in turn helps to clarify how characters on *The Simpsons* critique contemporary American Christianity. An initial notion to dispel is the idea that fiction has no instructive value. As McMahon writes, "Those who deny that literature can instruct found their skepticism in doubts about fiction's capacity to represent reality, as well as . . . the power of artful words to undermine rational thought."[14] On the surface, the argument that a cartoon cannot offer serious cultural critiques because it quite simply is not real seems to carry some weight. The show itself often pokes fun at the idea that, as a cartoon, it does not have to function according to reality's constraints.[15] However, the show's cartoon medium does not remove what Nussbaum understands to be the root of fiction's instructive ability: emotion.[16] Emotions demand a measure of discrimination,[17] which, in the case of *The Simpsons*, ascribes some responsibility to the viewer in order to understand the broader critical point. Lisa's response to Homer reminds the audience of this element. She injects emotion into the situation in order to make clear to Homer what is at stake in his decision. McMahon helps to clarifies the point: "When style that is abstract and cleansed of emotion is employed to describe reality that is concrete, complex, and infused with feeling, problems inevitably result. . . . This style misrepresents our situation and encourages misunderstanding regarding how we ought to live in it."[18] If *The Simpsons* created an analog of American culture that prohibited emotive ends, then the show would likely fail to receive viewer assent as an authentic representation of American culture. Lisa thus helps to authenticate how Homer's decision constitutes a shortsighted misunderstanding of the parameters involved in his choice.

The show's ability to present specific points in emotionally rich detail produces a deeply instructive social critique. For example, in "Homer's Enemy," Frank Grimes comes to work at the nuclear power plant. Grimes is a model employee who has worked for every success he achieves. This contrasts sharply with Homer, who embodies the paradox that lazy, oafish people can excel in America. Grimes becomes so frustrated with Homer that he ends up killing himself when, while imitating what he perceives to be Homer's self-proclaimed immunity from consequences, he grabs some high-voltage wires. The show then cuts to Grimes's funeral. Reverend Lovejoy begins to eulogize Grimes: "Frank Grimes, or Grimey as he liked to be called, taught us that a man can triumph over adversity. And even though Frank's agonizing struggle through life was tragically cut short, I'm sure he's looking down on this right now." Homer, meanwhile, is snoring in the front row. He must also be dreaming because he interrupts by saying, "Change the channel, Marge!" One would normally expect the crowd to chastise Homer for such an insensitive comment. However, the entire crowd, including Reverend Lovejoy, laughs. Lenny even says affectionately, "That's our Homer!" The collective response thus reveals an honest if inappropriate emotional quality in Springfield's Christian community. Homer is an endearing figure among Springfield's residents. His faults appear not to be serious enough to chip away at the embrace others offer him. Grimes may have been a hard worker, but the rest of Springfield does not accept him as one of its own. Tellingly, Reverend Lovejoy cannot help but laugh at Homer, who has certainly interrupted Reverend Lovejoy before. The solemn attitude one expects to see at a funeral is thus noticeably absent. Disrespectful though Homer's behavior may be, it generates an honest emotional response in the sense that he breaks up the monotony of a funeral for a person no one really likes. Homer thus enables a response that everyone at the funeral wants; they do not want to pretend that they are truly mourning anything.

The moment invites viewers to evaluate for themselves whether Homer deserves blame for his actions. The question, then, becomes whether a particular viewer will condemn Homer's interruption or recall a similar moment in his or her own experience when a similar comment would have been welcome. However one reacts, the point remains instructive. In this case, there can be no real mistake about what is going on at the funeral. An indictment lands squarely on those who empathize with Homer, or the crowd for that matter. The broader point questions what one should think of a Christian community that so completely runs against the grain of what it should say in such situations. Reverend Lovejoy pays lip service to the idea that Grimes died too young, but that cannot mask the more important reality at the funeral: no one cares about Grimes. When Christians attend a funeral but have no investment in their actions, they seem to tarnish the very faith community that brings them together in the first place.

The idea that a mirror can instruct viewers with respect to their religion is not new. In fact, the image of the mirror provides an important symbol in traditional Christian theology. It first appears in the Paul's First Letter to the Corinthians:

> For we know only in part, and we prophesy only in part; but when the complete comes, the partial will come to an end. When I was a child, I spoke like a child, I thought like a child, I reasoned like a child; when I became an adult, I put an end to childish ways. For now we see in a mirror, dimly, but then we will see

face to face. Now I know only in part; then I will know fully, even as I have been fully known.[19]

As a person who has committed his life to a Christian faith, Paul now recognizes what Jesus represents. In Jesus's message, and the Christian belief in Jesus's death and resurrection, Paul recognizes a transforming effect on life. Consigning one's life to this tradition symbolizes a death to a world apart from Jesus and the salvific atonement Jesus achieved for humanity.[20] The new life of a Christian allows one to "see in a mirror." That is, as a Christian one can see in Jesus's example how the non-Christian life leads to a spiritually empty existence. The corollary is that one can also see part of God in humanity's positive qualities as they emerge in a committed Christian ethic. Of course, one sees only dimly, a reminder that the Christian life is a process. Still, Paul's mirror provides a way for Christians to recognize how they now resemble what Jesus achieves through his atonement, just as one can still make out one's face when looking in a dim mirror. The image captures both the Christian elements that are present in a person's life, as well as qualities that still distort one's reflection.

That this cultural mirror makes viewers laugh is a large reason why *The Simpsons* has been successful for nearly two decades. Satirical efforts, such as *The Simpsons*, play an important role in how we understand our own cultural contexts. When one brings together both the postmodern and Christian notions of the self-reflective mirror, one can recognize how *The Simpsons* approaches its criticism of Christianity in America. For Wendy Wick Reeves, self-reflection, which is the foundational point in what the mirror symbolizes, allows satire to be an effective critical tool. Wick Reeves believes that *The Simpsons*, as a specific product of American culture, constitutes "a serious topic for discussion, despite its levity."[21] What often gets overlooked in humor is the subtlety with which it makes its points.[22] At first, one may not necessarily get the joke, so to speak. One can easily understand humor as intellectually deficient; what it lacks in meaning it must make up for through entertainment. However, humor can be as intellectually rewarding as other forms of social expression.[23] Wick Reeves suggests that laughter as a response may initially miss the deeper point, but in laughing one has absorbed the underlying meaning.[24] As a result, viewers have acquired information that can later clarify the important point, or rather what caused the laughter in the first place. Such moments, Wick Reeves summarizes, are invaluable in recognizing how humor can generate serious intellectual activity:

"Examining humorous art in its full complexity . . . can reveal not only clever manipulations, but also layered meanings and aesthetic sophistication that warrant our attention."[25] That *The Simpsons* exhibits clever jokes is a given, so it is the latter point, that humor provides a layered meaning, that needs to be explored in order to understand methodologically how *The Simpsons* critiques Christianity.

Humor provides the framework within which *The Simpsons* critiques religion. Moreover, it also allows viewers to recognize what is at stake in the points that the show addresses. Mark Pinsky recognizes the former issue in general terms but fails to realize the extent to which humor is an integral part of how *The Simpsons* levels its criticism against Christianity.[26] At the same time, Pinsky understands the role that humor plays in terms that do not lift out exactly how important humor is when exploring issues of faith. For example, Pinsky concludes: "A joking Jesus is not the same as a Jesus joke, which may be why, in the end, *The Simpsons* writers treat Jesus so gingerly."[27] Quite the opposite is true, however. *The Simpsons* writers deploy their Jesus jokes tactically and forcefully. Jesus jokes appear at crucial moments in broader criticisms about the Christian faith. For example, in "Thank God It's Doomsday," one can see the extent to which Jesus provides an excellent punch line. When Homer is talking to God about why no one believed his calculations about the apocalypse, God muses that humans are truly troublesome, a fact evident in what they did to Jesus when Jesus went to earth. The scene then cuts to Jesus sitting on a swing, twisting slowly, with a forlorn frown on his face. Jesus's crucifixion is the punch line, which is hardly a joking matter. However, this joke punctuates the show's broader point about how Christians neglect the basis for their faith tradition. Crucifixion would leave anyone a bit melancholic and *The Simpsons* uses this element of the Christian tradition to point out how problematic human behavior can be. Humor allows the show's writers to make delicate points with as much critical force as possible by using Jesus as a foil for humanity's ability to disappoint God.

Given that crucifixion jokes are inherently not funny, one would have a hard time reconciling the way in which *The Simpsons* uses the crucifixion, and the theological claim that this act redeems all of humanity, to suggest that Homer's sin is so bad that it practically nullifies the worth of Jesus's sacrifice on the cross. *The Simpsons* suggests as much in "Pray Anything" when Marge encourages Homer not to sue the church. Her argument rests on the past ways in which Homer has embarrassed the family. Marge pulls out an old church bulletin with the headline, "Jesus died for this?" Below the caption is a picture of Homer asleep, or more likely passed out, in the church pews. The reference is anything but "gingerly" treating of what Jesus's crucifixion represents. To suggest that the church, which is supposed to preach the good news of salvation offered by Jesus's sacrifice on the cross, would use the central tenet in Christianity to shame a member of that church makes a strong statement about how Christian communities will bend their beliefs to exert social influence. The doctrine of salvation holds that no one is beyond the reach of the grace God offers through Jesus's sacrifice.[28] To undercut this notion in the context of a joke illustrates that *The Simpsons* is willing to use humor about Christianity's most fundamental beliefs in order to pinpoint how Christians so often fail to understand, perhaps ignore, or flat out abuse what the doctrine entails when doing so is socially inconvenient.

True to its postmodern character, *The Simpsons* requires that the audience play an important part in translating such jokes. Through humor, the show offers a critical gateway that introduces the broader social concerns in the show's critique. That is, at times *The Simpsons* addresses an issue in Christianity as it exists in contemporary American culture that demands humor as a vehicle. Such criticisms strike nerves that are quite sensitive in America's cultural consciousness. This does not mean that *The Simpsons* will avoid the issue. Rather, such examples illustrate how humor provides a way to introduce a difficult point softly. The intended effect may be uncomfortable, but humor lets the audience experience the critique with a sense of "intimacy."[29] This strategy allows the show's writers to enable and even encourage the audience to recognize that they may, either intentionally or obliviously, belong to a Christian community that leverages its belief system to apply social pressure on those who may run against the grain of communal expectations. As Donald Capps explains, "A cartoon or a joke, insignificant as it may seem, may have a transformative effect that carries well beyond its immediate stimulus to laughter."[30] The willingness to call on Jesus and what he represents to Christians in order to be critical of Christians very much reflects this dynamic. While one could easily dismiss the joke as blasphemous, the writers' intent bores far more deeply into Christianity's flaws than it might appear on the surface. Homer's drunken actions are reprehensible; passing out in church is clearly inappropriate. However, the image bends critical attention back on to the church that will use such an image to shame one of its members at the cost of its belief system's integrity.

To anticipate a possible objection to the point above, and, in general, to the claim that *The Simpsons* is an inconsequential cartoon, a discussion of context is important at this point. To get the joke, one must be aware of the context in which the joke is made. As Ted Cohen explains, a successful joke depends upon "an implicit acknowledgment of a shared background, a background of awareness that both [the teller and the hearer] are already in possession of and bring to the joke. This is the foundation of the intimacy that will develop if your joke succeeds."[31] Yet again, the importance of context cannot be overlooked. *The Simpsons* relies on a shared cultural heritage with its American audience and it is this history that enables its social criticisms. The audience must recognize that Jesus jokes are normally taboo, so the presence of such a joke in the show alerts the audience that an important point is at hand. Moreover, the audience can recognize vis-à-vis personal experience that Christians do, in fact, use their beliefs to enact or enforce social distinctions. This shared foundation ultimately produces an "incongruity"[32] that brings into focus the criticism that the show offers in making the joke. James M. Wallace recognizes that such incongruity is a central component to the show's satirical strategy: "Incongruity serves to draw our attention to common human behavior (including, perhaps, our own) and to raise doubts about the appropriateness of that behavior. Such satire often challenges us to question 'ordinary' practices, habits and perspectives and to reflect on how the world might be improved."[33] When the viewer recognizes that *The Simpsons* recalls a social reality in his or her own culture,[34] that individual can recognize what is at stake in juxtaposing the fundamentally important doctrine of salvation with the petty concerns that so often emerge in a Christian church's social fabric.[35] If the viewer accepts the joke, then she or he will hopefully move to change the point in question. Perhaps next time someone in a congregation speaks ill of a fellow church member, the *Simpsons* fan will address the real incongruity: Christian faith often uses its core beliefs to marginalize its own.[36]

To say that *The Simpsons* exhibits a distinctly postmodern look at Christianity in American culture is to make a point that must be emphasized at the outset. The following analysis understands that, as a cartoon, *The Simpsons* approaches and critiques American culture in a specific way. Meaning in a broad sense is thus inherently fluid, but the pattern that produces ideas is consistent. The arguments that follow in subsequent chapters capture this process and suggest one way to under-stand how *The Simpsons* characterizes Christianity's role in contempo-rary American society and how the show interprets the consequent effects of Christian beliefs on American lives. While my points are symptomatic of what the show broadly tries to achieve by including Christianity prominently in Springfield's cultural identity, they are by no means the only possible conclusions.[37] As with the show's broad postmodern goal, what follows in this book is an attempt to provide a perspective that fans of the show can understand and relate to in order to recognize in *The Simpsons*, and thus in American culture, where Christianity fails. This project is not meant to be and thus is not exhaustive. The result will, hopefully, not argue that Christianity should become a cultural bystander. Rather, the following chapters ought to provide a departure point for helping Christianity retain its cultural relevance.

Chapter Two

Saints, Sinners, and Salvation: A Spiritual Survey of Springfield

"Nice try, God, but Homer Simpson doesn't give in to temptation that easily."

—Homer Simpson[1]

"Therefore it was called Babel, because there the Lord confused the language of all the earth; and from there the Lord scattered them abroad over the face of all the earth."

—Genesis 11:9

Impending disaster often reveals the true character of a person's faith. Springfield's residents are no exception. *The Simpsons Movie* provides a helpful look at how Christianity influences the ways in which people respond to moments of crisis. After an environmental disaster in Springfield Lake makes the town a national threat, the President of the United States approves a plan that encloses the entire Springfield in a glass dome. As an army of helicopters carries the dome toward town, an ominous shadow creeps along the ground. Reminiscent of an alien invasion, the silhouette induces panic among the townspeople. In an overhead shot, one sees the First Church of Springfield and Moe's Tavern in the same frame. At the climactic moment, the crowds in each establishment empty into the streets. Both groups, the faithful who are at church, as well as the drunks at Moe's, exhale a collective, terrified yelp.

What happens next captures in one brief but poignant image the complexity that defines Christianity's presence in Springfield. The churchgoers run into Moe's, while the drunks scurry into the church. Each group rejects its place of normal practice for the other, a switch that reveals much about their respective attitudes toward Christianity. The churchgoers may attend services dutifully on Sundays, but when disaster requires them to stand firm in their faith, they crumple and seek refuge in the type of place they otherwise condemn in the name of Christianity. Reverend Lovejoy leads the charge to the bar, an act that conflicts with his otherwise judgmental attitude toward alcohol.[2] On the other hand, the drunkards whose interests so often receive condemnation and who personally feel rejected by Christians seek solace in that very church.[3]

These diverse reactions point to a tangled Christian identity in Springfield. The way in which both groups respond to a moment that reveals their true feelings brings into focus two salient features that define Christianity on *The Simpsons*. First, those who represent a strong commitment to Christianity will, with their pastor at the helm, seek solace away from the church. This vacuous spirituality in a time of crisis lies at the heart of the show's criticism of Christianity. At the same time, the barflies' willingness to turn to Christianity in the face of disaster reveal that though secular concerns saturate the town's spiritual identity, even those who seem to lead the opposite of a moderate Christian lifestyle can still find value in what Christianity offers. Here, these two tendencies intersect at a specific point, but they move and shift constantly throughout the show's more than four hundred episodes. In this chapter, I will sweep through Springfield's streets to construct a portrait of Springfield's general Christian character.

Though they may not always be sincere in their Christian faith, Springfield residents seem to be committed to the idea of spirituality. "Thank God It's Doomsday" provides a clear example of the town's collective willingness to embrace Christianity. At the beginning of the episode, Homer, Bart, and Lisa watch a new Christian movie, *Left Below*. Homer is hooked; he completely buys into the message about the impending apocalypse. As a product of conservative Christianity, the movie depicts a society that suddenly experiences God's judgment on the world. A philandering husband faces God's judgment upon his un-Christian actions when his limo driver ascends to heaven, leaving the car to careen without a driver. A Buddhist monk is likewise doomed to experience the punishments that await those who do not accept the Christianity that the movie presents. Homer finds himself sufficiently scared to see signs of the rapture in the next few days. He encounters a man in a devil suit (who is part of an advertising stunt) and blood falling from a harpooned whale in the sky, two signs that convince Homer that he may soon end up like the unfortunate nonbelievers in *Left Below*. Homer's paranoia leads him to buy several books about apocalyptic thought in Christianity. Using these books, as well as a copy of da Vinci's *The Last Supper*, Homer is able to calculate that the rapture will arrive in Springfield within a week. He proclaims his findings to the town, which does not believe him at first. However, when Homer says that stars will fall from the sky and a blimp carrying celebrities crashes, thus validating Homer's prediction, the town hails Homer as a prophet. Based on his newfound spiritual authority, Homer tells the town to meet on the Springfield Mesa at the appointed time to make sure they are safe from the apocalypse. When that time arrives, everyone is present atop the mesa, but the apocalypse never happens.

The town's willingness to believe in Homer's prophecy illustrates several salient features that define Christianity in Springfield. First, the townspeople show a willingness to buy into Homer's apocalyptic message, a receptiveness that points toward some desire for spirituality in their lives. Homer turns out not to be a reliable prophet, if only because he makes a simple mistake in calculating the precise time and day the rapture will occur. Homer is many things in Springfield, but he is not a model Christian. Still, the entire town embraces Homer as a spiritual guide when his prophesy coincidentally comes true. This willingness to embrace Homer's supposed spiritual leadership captures the void in Springfield's Christian leadership. The mob mentality that causes the town to show up at Homer's door to ask him questions about the impending rapture exhibits a remarkable naïvete. Homer has no idea what he is talking about, but the mere appearance of spiritual authority is enough to endear him even to the town's committed Christians. Ned Flanders should recognize that Homer is not prophetic, but he, too, buys into Homer's prediction. To generalize, then, a relatively uninformed anxiety lies at the heart of the town's assumption about the veracity of Homer's prophecy. Most people seem receptive to elements of Christianity; they just need to be convinced. Homer accomplishes the latter, which points toward the brittle spirituality that characterizes Christianity in Springfield.

Most members of the Springfield community are at least open to the idea of Christianity, but at the same time some parts of the town exhibit a general suspicion toward the faith. In the hospital, a sign in a room reads *No Praying*,[4] a communal standard that Mayor Quimby echoes elsewhere when he tells a crowd, "Stop that! You can't pray on city property!"[5] Whether the sign reflects a doubt in prayer's efficacy or merely represents a social annoyance with the practice the episode does not make clear. What one can glean, however, is that the sign indicates a general secularization in Springfield's public life. A more in-depth example of Springfield's dismissive attitude occurs in "Sweet Seymour Skinner's Baadasssss Song." When a half-naked, greased Groundskeeper Willie and the Simpsons's dog, Santa's Little Helper, fall from the elementary school's ventilation system, Superintendent Chalmers fires Principal Skinner. Ned Flanders becomes the new principal at Springfield Elementary, but his tenure is short-lived.

Ned:	[over the PA system]: Well, cockly-doodly-doo, little buddies. Let's thank the Lord for another beautiful school day.
Superintendent Chalmers:	Thank the Lord. Thank the Lord? That sounded like a prayer. A prayer. A prayer in a public school! God has no place within these walls, just like facts have no place within organized religion. Simpson, you get your wish: Flanders is history!

Even though Flanders does not actually pray, his words ignite a reaction in Superintendent Chalmers that reveals just how suspicious some people are of religion as well as the unreasonable bias against Christianity as a legitimate intellectual belief system. While the separation of church and state is a hallmark of America's social history, practically the division is not as neat as Superintendent Chalmers would like it to be. Ned speaks as he always does; his diction indicates his generally cheerful and appreciative demeanor. His words seem no more harmful than the Pledge of Allegiance, in which students acknowledge their loyalty to a nation "under God." Still, the mere hint of religious activity within the school's walls elicits a reaction from Superintendent Chalmers that, much like the *No Praying* sign, characterizes Springfield's public suspicion toward Christianity.

Though a general distrust of Christianity pervades Springfield, its townspeople still recall their Christian heritage. Several moments arise when a character on *The Simpsons* will utilize language that makes apparent an awareness of the town's Christian roots. One of the more striking examples comes when Mr. Burns describes himself in Christian terms in order to explain his remarkable survival from a rockslide. In his own words, Mr. Burns "pulled a Jesus."[6] Mr. Burns's choice of words captures a more subtle but equally important component of Springfield's Christian heritage. The fact that Mr. Burns completely opposes Christianity makes the use of such lexical resources all the more telling. Even if he does not affirm the belief system, he recognizes the cultural relevancy of that belief system, at least historically speaking. He may not embrace Christianity on a spiritual level, but he can recognize the cultural value of Christian language. Mr. Burns invokes Jesus's name in order to declare his own remarkable power.[7] Thus, Christianity furnishes Mr. Burns with a comparative example to glorify his own decrepit nature, while at the same time violating the theological integrity of a key Christian belief.

Having discussed the communal attitude in Springfield toward Christianity, some brief remarks about the private faith lives of some of its residents will now prove helpful. Homer, arguably the show's central plot device, provides a clear example of several salient features that tend to define individual spirituality in Springfield. The first telling point about Homer is the sheer number of ways in which he diverts from Christianity's moral instructions. In his article "The Ten Commandments vs. The Simpsons,"[8] Jim Guida explores the ways in which the Simpson family, with Homer leading the way, routinely violates all of the Ten Commandments. A dream sequence in the episode "Homer vs. Lisa and the Eighth Commandment" drives this point home. Homer's dreams that he travels back to the Exodus story at the point when Moses receives the Ten Commandments on Mount Sinai.[9] When Moses goes up the mountain, mayhem breaks out and the Israelites neglect any sense of morality. Of course, The Simpsons characterizes one of the ringleaders as Homer, which reinforces the extent to which Homer rejects Christianity's moral guidelines.

Homer does not just violate the Ten Commandments, he does so in a way that exhibits another list in the Christian tradition: the seven deadly sins. At one point or another, Homer embodies all seven sins: sloth, greed, wrath, envy, lust, gluttony, and pride.[10] For brevity's sake, a brief discussion of the final two listed should provide clear enough evidence that Homer's life is steeped in sin. One need not look very far to find examples of Homer's gluttony. According to Diogenes Allen, gluttony reflects an inability to exercise control over one's appetites.[11] This conception does not deny the enjoyment that comes with eating; thus, one cannot label Homer sinful based solely on appetitive desires. Allen, however, makes clear that gluttony indicates excess: "Because the gratification of appetites is pleasurable, we have to make an effort to restrain them . . . . If we cannot control our appetites, it is unlikely that we can ever be strong enough to give up anything for the sake of another person or do something for the sake of another when it runs counter to one of our appetites."[12] Defined in these terms, gluttony may just be Homer's calling card. In "King-Size Homer," in fact, Homer purposefully embraces gluttony to gain enough weight to qualify for a medical disability. Homer clearly fails to moderate his appetite, even when Marge implores him to stop his plan to eat his way to disability. When Homer is about to cross the three-hundred-pound threshold, Maggie offers him a donut made out of Play-Doh. Bart is unsure about whether Homer can safely eat Maggie's offering, so he consults the packaging. His fears allayed, he then tells Homer, "Dad, it's nontoxic." The warning is a moot point; Homer is already licking his fingers clean by the time Bart assures him that the Play-Doh is safe to eat.[13]

While Homer is certainly a glutton, his tendency toward pride strongly resembles a traditional Christian notion of sin that reveals far more about Springfield's spiritual climate. Pride is often understood as the root of sin. Allen describes pride in terms of "self-understanding and self-evaluation."[14] That is, when Christians regard their successes as the results of their own actions, while at the same time blaming their failures on others, they skew their faith by denying their identities as created beings. The corollary result is that God's authority over their lives is dismissed. In "Simpsons Bible Stories," this tendency becomes readily apparent. Marge daydreams about the Garden of Eden story.[15] In her imagination, Homer plays the role of Adam and Marge plays the role of Eve. True to form, Homer/Adam clearly fails to moderate his appetite and manifests his self-interest immediately after he eats several apples from the Tree of Knowledge. Homer not only defies God, but he does so with excessive disregard both for God's prohibition and potential consequences. When God asks what happened, Homer/Adam says nothing while he kicks his eaten apple cores into a bush. He is responsible, but he does not claim responsibility for his acts. This dynamic underscores how pervasive Homer's pride can be. Just as he does during the course of a normal day, Homer/Adam projects his own interests in the garden at Marge/Eve's expense.[16]

Throughout The Simpsons, there is little doubt that Homer thinks rather highly of himself. A good example occurs in "Sleeping with the Enemy." When Lisa confides to Homer that she thinks she is fat, Homer explains that all Simpsons must deal with "the Simpson butt." Homer then offers some advice to Lisa that might help her disguise this genetic trait. He ties a sweatshirt around his waist to make himself look thin. In a bizarre sequence, the sweater's effect generates a self-attraction that causes Homer to pretend to hug and kiss himself. He looks so good that he now finds himself sexually attractive, a transition that very much characterizes the sin of pride. Of course, Homer is still quite fat, but he finds himself irresistible all the same, which points to the delusory nature of his pride. The effect is so strong that Homer then encourages himself to have a sandwich, which he promptly pulls out. Homer's pride meets Homer's gluttony, which, once mixed, manages to horrify Lisa, who usually remains on an even keel in the face of her dad's flaws.

Homer's pride is usually apparent in his actions, but it also manifests itself in a tendency that underscores how Christians in Springfield tend to glorify themselves at God's expense. In several instances, Homer is described in messianic terms, a characterization that dilutes God's power in order to accommodate Homer's false sense of importance. In "Kiss Kiss Bang Bangalore," Homer takes over as boss of Mr. Burns's new power plant in India. The new position is quite a promotion for Homer, whose authority over the new plant causes him to declare himself a god. This newfound divine authority, despite its self-appointment, demands an appropriate change of personal information, so Homer promptly orders new business cards. Though his cell phone number is the same, Homer announces that he has been promoted "to God." Homer not only abuses his workers' own belief system, he also glorifies himself in a way that echoes the pride that is so pervasive in sin.[17] By suggesting that, and then acting as if he really is God, Homer follows in Mr. Burns's footsteps. He devalues who God is and what God represents in order to indulge the self-driven notion that he is godlike. This strategy captures precisely the kind of self-deception that feeds pride, which is a sin that abounds in Springfield.

It is possible to dismiss Homer's excessive self-deification while in India as merely the product of a particular set of circumstances wherein Homer really does exert a unique influence. Even if this were to excuse the way in which he glorifies himself, it would not explain the instances in Springfield when Homer takes on a messianic role in other peoples' eyes. In "Homer the Great," Homer is, quite literally, the chosen one, though his eventual unpopularity suggests that his abilities may not ultimately satisfy the group's needs. Perhaps more tellingly, at the conclusion of "Thank God It's Doomsday," Homer has just returned from heaven after being the only person to escape God's judgment during the rapture. While in heaven, Homer is able to negotiate several favors with God, which not only save his family from God's judgment but also restore Moe's Tavern to its rightful state, a dank, dark bar. Homer thus communicates with God in a way that recalls a role Christianity traditionally ascribes to Jesus. In heaven, Jesus is supposed to be the one who intercedes with God on behalf of others. When Homer assumes this role, the show develops further the notion that in the context of *The Simpsons*, Homer is perceived as spiritually significant in the eyes of his peers. Moreover, he has no problem acting as though he really were entitled to special privileges. To emphasize the point, the episode concludes by depicting Homer at the center of his fellow barflies, his arms outstretched, in a clear allusion to Leonardo da Vinci's *The Last Supper*. In the context of the particular episode, the suggestion that Homer is a messiah among Springfield's residents seems apt. After all, Homer's plea convinces God to reverse the apocalypse. Episodes such as these suggest that in Springfield, a tendency to replace God, or at the very least to understand certain individuals as partially godlike, points toward a Christianity that bends itself to fit a social context.

The willingness to elevate oneself, or be elevated, to godlike status may seem incidental. Perhaps such moments on *The Simpsons* are little more than sight gags. However, in "The Joy of Sect," one finds a rational, intentional example of how Springfield's residents will compare themselves to God. With the excitement of the Movementarians sweeping through Springfield, Mr. Burns spies an opportunity to deify himself. He adorns himself with an artificial physique that casts himself as a Greek god. He then tells his workers that they "may now praise me as the Almighty." In so blatantly hiding his withered body, Mr. Burns reveals the extent to which he must artificially embrace the notion he wants to convey. Only when he literally hides who he really is can he claim to be divine. Moreover, the charade is painfully obvious from the beginning. Everyone knows that Mr. Burns lacks any qualities that could be associated with a Greek god, much less the Christian God. As though the real God wants the last laugh, Mr. Burns's costume catches fire immediately following his blasphemous proclamation. Thus his self-delusion, and his attempt to broadcast this delusion to his workers, comes undone in a way that amplifies the façade.[18] Mr. Burns's willingness to present himself as godlike is a conscious attempt to create in the minds of his workers an image which the workers easily recognize as false. Thus, God becomes a touchstone of self-aggrandizement rather than an object of sincere worship. Self-deification constitutes an extreme form of pride. That Homer, Mr. Burns, and others will conceptualize themselves as such captures the extent to which Springfield's residents can employ their faith to dismantle God in order to glorify themselves.

Though Homer and Mr. Burns embody these sinful tendencies, Marge seems to offer a counterweight to Homer's moral depravity. Many consider Marge to be the show's moral and spiritual anchor.[19] According to Gerald Erion and Joseph Zeccardi, "Marge stands as a remarkably stable touchstone of morality. To resolve her moral dilemmas, Marge simply allows reason to guide her conduct to a thoughtful and admirable balance between extremes."[20] For the most part, such praise is warranted. Especially when compared to Homer, Marge seems to offer a positive foil, both for her kids and for the town in general. When Lisa protests that Homer is stealing cable, Marge is the first one to sit with her daughter on the lawn in protest.[21] When Homer wants to skip church, Marge refuses to compromise her faith.[22] In fact, she asserts that faith in absolute terms: "Homer, please don't make me choose between my man and my God, because you just can't win." Whereas Homer will reject Christianity for the slightest inconvenience, Marge recognizes such ludicrous ideas for what they are. Even when Mr. Burns brings Lisa a check that would make the family multimillionaires, Marge refuses to encourage Lisa to accept the money, a tacit but clear endorsement of her morality.[23] Marge's ability to apply practical reason to moral questions, which Erion and Zeccardi rightly see as an embodiment of Aristotelian virtue,[24] best suits the intersection of faith and social reality in Springfield. She manages to make her Christianity relevant, both in her morals and in her commitment not to sacrifice her personal faith.

Though Marge is a committed Christian and perhaps Springfield's moral exemplar, she, too, reveals that even the strongest spiritual pillars in Springfield have cracks. When pressed enough, Marge will compromise certain values that call into question her resolute moral character. Marge is notoriously bored at home; her identity grows out of doing chores.[25] She can address the boredom by exploring small business ventures, or by volunteering, but neither tendency addresses a deeper issue for Marge: loneliness. Granted, she has Maggie, but her condition clearly leads her to set aside her otherwise strong moral beliefs. A clear example of how loneliness unravels Marge's morality occurs in "The Last of the Red Hat Mamas." In this episode, a local women's group offers Marge membership, but with conditions.[26] She must help the group break into Mr. Burns's mansion to steal some Fabergé eggs. At first, Marge resists. She explains that even though Mr. Burns may be selfish, that does not justify breaking into his house. Despite her moral stand, Marge soon casts her moral objections aside. She is willing to "do what is wrong" to join the group, which hardly constitutes an embodiment of Christian morality in the face of temptation.

Prayer offers another example of how Christian faith in Springfield exhibits a quality that suggests a self-serving interpretation of what it means to be a person of faith. Many of the show's main characters pray at some point, and a pattern emerges, which with few exceptions reveals a specific expectation of how God will answer such prayers. Take, for example, Ned Flanders, who prays consistently. Despite his outward devotion, many of Ned's prayers suggest that God is a kind of servant for Ned's needs. While filming a scene from *Exodus* for the Springfield Film Festival, Ned places his son Todd in a basket to recreate the moment when Moses's mother did likewise.[27] A rushing current threatens to send the basket downriver, with Todd in it, so Ned prays, "Flanders to God, Flanders to God, get off your cloud and save my Todd!" God responds immediately: lightning strikes a tree, which causes a branch to fall and block the river. The basket carrying Todd stops and all is well. Ned appreciates the help: "Thanks, God." Though contrived, the example suggests that prayer, when appropriately presented, has efficacy.

More important, when Ned prays, he seems to have God's immediate attention. Ned does not ask for something trite; he sincerely wants God to save his son. Given these circumstances, one could argue that God does answer prayers on occasion, so long as the prayers are sincere.[28] This kind of interaction happens again at the bowling alley when Ned's team, the Holy Rollers, plays Homer's team, the Pin Pals.[29] True to form, Homer begins to taunt Ned when the two neighbors compete.[30] Homer's bravado seems to distract Ned in one particular frame, as Ned uncharacteristically leaves one of the pins standing. Homer mocks Ned: "God-boy couldn't get a strike!" In response, Ned simply turns his eyes to the sky and asks God to help: "It's me, Ned." The prayer works, the pin falls, and one is left with the impression that God really does do whatever Ned wants. This second example complicates the role prayer plays, as Ned does not ask God for help with something that relates to Ned's faith. Other than the demographics of Ned's team, which includes his wife and the Love-joys, his prayer occurs in a wholly secular context in a spiritually inconsequential situation. The result is something akin to praying for victory in the lottery. To suggest that God will help Ned during a bowling game characterizes prayer in a way that belittles God. If God truly cares about knocking down Ned's bowling pins, one would have a difficult time explaining why God does not seem to care about other, more serious problems in Springfield.

Ned's prayer in the bowling alley exhibits two distinct qualities. First, Ned does not pray in a way that genuinely reflects the concerns of his faith. The most famous prayer in Christianity, the Our Father, focuses on God's authority over humanity and thus demands a measure of humility in the one who prays it. Ned's request for a little extra help in the bowling alley does not resonate with this approach. Even the argument that Ned is humble and thus God responds does not work, as Ned's prayer seems to be a move of one-upmanship in response to Homer's taunts. Moreover, Ned's prayer is entirely self-serving and thus does nothing to acknowledge God's qualities. Ned does not approach God in thanksgiving or humbly. Rather, he prays with a clear expectation that his requests will be met.

If Ned Flanders does not pray sincerely, one should have little hope that the Simpson family will do any better. Still, Homer prays quite frequently. The content of his prayers, however, is even more self-serving than that of Ned's. *The Simpsons* links these two extremes of Christian faith in the episode "Pray Anything." In the opening scene, Ned prays for guidance during a contest to make a half-court basketball shot. Once again, God seems to answer Ned's request, as Ned sinks the unbelievable shot. Consequently, he receives a handsome check as his prize, which he promptly donates. Throughout the entire vignette, Homer is beside himself, but he soon realizes how he can learn from Ned's example. Homer soon convinces himself that prayer can provide for his every desire. He starts to pray regularly but only for things that indulge his appetitive desires. Perhaps the best example comes when Homer is driving down the road and he feels a bit hungry. He prays that God will generate a new kind of snack. What happens next seems to confirm for Homer that God answers such prayers at a moment's notice. A truck carrying fudge crashes into a truck carrying bacon. The two mix and, without having to slow down, Homer can pick the new snack, fudge-covered bacon, off his windshield. The answered prayer is purely coincidence, but in Homer's mind it is proof that God obliges all requests. Moreover, God does so in a way that appeases even the most uncommitted Christian. In another prayer from this episode, Homer says "chop-chop" to conclude his request, an epilogue that gets to the heart of how Springfield's Christians tend to understand prayer. In scenes such as these, God is treated as a kind of metaphysical butler who will take care of every need. In one sense, this approaches the truth, as Christianity does understand God to be a source of provision. However, what kind of help people understand themselves to need offers another manifestation of the secularized, sinful concerns that seem to define the general attitude toward prayer in Springfield.

Even Marge is not above this kind of prayer. In "Homer Defined," she finds herself in need of divine help. The crisis seems real enough; a nuclear meltdown is about to destroy Springfield. Despite the threat she faces, Marge finds herself at a loss for words when she tries to convey to God how sincere she is in asking for help. "Dear Lord, if you spare this town from becoming a smoking hole in the ground, I'll try to be a better Christian. I don't know what I can do. Hmmm. Oh. The next time there's a canned food drive, I'll give the poor something they'd actually like, instead of old lima beans and pumpkin mix." Though Marge requests something significant, one can question her sincerity. What she offers in exchange for God's help reveals a desire to invest as little as possible to get what she needs. The value of the canned foods she offers to donate pales in comparison to what she wants. Additionally, Marge reveals that she is already out for the least intrusive moral position with respect to her bargaining chip. Her willingness to skimp on charity betrays that she takes care of her own needs first, which points back to her motivation for praying in the first place. For Marge, then, prayer is not necessarily a sincere attempt to commune with God. Rather, like so many others, she offers prayer when doing so will be personally beneficial.[31]

The disconnect between the Christian notion that God can help with life's struggles and the way in which characters on *The Simpsons* ask for such help comes sharply into focus when one considers another consistent quality of Christian faith in Springfield. Nearly everyone in Springfield seems to believe in a kind of afterlife, and they frame their understanding in terms that resonate with traditional Christian ideas about heaven. For example, in "Thank God It's Doomsday" most of Springfield's residents show a willingness to turn toward a spiritual leader. The problem, of course, is that they perceive Homer to be the best person for the job. They mistakenly think Homer can provide the answers they seek, but at the very least they exhibit a corporate desire for leadership. While these same people rarely, if ever, nurture that same desire for spirituality in their day-to-day lives, they remain capable of remembering that Christianity can be relevant.

In "Bart's Comet," this ability emerges more forcefully. As a comet threatens to destroy the town, Ned and his family retreat to the bunker they long ago stocked just in case such a situation arose. Word gets around that Ned has the bunker, and before too long, everyone has crowded into the shelter. Unluckily, there is not quite enough room; one more person has to leave in order to close the door. Ironically, Ned is deemed to be the only person the town can sacrifice, so he bravely accepts the town's decision to eject him from his own bunker. While the crowd attempts to pass the time, a kind of spiritual awakening occurs. The entire group gradually realizes that they ought to wait with Ned for the comet to strike Springfield. Ned's personal faith shines in this moment; he seems to be at peace with the apparently inevitable destruction he faces. Importantly, the rest of the town likewise feels confident enough in Ned's example to join him. They may not all connect the dots with a specific spiritual interpretation of the event, but they do recognize in Ned something that they lack. Given his obvious faith, one can venture to guess that those who eventually leave the bunker to be with Ned connect his bravery with his Christianity. These moments on *The Simpsons*, though fleeting, repel criticism that the town rejects all legitimate spirituality. Flawed though its institutions and leadership may be, Christianity can, and every now and then does, enrich the lives of Springfield's residents.

Broadly speaking, one can thus characterize Springfield's collective commitment to Christianity as lukewarm. At the same time, individuals act in such a way that recalls the town's Christian heritage. Springfield's Christians go to church, even if a firm underlying faith is rare. They may hitch their spirituality to the most immediate source of inspiration they can find or, more appropriately, the one that will pay out quickly, but at the very least they are willing to embrace, however momentarily, the notion that Christianity can generate a positive effect in their lives. Though one can characterize Springfield's Christian identity and subsequent culture as lacking sincerity, one can never dismiss it entirely as irrelevant. This tension provides the foundation upon which *The Simpsons* constructs its critique of how American culture understands and embraces its Christian heritage and current faith. The subsequent chapters will now explore specific spiritual, theological, and cultural elements of Christianity's presence in Springfield that define the town as reflecting accurately how Christianity functions in contemporary American society.

Chapter Three

A True Class Act: God in *The Simpsons*

"Part of this D-minus belongs to God."
—Bart Simpson[1]

"But if God so clothes the grass of the field, which is alive today and tomorrow is thrown into the oven, how much more will he clothe you—you of little faith!"
—Luke 12:28

"Dear Lord, as I think of you, dressed in white, with your splendid beard, I am reminded of Colonel Sanders, who is now seated at your right hand, shoveling popcorn chicken into thy mouth. Lord, could you come up with a delicious new taste treat like he did? I command you!"[2]

While driving down the road, Homer practices his newfound strategy for solving his problems through prayer. This particular attempt reveals a multilayered portrait that characterizes how residents in Springfield conceptualize God. Homer pictures God in stereotypical terms: an old man with a long white beard. This image understands God in terms that are similar to the appearance of other Springfield residents. God is distinctly human and though God may be somehow different insofar as God is divine, what matters to Christians on a day-to-day basis with respect to God is how this deity can resonate with their own experiences. Since Homer likes fast food, it makes sense that he would imagine God as a deity who likes the same thing. Perhaps more important, the right-hand seat, which Jesus traditionally occupies, now belongs to Colonel Sanders.[3] God does not listen to intercession from this seat of honor; God eats popcorn chicken. In this substitution, Homer pictures God not as the creating and redeeming deity that lies at the heart of Christian theology. Rather, God exists in terms that reflect Homer's immediate concerns. Homer does not pray to the Christian God; Homer prayers to a deity who understands what it means to be hungry.

When one digs more deeply into Homer's prayer, one finds several significant points that characterize how many Americans understand God in their cultural context. God thus comes to reflect cultural values rather than embody traditional notions of who God is. In the above example, Homer reifies his own appetitive desires into a divine portrait in order to justify such desires. The critical point here is that Homer fails to recognize the theologically inconsistent image he offers. More importantly, the way in which Homer negotiates with God captures one of the defining characteristics in many a Christian conception of God. First, Homer thinks of God only at a moment when so doing will help resolve an immediate need. If Homer were not hungry in a place where food is not readily accessible, then Homer would in all likelihood not think about God. Such a "functional"[4] account of who God is for the average Christian reveals a lack of a serious commitment to his or her faith. Christianity suggests a lifelong and life-affecting belief system. For Homer, God matters only when Homer can call in a favor. That is, God is a divine convenience, not a living deity who interacts with a faith tradition and redeems people from their fallen nature. Moreover, the creative power that Homer invokes refers back to a key Christian belief, but in a way that sacrifices the belief's theological integrity in order to adapt God to his particular needs. Homer recognizes, or rather remembers vaguely, that God has creative powers. Christianity holds that God created the world out of nothing and it is this ability that Homer wants God to exercise. Homer's ability to phrase his request in terms that recall such an ability speak to his participation in the Christian tradition as well as his ignorance of what the tradition really means. Thus, Homer lifts out from his faith tradition God's creative power, but he does so in a way that dilutes the theological significance of God's creative act. Homer then concludes his prayer in a manner that underscores the way in which he subordinates God to specifically human actions and abilities. By commanding God to create a new snack, Homer attempts to control that creative power and in so doing inverts the traditional paradigm of God as creator and humanity as created. Whereas humans should be understood as the product of God's creative act and thus subordinate to God's power, Homer understands himself in terms that deny what Christianity otherwise asserts.

The notion that God will respond to human commands provides the basis for how many Christians conceptualize an understanding of God. Importantly, this dynamic does not reject God's existence. Homer conceptualizes God in a theologically flawed manner, but he does not doubt at any point that God actually exists. It is this point that *The Simpsons* focuses on most strongly when exploring how American Christianity understands and responds to its notion of God. The show takes as a given God's existence and, moreover, tends to characterize God in positive terms.[5] What matters, then, is the way in which characters on *The Simpsons* articulate their beliefs about the Christian God. How the show portrays God is not the primary concern of this chapter. Rather, how residents of Springfield incorporate that portrayal into their lives will be the focus of this exploration of God's role on *The Simpsons*. The ways in which different characters pray to, respond to, and talk about God reveal not only a clear recognition that God exists, but also a confused notion of how that existence affects their lives. In these moments, the show suggests that much is at stake in how Christians fail to realize the theological implications of believing in the Christian God. Consequently, such conceptions reveal much about many Christians' laissez-faire spiritual commitments in contemporary American culture.

At the outset, a few basic points about how Christian theology traditionally understands God will prove helpful to understanding more fully how *The Simpsons* portrays God. In broad terms, the Christian conception of God embodies the three Os: omnipotence, omnipresence, and omniscience. The first, omnipotence, is the quality most commonly presented in *The Simpsons*. Omnipotence claims that God is all-powerful and thus God can act however God wants to act. In Christian theology, this quality emerges strongly in the doctrine of creation, which asserts that God created the world ex nihilo, or out of nothing. Moreover, God's omnipotence allows God to enable actions that would otherwise be impossible. Perhaps the strongest example in Christian theology comes with Christianity's central faith claim: Jesus rose from the dead. Because God is all-powerful, God can override physical laws to which all humans are subject, such as death's finality. The obvious question of how God can do this points to a fundamental part of Christian doctrine. According to Daniel Migliore, "Christian theology begins, continues, and ends with the inexhaustible mystery of God. . . . The central task of Christian theology, therefore, is to clarify the understanding of God that is proper to the Christian faith."[6] The search to "clarify" who God is and what God does underscores much of Christian thought. Moreover, God's mystery indicates that part of God remains hidden from humans. Thus, one must continually question whether one understands God in a way that is consistent with what one does know about God. For Migliore, this search "is not self-consciousness by awareness of the reality of God."[7] That is,

God's role in the Christian faith is not human-centered; human experience does not define who God is. Rather, Christians must seek to clarify who God is within the context of their own individual experiences. While this paradigm risks making God wholly relative to a particular situation, the litmus test always remains whether a particular interpretation squares with what God has revealed to humans. A personal journey to understand God's mystery thus requires an important interpretive element in how Christians understand their faith commitments.

The notion of God as embodying mystery thus constitutes a foundational point in exploring how *The Simpsons* portrays God, both literally and symbolically. When God appears on the show, the writers never reveal God's face, which upholds a biblical precedent that God does not reveal God's face.[8] Inherent in the notion of mystery is a distinct limit on the ability of human knowledge, experience, and language to understand and articulate perceptions and attitudes about God. In Springfield, these limits are very much in place, as viewers are not permitted to see a complete portrait of God. Consequently, an element of uncertainly marks how Springfield's Christians understand God. In the following exchange, one can see how this mystery affects Homer:

Marge: Homer, you don't have to pray out loud.

Homer: But he's way the hell up there![9]

Homer's irreverence is laughable yet understandable. Given his limited scope of knowledge about God, he analogizes as best as he can. To Homer, God is a being who lives in heaven, a distant place in the clouds, so naturally he should pray loudly enough for God to hear. The theological significance of this moment passes quickly, but it announces two important characteristics that frame Homer's ability to relate to God. First, his language characterizes God in terms that emerge out of Homer's own experiences. Second, when Homer addresses God, he does so based on the image of God that his cultural experiences have generated. Thus, Homer's image of God demands that Homer yell in order to pray appropriately, because volume is the only reasonable solution to the communicative challenge that Homer's conception of God creates.

By praying loudly, Homer reveals two important characteristics that Christians often exhibit in their personal understanding of God. First, Homer conveys an interpretive problem that many must struggle with: God so often seems to be physically distant. Doctrinally, God is always present, but in actual life experiences this theological assertion is not always tangible, as individuals can easily understand God as being absent in a particular moment. In "And Maggie Makes Three," Homer reveals just how easy it is to mistake whether or not God is present when one's own expectations define how one understands God. Having paid off his debts, Homer quits his job at the power plant in order to work at the Bowl-A-Rama. In Homer's mind, everything is perfect. However, he doesn't yet know that Marge is pregnant with Maggie, which means Homer will need to get his job at the power plant back. When Marge tries to tell Homer what is going on, a revealing conversation occurs:

Marge: Homey, I . . .

Homer: Can't talk, praying. Dear Lord, the gods have been good to me and I am thankful. For the first time in my life, everything is absolutely perfect just the way it is.

Marge: Mmm.

Homer: So here's the deal: You freeze everything as it is, and I won't ask for anything more. If that is OK, please give me absolutely no sign.

[Homer pauses. He perceives no sign.]

Homer: OK, deal. In gratitude, I present you this offering of cookies and milk. If you want me to eat them for you, please give me no sign.

[Again, Homer pauses and perceives nothing.]

Homer: Thy will be done.

[Homer begins to eat the cookies.]

Homer insulates himself from what is going on around him. He prays with a certain set of expectations about whether or not God is present. On the one hand, Homer believes that God is listening to his prayer, but his understanding of God's presence is limited insofar as he does not acknowledge what could very clearly be considered a sign of God's presence. Homer assumes that because God provides no obvious sign, which is to say a sign that affirms what Homer wants God to affirm, his prayer has been answered. His self-defined perfect existence requires that God not intercede, which acts as a foil to God's seemingly obvious presence in the fact that Marge is pregnant. Of course, Marge constitutes the sign that Homer prays for, but he does not perceive this because he presupposes that God is not actually going to interrupt his perfectly comfortable life. Homer provides a tangible point of reference that indicates the problem with making assumptions about God when God's mystery may or may not affirm what one hopes will be the case. Based on a limited set of expectations concerning God's character, Homer feels safely distant from the possibility that God will immediately interrupt the perfect existence he has carved out for himself. At the same time, *The Simpsons* makes clear that Homer's naïve expectations actually lead him to miss an obvious reality: the very thing he values so much has been turned upside down.

God's mystery tends to cause confusion among Springfield's residents, but the basis for such mix-ups still reflects a general awareness of God's identity. For example, in "Dead Putting Society," Homer and Ned Flanders bet on whose son will win the local putt-putt competition. Just before the final round, Homer sees the Flanders family praying. Homer calls out, "Hey, Flanders, it's no use praying. I already did the same thing and we can't both win." Though Homer is mocking Ned, his taunt is logically consistent. God could not answer a prayer for victory from both Homer and the Flanders family. By definition, there can be only one winner. Thus, Homer is correct to assert that because he already prayed for victory, God cannot help if Flanders is praying for the same thing. The problem, of course, lies in the parameters that Homer establishes. He bases his prayer and his subsequent taunt on God's relevancy to his particular desire to win the bet. Such a shortsighted viewpoint ignores the larger theological picture. Belief in God has nothing to do with the particular circumstances of the local putt-putt game. To suggest that God would involve God's self in such things reveals a limited understanding of God. The Flanders family represents this side of the question and thus offers the foil to expose the limits of Homer's theological awareness. Ned tells Homer that he was praying so "no one gets hurt." Homer would do well to realize that belief in the Christian God transcends such petty concerns. As Ned makes clear in his own prayer, inherent in God's identity is concern for all people, not just the first person to ask for special treatment in a given situation.

Another example will help to clarify how characters on *The Simpsons* develop their understanding of God in a distinctly limited capacity. In so doing, they fail to understand fully an appropriate Christian understanding of God. In "Homer's Triple Bypass," one hears the Sunday school teacher conclude that God "causes train wrecks." On the one hand, the teacher's comments recognize that God has the power to interact with the world and cause calamity. Given biblical precedent, such as when God floods the earth,[10] the conclusion is to some degree understandable. Homer echoes this understanding of God's destructive power in "Dude, Where's My Ranch?" While vacationing at the Lazy I Ranch, Homer destroys a beaver dam in order to give the land back to the Native Americans who have been displaced by the ranch. As he watches the water sweep the beavers' home away, Homer comments that he now knows "how God feels." By alluding to the biblical story of the flood, Homer makes clear that he is aware of God's destructive power as told in the Bible. Thus, he reiterates the awareness within Springfield's Christian community that God has shown a willingness to mete out devastating actions in the world. In both cases, invoking God's destructive power in a way that requires God to script singular instances does not fit with the broader Christian conception of God's character. To suggest that God brings about suffering, death, or destruction creates a challenge that is not easily met. One would have to postulate some "higher purpose" to God's actions for intentionally causing a train to crash. Such arguments are flimsy at best and reveal the limits of human reason when trying to understand God. When one claims to understands God's agency, especially when the results of that agency produce disastrous outcomes, one is running against the grain of God's relationship to humanity. To claim that human knowledge can access God's motivations, or to suggest that humans can act with similar authority in their world, is either to grant more power to human knowledge than actually exists or to debase God's power. Both the Sunday school teacher and Homer understand loosely the extent of God's dominion, but they endorse this theologically flimsy point in a way that reveals their limited understanding of who, exactly, their Christian tradition understands God to be.

In their book *Metaphors We Live By*, George Lakoff and Mark Johnson provide a framework that can delineate clearly what is at stake in Homer's prayer for a new snack, as well as the general confusion about God that other characters on *The Simpsons* express. As an extended analogy for American culture, the show invites an analysis based on metaphor. Given the above components in traditional Christian theology concerning the doctrine of God, metaphors offer a handle for clarifying how *The Simpsons* characterizes American society. When faced with a complex topic, oftentimes a good strategy to begin discussion is to explain an unfamiliar idea in terms of familiar things. According to Lakoff and Johnson, this communicative strategy is so ingrained that, more often than not, people are not aware that they use metaphors to communicate.[11] For example, to picture God as an old man with a white beard is to understand God in a specific way that people (in this case, those who view the show) can understand from their own experiences. The image of God as an old, bearded man connotes qualities in the person of God such as wisdom and authority. God in the abstract may not be easily understandable, but most people can identify the metaphor of an old man as having specific qualities, which in turn helps to clarify who God is as God interacts with humans.

By presenting God consistently through the metaphor of an old man with a white beard, *The Simpsons* structures the notion of God in a particular way. The metaphor produces a notable effect: it prescribes a specific range of possible responses to the metaphor. As Lakoff and Johnson state, "[W]e conceive of [things in a particular way]—and we act according to the way we conceive of things."[12] The metaphor used to clarify an idea subsequently and necessarily directs how people respond to the possible meanings contained in the metaphor. Thus, when Homer understands God as an old, bearded white man, much like Colonel Sanders, the metaphor inevitably produces a certain range of conceptual possibilities with respect to God's character. One should not be surprised, then, that Homer makes the jump to picturing God as eating lots of popcorn chicken. Likewise, if Homer uses a metaphor of God as physically distant to frame his prayers, then he will inevitably pray loudly to overcome the implications of the metaphor he uses.

These systemic qualities in metaphors help to clarify how people understand God and consequently suggest certain qualities about God. Language must be logically or contextually consistent to enable communication between the speaker and the listener.[13] Systemically, the metaphor of God as an old man conveys the notion of God as a fatherly figure.[14] In Homer's experience, a caring father is noticeably absent, so he naturally desires a fatherly influence who will, first and foremost, offer emotional support.[15] Consequently, he seeks in his metaphors to understand God in a way that counteracts this shortcoming in his own father.[16] In "Homer the Heretic," one finds an especially revealing example of how the metaphor of God as a supportive father figure produces certain reactions that, at first, may be puzzling; however, when clarified through Lakoff and Johnson's emphasis on systemicity, these reactions make perfect sense. During his dream, Homer converses with God about why he has stopped going to church:

God: Thou hast forsaken my church!

Homer: Uh, kind—of . . . . b-but . . .

God: But what!

Homer: I'm not a bad guy! I work hard, and I love my kids. So why should I spend half my Sunday hearing about how I'm going to hell?

God: [after pausing for a moment]: Hmm. You've got a point there. You know, sometimes even I'd rather be watching football. Does St. Louis still have a team?

Homer: No, they moved to Phoenix.

God: Oh. Right.

God's interest in football presents an interesting point for discussion. Some might argue that in talking to Homer about football, God somehow comes across as less powerful. After all, if God knows everything, then surely God would know that St. Louis's football team moved. It is important to remember, however, that God appears in the dream as a product of Homer's imagination. God's reflects the qualities that Homer desires and thus provides the basis for his conception of the divine. That is, Homer pictures God in a way that produces several salient points for consideration. First, Homer desires a God who is sympathetic to the challenges of everyday life. Homer does not blame God for his having to raise a family, go to work, and the like. Rather, Homer presents what he feels to be an obvious complaint. If he does his best to live a good life, why should church provide a source of negative reinforcement? God's response does not suggest God loses an argument in conceding Homer's point. Rather, God says what Homer wants to hear. By using a metaphor that conveys God as having sympathy, Homer can anticipate and ultimately receive the response that his own experience demands. Second, by talking about football God provides Homer with some spiritual reassurance. In response to the frustration captured in the previous point, Homer seeks comfort from God in a way that allows Homer to forget his weekly frustrations. For Homer, God should offer comfort, which, on Homer's terms, requires an interest in football.

A metaphor's systemic consistency allows people to understand better an abstract topic such as God by focusing on particular aspects of the idea.[17] Inherent in the notion of the metaphor is that one does not describe something completely in terms of another. Sallie McFague recognizes in this limitation a fundamental tension in conceptualizing God: "[One] feel[s] conviction at the level of experience, at the level of worship, but great uncertainty at the level of words adequate to express the reality of God."[18] The "partial"[19] structure that a metaphor brings to a concept allows flexibility in adjusting the meaning one wishes to convey. Based on the initial structure, one can then adapt the metaphor to emphasize a particular point.[20] For example, in "Thank God It's Doomsday," Homer ascends to heaven and finds himself in a place that very much resembles a five-star resort. A host angel greets him and shows him around. He has a flat-screen television that provides ready information about heaven. He can even wish for whatever he wants and that thing will happen immediately.[21] Most important, when Homer has a complaint, he visits God, who acts as the resort's general manager. By using this metaphor, *The Simpsons* fulfills Homer's expectation that God will listen to Homer's feedback about heaven in order to enact any changes that would make the stay more comfortable.

The metaphor of God as a resort manager thus resonates with the broader metaphor for God on *The Simpsons*. Once again, God is the old man, which includes the wisdom and service-minded attitude that one would need to run the most inclusive resort around. The basic metaphor of God as an old man thus allows the show to "extend"[22] the metaphor to a different situation. Continuity between episodes exists in the initial metaphor and, based on this metaphorical structure, the particular need in "Thank God It's Doomsday" that God be appropriately present and involved in managing heaven as a resort follows naturally. Consequently, what God provides to Homer in heaven helps to explain not only who Christians often understand God to be in general, but also what the popular imagination anticipates God to provide in the afterlife.

The notion of God as heaven's general manager builds upon a primary structuring metaphor, but the metaphor's accuracy in the context of *The Simpsons* relies on the show's other moments when this metaphor for God emerges. That is, the image of God as an old man, or as heaven's general manager, requires a specific context in which the metaphor has communicative value. Christianity traditionally has characterized God in terms that appear in *The Simpsons*. American Christianity often utilizes the image of God as an old man because structuring metaphors ultimately grow out of "our physical and cultural experience."[23] *The Simpsons* can safely represent God as an old man, or a resort manager, because American culture is both patriarchal and capitalist. Despite recent diversity in America's corporate, political, and religious leaders, by and large older men occupy the country's highest leadership roles. Thus, the metaphor of God as an old man reflects a cultural bias toward patriarchal leadership in American social institutions.[24] Moreover, as members of a consumer society, Americans very much relate to the idea that God should act in a way that reflects their consumptive lifestyle. God should run a resort that has nice televisions, gracious hosts, and afford one the freedom to imagine whatever would make one's stay more comfortable. Importantly, this same general manager is available to speak to any guest, which ensures that a Christian's needs are met with precise service. Overall, the God that Homer encounters in "Thank God It's Doomsday" represents general cultural attitudes about God. Americans want their deity to serve them. This captures a significant expectation that God must accommodate individual desires, a relational dynamic that grows out of the consumptive values that define so much of American culture.

Metaphors, then, help to clarify concepts that might otherwise be too vague. Moreover, people will use their personal experiences and expectations to provide the basis for metaphors for God. Though the cultural values that are embedded in a particular culture's metaphors are representative (just as metaphors themselves are representative), Lakoff and Johnson make clear that the cultural values contained in a metaphor must be consistent with that culture's beliefs. The metaphor does not generate meaning; rather, it reflects specific attitudes from particular experiences that give rise to the metaphor.[25] With respect to metaphors for God, *The Simpsons* proves to be instructive on this point. God comes across as an old man, which reflects certain cultural values. That God on *The Simpsons* is an old *white* man is also significant. Conceiving of God as such reflects another significant cultural value in American Christianity. American culture, especially its wealth and consequent consumerism, grows out of a racially oppressive history. Much of mainstream American culture requires slavery, expansion, and other acts that clearly benefited white Americans.[26] America's current economic prosperity, which drives its consumptive cultural practices, is built upon the foundation of wealth that slavery played a significant role in developing.

In Springfield, one can see a cultural makeup that very much reflects America's race issues. On *The Simpsons*, minorities are disproportionately represented. For example, Carl Carlson, Dr. Hibbert, and Lou the cop are the only consistently recurring characters who are black.[27] In "Milhouse of Sand and Fog," *The Simpsons* calls attention to Springfield's racial composition to critique the broadly endorsed cultural metaphor of God as an old white man. When Marge needs to find Dr. Hibbert on Sunday morning, he is not to be found in the First Church of Springfield, where he normally attends services. Rather, Dr. Hibbert and his family are at Springfield's black church. The Simpson family goes to find Dr. Hibbert and, when they arrive, they see a black congregation that is full of energy. The contrast between the black church and the typical church experience at the First Church of Springfield, which is to say worshipping at the stereotypical mainstream Protestant church, is striking. Bart sees the energy and exclaims, "Black God rules!" Whereas God usually exhibits a measured stoicism, and the First Church of Springfield usually lacks spiritual pop, Bart recognizes an immediate vibrancy that is a hall-mark of black churches in America.[28] Bart's words capture a hidden but very real element of cultural influence that determines a metaphor's value. American Christianity often ignores issues of race, even as it speaks in terms of the universal nature of Christian beliefs. Consequently, metaphors for God incorporate subtextual but very real racial attitudes in American culture.

Cornel West argues that identifying these underlying racial attitudes in American culture is a critical task in liberating blacks from the effects of America's racist past. West writes, "The uncritical acceptance of self-degrading ideals that call into question black intelligence, possibility, and beauty not only compounds black social misery but also paralyzes [the] black middle class."[29] The dull, disinterested Christianity found in Springfield's main church lacks the energy that defines the town's black church, yet the black church remains hidden in Springfield's social fabric in every episode except "Milhouse of Sand and Fog." Despite its spiritual vibrancy, the black church remains a part of American Christianity that mainstream denominations often ignore. This glossing over of a spiri-tually thriving and culturally relevant place of worship is complicit in broader social patterns that uphold racial distinctions in American cul-ture. In West's opinion, understanding the black church as invisible will harm an already difficult social experience for blacks. Moreover, rele-gating the black church to Springfield's fringes disallows the possibility that more people from the First Church of Springfield will recognize, as Bart, does, that the Black God thrives spiritually.[30] Thus, in presenting an alternative metaphor for God, The Simpsons adds another layer to the cultural coherence that generates such metaphors. A common main-stream Christian conception of God is not merely the picture of a caring old man. God must be an old white man so as to uphold the broad practice in mainstream Christianity of ignoring obvious hypocrisy and inconsis-tency in how that same culture often distances itself from its own racist past. In Springfield, the black church's pews are full, but the majority of those black residents never appear in Springfield's streets. The Simp-sons, then, points out that while the stereotypical Christian experience accepts God as given, the way in which those experiences unfold represent a prevalent and problematic quality in mainstream Christianity. Metaphors for God must be coherent, but as this point makes clear, American Christianity often produces coherence by ignoring a prob-lematic element of its own past.

As representative of American Christian beliefs, metaphors for God on The Simpsons underscore a broad pattern in how mainstream

Christianity understands God. The tendencies one sees on the show point toward a general cultural attitude that conflates God and broader social values. God's authority over humans disappears and people begin to understand themselves as coequal with God, or even more powerful than God. To return to the metaphor of God as general manager, one can see in Homer's ability to negotiate with God the notion that God exists to serve humans. Likewise, most prayers to God on *The Simpsons* reveal this kind of approach. Springfield's Christians often do not revere God. Rather, God in the cultural conscience exists less as a creating and redeeming authority and more as a benchmark to measure human achievement. For example, in "Hello Gutter, Hello Fadder," Homer understands himself to be on a par with God:

Lisa: Dad, what she's saying is, you've had your moment in the sun and now it's time for you to gracefully step aside.

Homer: Lisa, I know what's going on here. They did it to Jesus, and now they're doing it to me.

Marge: Are you comparing yourself to Our Lord?

Homer: Well, in bowling ability.

When the town tires of Homer's self-promotion after he bowls a perfect game, Homer needs to elicit sympathy. To do so, he casts himself in messianic terms in order to argue that Springfield's residents have marginalized him. In his mind, he has done nothing wrong because he, like Jesus,[31] can bowl a perfect game. The comparison is, of course, absurd, and Marge recognizes as much in the argument that Homer makes. Still, that Homer uses this strategy reveals his lack of appreciation for who God is. In this particular conversation, Homer ought to invoke Jesus in terms of needing Jesus's forgiveness for what he did. However, Homer uses Jesus to help explain to Marge that he was justified in skipping work to go bowling. Jesus, then, ceases to be a foundation for Homer's faith and becomes a measuring stick to establish what Homer needs.

The extent to which Christians will demean or ignore God's authority over their lives becomes apparent when Ned Flanders faces temptation. While dating Sarah Sloane, Ned cannot decide whether or not to have sex.[32] When facing temptation, he states, "I better ask the big guy." Given that Ned represents the Evangelical community, one would assume that "the big guy" refers to God. However, Ned turns to Homer and asks what he should do.[33] One would expect Ned to rely on his faith when he faces temptation, but he finds more relevant spiritual advice by ascribing to Homer a semi-divine identity. Homer thus comes across not as the antithesis to most of what God represents in Christian faith, but rather as a person who can provide something for Ned that God cannot offer. Homer's ability to provide answers in a secularized context points to the way in which Christians reject God's authority over their lives.

This tendency ought to alarm those who wish to uphold traditional Christian doctrine. The willingness and practice of understanding humans as equal to, or better than, God undercuts a fundamental part of Christian belief. That such a move happens so frequently on *The Simpsons* illuminates the extent to which a personal relationship with God, which traditionally plays a foundational role in personal and corporate belief, no longer permeates the daily life of many American Christians. Though Christianity traditionally understands God's creation of the world as necessarily claiming humans to be special beings, this privileged status too often pushes aside what the faith tradition stands for; in its place is a notion of God that serves to sanction secularized concerns. Such spiritual convenience is symptomatic of a sick faith. During the Reformation, the extent to which the Christian Church and its doctrines became co-opted for purposes other than worshipping God produced a renewed emphasis on correctly understanding humanity's relationship with God. *The Simpsons*, then, sounds an alarm by exposing the shortsightedness of these common conceptions of God.

On the one hand, the need to use metaphors to discuss God demands that humans turn to their own experiences to find resources to articulate who God is or what God means to human life. The risk, which exists throughout Christianity and becomes apparent on *The Simpsons*, comes when people's experiential resources produce metaphors that do not uphold the integrity of God's character as understood in the Christian tradition. Though *The Simpsons* critiques American Christianity for this diluted commitment to God, it is careful not to become complicit in this attitude. In "Mr. Plow," Homer buys a snowplow to make some extra money and business quickly booms. Seeing Homer's success, Barney buys a bigger, better plow and thus cuts into Homer's business. To remove competition, Homer calls Barney and pretends to be a customer who needs his snow plowed in a dangerous area. Barney takes the job and, sure enough, he becomes trapped when an avalanche buries his truck.

Homer eventually has a crisis of conscience and rushes out to save his friend. Having done so, Homer praises his newfound ethic and the invincibility that such human action exhibits. He exclaims, "When two best friends work together, not even God himself can stop them." Once again, Homer's own perception of reality overrides God's authority. Homer's comment captures the general attitude about God's authority in Springfield insofar as he understands his actions to be immune to God's interference. However, the show follows Homer's assertion in a way that reestablishes God's authority. In response to Homer's claim, God bellows from the clouds, "Oh, yeah?" A ray of sunshine breaks through the clouds and melts all the snow. God has the last word in a way that reminds Homer and the show's viewers that the Christian notion of God as creator always carries with it the possibility that God can reassert God's authority.[34] When all is said and done, God retains authority over Homer's life, which makes clear that anyone who claims otherwise is mistaken. Here and elsewhere throughout the show, God gets the last word. Springfield's residents may go through life thinking the opposite, or not thinking about the issue at all, but they never truly displace God's authority in their world.[35]

Chapter Four

Re-reading the Good Book: Biblical Representation and Authority in *The Simpsons*

"A real preacher knows how to bring the Bible alive, through music, and dancing, and Tae Bo!"
—Bart Simpson[1]

"In the beginning was the Word, and the Word was with God, and the Word was God."
—John 1:1

"This book doesn't have any answers!"[2]

So says Homer about the Bible when disaster threatens Springfield. At the end of *The Simpson's Movie*, when facing their doom, Homer and his family head to church in hopes that they might find some kind of encouragement. Such a spiritual crisis would seem to be precisely the kind of moment to which the Bible could speak. When all else fails, Christians should be able to turn to the Bible for answers.

Homer's frustration captures precisely the attitude that pervades much of the American Christian landscape with respect to the Bible. On the one hand, the Bible tells the "foundational"[3] story of a God who not only interacts with the world but also redeems that world from its fallen nature. The New Testament expresses the notion that the downtrodden have hope, God loves the world, and that through Jesus Christ's redemptive work, no one need remain outside the hope of eternal salvation. Such assurances ought to present hope to Homer in the face of death. That Homer looks to Christianity's scripture and finds nothing he deems to be valuable speaks to the way in which the Bible's relevance in contemporary American culture has fathered. The disconnect between what the Bible says and how Christians understand that message appears frequently throughout *The Simpsons*.

A new approach to the Bible constituted a landmark shift that emerged during and after the Protestant Reformation. Through the reformers' emphasis on reading the Bible in vernacular languages and the spread of the printing press, laypeople suddenly had access to Christianity's authoritative text. Previously, the Bible remained the effective property of the educated, which is to say those who could afford to learn Latin. The Bible's "liberating message"[4] was now available to anyone who could read. People no longer had to rely on priests to interpret a story that "was experienced not as an arbitrary or despotic authority but as a source of renewal, freedom, and joy."[5] The Reformation recalibrated the Bible as relating directly to Christians' lives, but this new emphasis did not dilute the Bible's authority as the foundation of Christian belief. The individual could now interpret the Bible vis-à-vis her or his own religious experience. In a world where religious authorities quite literally charged for access to biblical truth, the notion that everyone could and should interact with the Bible on his and her own terms liberated Christianity by grounding biblical authority in the everyday lives of Christians who otherwise had to depend on a priest to dispense their salvation.

A corollary quality in this new dynamic arose when a wider reading public encountered the Enlightenment's intellectual revolution.[6] If each person must be responsible for reading the Bible for him- or herself, a maze of possible interpretations presented an inevitable challenge to interpretive legitimacy. The infusion of lay interpretations diluted a sense that the Bible presented definitive statements on particular concerns. Lifting out passages from the Bible and using these passages to support an idea became an interpretive strategy that did not always treat the Bible with appropriate concern for its broad role in Christian theology or uphold the Bible's literary integrity. This strategy, which is colloquially known as proof-texting, risks using the Bible as a resource of convenience, not as a sacred text. Despite its role in Christianity, the Bible did not "have immunity from the wider cultural critique of authority."[7] Given the way in which *The Simpsons* critiques most notions of cultural authority, it is not surprising, then, that the Bible's role in Christianity, as well as in society, should receive critical attention on the show.

A basic synopsis of a Reformed understanding of the Bible will prove helpful in understanding how *The Simpsons* understands and thus characterizes Christianity's sacred text. Daniel Migliore summarizes succinctly what the Bible means to Christianity: "The Bible is a unique witness to the sovereign Grace of God at work in the history of Israel and above all in the life, death, and resurrection of Jesus."[8] With respect to this summary, the following distinction is important. The Bible is not in itself an object of worship in Christianity; the Bible tells the story of how God interacts and redeems the world through the person of Jesus. The Bible therefore is not the ultimate foundation for Christian beliefs. Rather, the Bible attests to a particular understanding of God as God reveals the story to a particular community. Thus, the Bible offers an affirming account of God's interaction with the world, and Christianity in particular recognizes that in the person of Jesus, God redeems the world. However, Migliore is clear that while the Bible reveals a foundational part of God's identity, it also does not make known God's entire being. Additionally, one should also remember that the Bible remains a dynamic literary document that can be interpreted in many different capacities. That is, the Bible remains a testament to Christian beliefs, but one should not forget that individuals and communities access that story within the framework of human language. Thus, one can understand the Bible as divinely inspired, but one should recognize that God did not and indeed could not have written the Bible in a literal sense.[9] God is revealed only partially; the Bible is not God's definitive biography. Rather, the Bible requires the individual and the community to recognize that claims about God and how that image relates to his, her, or their own experiences are interpretive exercises. Responsibility for interpreting the Bible faithfully falls into the hands of people who may or may uphold the Bible's integrity as a sacred text. Problematically, as soon as the burden to interpret the Bible becomes an individual's responsibility, the risk of misinterpretation or, worse, active manipulation, arises.

These particular problems summarize to a large extent the way in which *The Simpsons* understands the Bible. The show characterizes Christians in a way that problematizes the task of interpretation. Quite simply, many Christians are, to some extent, ignorant or self-serving when it comes to interpreting the Bible as an authoritative text in a particular cultural context. While most Christians recognize that the Bible plays an authoritative role in their religion, they also do not understand the salient points, both in a narrative and theological sense. For example, in "Marge Be Not Proud," Homer learns that Bart shoplifted a video game. To punish Bart, Homer appeals to what the family learns about the Bible at church in a way that captures the partial ignorance with which many Christians approach the Bible and reflects the consequences with respect to interpretation:

Homer: Haven't you learned anything from that guy who gives those sermons at church? Captain Whatshisname? We live in a society of laws. Why do you think I took you to all those Police Academy movies? For fun? Well, I didn't hear anybody laughing! Did you? Except at that guy who made sound effects. Where was I? Oh yeah, stay out of my booze.

Homer appeals to someone else's interpretation rather than his own for guidance. His general ignorance illustrates how Christian responsibility to read and interpret the Bible regresses. Rather than draw on his own understanding, Homer appeals to what Reverend Lovejoy has to say about the Bible. Homer recalls vaguely what the Bible should say about the situation, but his interpretation is ultimately twice removed from the actual text. Of course, the Bible is clear on the issue of stealing,[10] but Homer cannot recall any specific information. His memory about the Bible's stance on stealing is as hazy as Bart's. Thus, Homer turns to a different authority in hopes of offering some stern advice. Importantly, the next set of guidelines has nothing to do with Christianity. Homer, then, appeals to an inconsequential movie. He thus concludes with a point that illustrates how quickly the Bible becomes irrelevant with respect to contemporary American culture. Homer initially appeals to the Bible's moral authority because he remembers vaguely that he ought to do so, but he fails to connect any more dots with respect to the specific situation in which he finds himself. Even a basic awareness of what the Bible says about theft is absent, and Homer cannot make clear to Bart why stealing is problematic. The result is that Christianity's moral authority as conveyed in the Bible becomes irrelevant when it ought to be the primary influence in Homer's discipline.

Homer's vague knowledge about the Bible characterizes the general biblical ignorance that is pervasive throughout *The Simpsons*. As Migliore notes, "An appeal to the Bible . . . should not be considered an alternative to serious reflection."[11] Homer understands that the Bible provides Christianity with moral guidance, but his limited awareness betrays a lazy and thus ignorant response to the Bible as a relevant moral text. This kind of appeal to the Bible in order to provide an authoritative moral argument occurs frequently in *The Simpsons*. In "The Otto Show," Marge responds to Homer's desire to throw Otto out of the house with a seemingly appropriate verse from the Bible: "Doesn't the Bible say, 'Whatsoever you do to the least of my brothers, that you do unto me?'" On the surface, Marge understands the underlying message in the Bible, that as a Christian she is supposed to love those in need. However, she proves to be inconsistent on this point in "It's a Mad, Mad, Mad, Mad Marge." In this episode, Marge initially welcomes Becky, who is an attractive young woman, into her home. Becky endears herself to the family and genuinely helps Marge. However, Marge soon becomes jealous and accuses Becky of being out to ruin her family. Consequently, Marge wants to throw Becky out of the house. In this case, upholding the biblical imperative to provide for her neighbor trumps Marge's desire for personal comfort. Thus, she does an about-face and rejects the very things she endorses in "The Otto Show." Marge, then, echoes the notion that a faith-based moral responsibility is relevant only so long as it does not infringe on the ease of day-to-day living. The hypocrisy that Marge exhibits in these two episodes underscores the way in which Christians fail to appreciate the Bible's authority. Whereas the Bible's moral imperatives should be applied evenly and consistently, Marge only embraces the Bible's moral authority when doing so is not overly inconvenient.

In "The Otto Show," Homer responds to Marge in a way that betrays his own ignorance. Rather than embrace Marge's appeal to the Bible, Homer distorts the same moral authority for his own purposes. "Doesn't the Bible also say, 'Thou shalt not take moochers into thy hut?" Two salient features emerge in how Homer responds to Marge. First, he, too, appeals to the Bible to support his own position, but his citation does not actually exist. Rather, the authority that the Bible represents is what matters to Homer. He appeals to the Bible's cultural authority in order to provide a rebuttal to Marge's claim. Homer recognizes that Marge is appealing to a specific moral authority, so Homer must do likewise if he is going to win the argument. The text he cites may not actually exist, but Homer's appeal conveys that he knows enough about the Bible's cultural authority to mirror Marge's own invocation.

More tellingly, Homer does not seem to be aware that his response is inaccurate at best. As Gerry Bowler remarks, "Homer's Bible ignorance is pretty comprehensive."[12] Though Bowler is right to an extent, he understands Homer in simplistic terms that obscure the more problematic point in what Homer does know. Homer is aware that the Bible represents a moral authority that nothing else can trump. This general awareness of the Bible's role in Christianity reflects a quality often present in Christian discourse about moral issues. Homer invokes the Bible not to appeal sincerely to something he truly believes in; instead he realizes that the Bible constitutes an untoppable tactic in his argument with Marge. In this case, ignorance might be preferred, if only to break the cycle of massaging the notion of the Bible as a moral authority to be used in service of a particular interest. Too often, the goal in such situations runs against the Bible's moral grain. An uninformed awareness reveals the extent to which Homer and indeed most of Springfield's Christians understand their sacred text only as something to call upon when convenient. Thus, the Bible becomes a way to enforce one's own beliefs in a particular situation rather than providing sincere moral guidelines.

Even Reverend Lovejoy, who ought to cite the Bible with due humility and reverence, acts in a similarly problematic way. In "Homer the Heretic," Marge invites Reverend Lovejoy to dinner in hopes that he will help convince Homer to return to church. In the ensuing dialogue, Reverend Lovejoy appeals to the Bible in order to convince Homer that he ought to reconsider his decision to reject Christianity. "Homer, I'd like you to remember Matthew 7:26: 'A foolish man who built his house on sand.'" He offers sincere advice from the Bible that addresses the situation on the situation's own terms. With respect to Homer's lapsed faith, the verse that Reverend Lovejoy offers seems relevant. Homer's decision is foolish and he is risking severe spiritual consequences. Reverend Lovejoy's advice, then, at first glance suggests that he appeals sincerely to biblical authority.[13]

Were this exchange symptomatic of how Reverend Lovejoy generally refers to the Bible, one could find some hope for the idea of biblical authority in Springfield. Reverend Lovejoy turns to the Bible for support that speaks directly to Homer's situation. Despite his apparent good intentions, however, Reverend Lovejoy also tends to exhibit similarly problematic appeals to the Bible's authority in society. As Springfield prepares for Whacking Day,[14] Lisa implores Reverend Lovejoy to speak out against killing snakes. Reverend Lovejoy turns to the Bible to answer her question. "And the Lord said, 'Whack ye all the serpents which crawl on their bellies and thy town will be a beacon unto others.' So you see Lisa, even God himself endorses Whacking Day." When Lisa asks to see the Bible to verify Reverend Lovejoy's citation, he refuses to show her. Yet again, the Bible provides a way to justify actions that one would otherwise not do. The Bible does not sanction killing snakes for sport. Because he has exhibited appropriate knowledge of the Bible elsewhere, one cannot dismiss Reverend Lovejoy's proclamation against snakes as a naïve appeal to biblical authority. Rather, Reverend Lovejoy trusts in Springfield's general ignorance about the Bible to endorse an otherwise questionable activity. Even worse, Reverend Lovejoy justifies killing snakes by echoing Homer's problematic appeals. Reverend Lovejoy simply makes up a verse, a tactic that relies on the moral currency that the Bible has in American culture.

Unfortunately for Reverend Lovejoy, Lisa is more familiar than most with what the Bible says, so she seeks to verify the accuracy of his claim. Exposed, he reverts to a strategy that recalls troubled times in Christian leadership. In the face of skepticism about his interpretation, Reverend Lovejoy treats the Bible as a privilege; as an ecclesial authority, only he should have the freedom to look at the actual passage. It is significant that Reverend Lovejoy couches this strategy by providing Springfield with a townwide imperative to whack snakes. By doing so, the town can be an example to others of a Christian society.[15] Reverend Lovejoy distorts the Bible's content to endorse an action that the town needs to be endorsed, and in doing so he frames his misrepresentation in terms that aggravate the abuse of moral authority that the Bible represents. The image of the city on a hill appears often in American history as an imperative to exhibit Christian morality as a nation.[16] By whacking snakes Springfield is not fulfilling its Christian duty in more than one way. The true problem is that only Lisa recognizes what is at stake when Reverend Lovejoy claims that the Bible endorses Whacking Day. Only Lisa realizes clearly that Reverend Lovejoy's appeal to biblical authority is problematic because its leads to a communal endorsement of a barbaric practice.[17] Given America's problematic past endorsements based on biblical precedent, the response seeks to raise suspicion. As soon as an ecclesial leader claims exclusive knowledge of the Bible, ironically enough immorality is likely not far away.

Throughout *The Simpsons*, the desire to use the Bible to legitimate one's personal opinions is a common strategy. By itself, this tendency would be instructive about the extent to which Christianity has lost a sense of what the Bible truly means to its identity as a faith community. *The Simpsons*, however, aggravates the problem by portraying the way in which Springfield's Christians focus on a particular theme in the Bible. In "Secrets of a Successful Marriage," Marge seeks Reverend Lovejoy's advice on what she should do to fix her marital problems. The following conversation is revealing:

Reverend Lovejoy: Marge, get a divorce.

Marge: But, Reverend, isn't divorce a sin?

Reverend Lovejoy: [holding up a Bible]; Have you ever read this thing? Everything's a sin. Technically we're not allowed to go to the bathroom.

Reverend Lovejoy summarizes the Bible's moral content in a way that is doubly problematic. He once again speaks about the Bible in terms that require only a basic familiarity with its content, a quality that defines how *The Simpsons* generally characterizes Christian understanding of the Bible. Moreover, and more tellingly, Reverend Lovejoy focuses on a particular aspect in summarizing the Bible's content as it relates to Marge's predicament: judgment. That is, Reverend Lovejoy points Marge to the broad thematic content of the Old Testament. The hallmark of this part of the Bible is the notion that God provides specific rules of conduct for the Israelites and when the Israelites fail to uphold God's commands, they face punishment. This notion, that God establishes laws and consequences for failing to uphold said laws, is part of the Christian tradition, but in a way that ushers in the thematic emphasis of the New Testament: salvation. God is vengeful in the Old Testament, but in the New Testament God changes course. Through Jesus, God acts in a way that emphasizes forgiveness for all those who believe.[18] A general tendency within Springfield is to focus heavily on the issues of prohibition, judgment, and God's punishment that pervade the Old Testament. Reverend Lovejoy does not counsel Marge in a way that recalls God's love; he does not assure her that God will forgive her.[19] Rather, he asserts the Bible's judgmental content, which leaves Marge with little moral direction.

The notion that the Bible constitutes the ultimate moral authority in Christian society becomes problematic when Christians understand the Bible only as presenting God as a judging, vengeful deity. Interpreting the Bible as such runs counter to the very notion of who God is as traditionally conceived in Christianity. If one recalls the notion that the Bible ought to be a foundational source of joy for Christians, then the tendency to restrict such joy and focus instead on God's judgment becomes problematic. The belief that God ultimately embodies love is the theological point that defines Christianity's unique belief system.[20] Culturally, however, Christianity tends to revert to its shared roots with Judaism. Reverend Lovejoy's response to Marge embodies this point fully. Even though Christian thought distinguishes clearly between the Old and New Testaments, in practice Christians often collapse the two thematic elements in singular symbolic authority. That is, in contemporary culture, the notion that the Bible provides society with a foundational moral authority tends to forget the strong thematic demarcation between the Old and New Testaments.

The two salient features that define the Bible's role in Springfield, a general awareness of its role in Christianity but a marked ignorance of specifics, emerge throughout *The Simpsons*. Often, various characters refer to the Bible to address a particular concern, but they do so in a way that reveals more often their own interests or interpretations of what the Bible means rather than a sincere appreciation for Christianity's sacred text. The show clearly incorporates these distorted notions of the Bible into Springfield's religious fabric, a consciousness visible in "Simpsons Bible Stories." In this episode, one can see clearly how various characters interpret the Bible in the context of their contemporary society and personal experiences. During the Easter service, Reverend Lovejoy finds a chocolate bunny in the collection plate.[21] In response, Reverend Lovejoy announces that the congregation needs "a hefty dose of the Good Book." He then proceeds to read different passages from the Old Testament. Reading exclusively from the Old Testament on Easter Sunday embodies the Christian tendency to emphasize God's judgment rather than God's forgiveness. "Simpsons Bible Stories" thus portrays the specific biblical scenes that Reverend Lovejoy reads as various members of the Simpson family imagine them. The following discussion will focus on the first two biblical stories presented in "Simpsons Bible Stories."

The first biblical vignette tells the Garden of Eden[22] story as Marge imagines it. Her daydream begins with her amazement at the beauty of the garden. Everything is idyllic; even the resident lion sits next to the resident lamb[23] with a smile on its face. When Adam, characterized as Homer, meets Eve, characterized as Marge, the two experience all that paradise has to offer. However, when the climactic moment arrives, Marge's imagination veers away from traditional readings of this story. Marge/Eve is not the first one to eat from the Tree of Knowledge. In fact, while Marge/Eve protests to the snake that God forbade her and Homer/Adam from doing so, Homer/Adam eats the entire plate of apple slices that the snake offers. The following conversation ensues.

Marge/Eve:	Please stop eating that. God's going to be furious.
Homer/Adam:	You're pretty uptight for a naked chick. You know what would loosen you up? A little fruit.
Marge/Eve:	[hesitantly]: Well, it is a sin to waste food.
Homer/Adam:	You're always talking about how we need to do things together.

Marge/Eve: [taking a bite from the apple]: Mmmmmm,
              this could really spice up those pies I've been
              making.

This conversation makes clear how Marge interprets the Garden of Eden story in light of her own experience as a woman. In contrast to traditional renditions of the narrative, Homer/Adam is the one responsible for disobeying God's order. As a woman, Marge understands how society in general and the church in particular blame women for being morally inferior.[24] In Marge's imagination, men, and especially Homer, lack the moral fortitude to resist temptation. Moreover, Homer/Adam uses sexuality to tempt Marge/Eve, a move that captures a similar concern for Marge as a woman. In fact, Homer/Adam's first comments lay the groundwork for this later temptation. One of the first things he says to Marge/Eve is a clearly seductive comment: "God must have made you out of my sexiest rib." Homer/Adam's focus on sexuality remains consistent, which reiterates the way that Marge's individual experience affects how she understands this particular biblical passage. For Marge, sexuality pervades life in the Garden of Eden even before anyone eats the apple. This inverted notion obscures the traditional narrative in the Bible, which holds that awareness of human sexuality is a post-Fall condition. In Marge's interpretation, her experiences as Homer's wife very much guide how she understands a biblical text. Sexuality as a manipulative tool is so pervasive in her experience that it precedes the Fall. Marge punctuates this feminist frustration by imagining her condition as a traditional homemaker once she eats the apple.

Following this conversation, Marge's imagination expands the way in which her personal understanding of the Eden story diverges from a traditional Christian reading of the biblical text. In Marge's interpretation, God appears, furious, and, pointing his finger directly at her, asks if she ate from the tree. As Marge/Eve struggles to respond, Homer/Adam kicks the apple cores he has eaten into a bush. Marge/Eve confesses that she did eat the apple and God responds that she had better "high-tail it out of this garden." Marge/Eve then implores Homer/Adam to say something, but he responds in a way that Marge understands to be characteristic of men when faced with a sincere call for support: "I, um, think we should see other people." He then slinks away and Marge/Eve faces expulsion from the garden. This point echoes the biblical text, but importantly Homer/Adam does not initially face the same punishment. The separation amplifies the aggravation that Marge feels as a woman; too often she is left to deal with the consequences of Homer's actions. In her imagined version of the Eden story, Homer/Adam purposefully rejects the idea of standing up for Marge/Eve, which would necessitate that he take responsibility for what he has done. The image of Marge/Eve trudging out of the garden, while Homer/Adam watches from his perch in paradise, captures a feminist critique of this biblical passage. Though Homer/Adam deserves blame, he receives none, which mirrors the traditional cultural reading of this story.[25] Marge's imagined version, however, makes clear that, as a woman, she is the one who must bear the brunt of the moral blame for what happened in the Garden of Eden.

Homer/Adam eventually feels remorse and gets a unicorn to dig a hole so Marge/Eve can sneak back into Eden. The unicorn dies from its efforts, and God soon discovers that Eve has managed to return to the garden. Facing banishment, Homer/Adam tries to change God's mind with the only overtly Christian line in Marge's daydream: "God is love, right?" God ignores the point and flicks Homer/Adam out of Eden. Marge/Eve tries to defend herself, but before she can present her argument, God flicks her out as well. Marge/Eve then lands on Homer/Adam in a clearly sexual position. "Oh, this must be that pain thing," he laments. Homer/Adam's response reveals the nature of sexuality as Marge understands it: a source of pain. As Homer/Adam complains, Marge/Eve tries to comfort him: "I'm sure God will let us back in soon. I mean, how long can he hold a grudge?"

In the wake of the Fall, one can see clearly the way in which Marge's imagined version of the Garden of Eden story reflects the show's general approach to the Bible. Homer/Adam behaves selfishly, which reflects Marge's earlier frustration with the gender inequality that many interpretations of the story imply. Thus, Marge is broadly aware of the story's traditional version, even if she asserts a feminist critique of the traditional narrative. Her imagination ultimately dovetails with the more common cultural reading of the story. Eve traditionally takes the blame for the Fall. This general familiarity, however, gives way to a broader ignorance, presented in Marge's daydream in her comments about God holding a grudge. Marge/Eve's comment, then, exhibits a naïveté when one remembers that the episode conveys Marge's imagined understanding of the story. As a Christian, Marge should know that God ultimately forgives the mistake, but this awareness does not creep into her imagination. Marge/Eve's open-ended wonder misses the point, which suggests that Marge herself may have doubts about the efficacy of Jesus's death and resurrection.[26]

The second vignette offers a similarly striking example of how the Bible becomes distorted in an individual's mind. In this scene, Lisa imagines the story of the Israelites' captivity in Egypt.[27] Much like Marge's, Lisa's daydream reveals a general awareness of what is at stake in the story. However, the details echo the show's broader points about how individuals can interpret the Bible in ways that are not consistent with the text. Lisa's version provides another example of how an individual's experiences influence the way that person imagines the Bible. Specifically, Lisa imagines herself as a slave under Pharaoh's control who, along with the other slaves, suffer as they build Pharaoh's tomb. When Pharaoh comes to check on the project's progress, he is shocked to see that someone has graffitied his tomb with an unflattering portrait and the caption "King Butt." When Pharaoh asks who is responsible, a burning bush points to Bart and says, "He did it." The burning bush is an important element in the Exodus story,[28] but here Lisa's imagination distorts its significance. In the Bible, God speaks through the bush to encourage Moses to lead the Israelites out of captivity. Here, however, God plays a significantly different role: God rats out Bart. As the product of Lisa's imagination, this detail seems in line with God's power, as she seems to be happy to see her brother suffer the appropriate consequences for his actions. What is out of sync, however, is the fact that Lisa's imagined story brings about more harm on a particular person. God may be vengeful, but *The Simpsons* makes clear elsewhere that turning in one's friend is not an admirable act.[29] Thus, Lisa is willing to tweak how she understands the story to ensure that Bart receives a punishment that she feels he deserves.

Based on how Lisa interprets the Exodus story, a corollary point emerges. Because the bush plays a different role in Lisa's imagination, someone else must inspire Moses to assume his leadership role. In her daydream, Lisa performs this task herself, which projects her self-imagined authority. Even though she is among the slaves, Lisa cannot help but understand herself as somehow superior to her peers. In fact, when Moses first goes to see Pharaoh, Lisa not only accompanies him, she quite literally has to tell him what to do.

| Lisa: | Excuse me, Pharaoh, I think Moses here has something to ask you. [nudging Milhouse/Moses]: Go! |
| Milhouse/Moses: | [mumbling]: Let my people go. |

Pharaoh:	Let your people go? I've never heard such insolence. You call yourselves slaves?
Milhouse/Moses:	[after he and Lisa have been thrown out of Pharaoh's tent]: Well, the ball's in his court now. [Lisa rolls her eyes in frustration.]

There is little question that Lisa provides the catalyst for the coming exodus from slavery. Milhouse/Moses proves to be a poor leader who is incapable of bringing about his people's freedom. Lisa can only roll her eyes at his inabilities. Lisa thus recasts the Exodus story in terms that are amenable to her own self-perception. The biblical text does state that Moses first visits Pharaoh with his brother Aaron at his side, but Moses does not come across as inept. In Lisa's version, however, she clearly plays the role of antagonist and hero because Milhouse/Moses proves to be wholly ineffectual.

When the plague of the frogs comes to Pharaoh, Lisa's interpretive pattern proves to be consistent. Lisa directs Milhouse/Moses to drop frogs on Pharaoh and when Pharaoh interprets the frogs as a gift from Rah to eat, Lisa is the one who clarifies what actually happened. Subsequently, she, and not Milhouse/Moses, warns Pharaoh, "There's lots more planned. And there's nothing you can do about it!" This leadership continues throughout the escape from Pharaoh. Even though Milhouse/Moses eventually urges the Israelites to escape with him, his bravery lasts until he sees Pharaoh pursue him. He then gives up. "Screw this. I'm converting." As he begins to pray to Rah, once again Lisa tells him to stop and urges him, "Moses, lead your people." Milhouse/Moses then does what Lisa says and the slaves escape. However, there is little doubt that Lisa helps the slaves to flee. Thus, she not only provides guidance to Milhouse/Moses, she also acts as a de facto liberator for the community of slaves.

Throughout the narrative, Lisa is unquestionably the protagonist. Significantly, in Lisa's imagination, she, and not God, is the one who enables the events to unfold. Lisa's agency produces the plague of the frogs, and the parting of the Red Sea is likewise a result of her plan. Her insight, not Moses's, allows the Israelites to escape. Moreover, she is the only one who can help Moses accomplish what the Bible says he accomplishes. Lisa's imagination, then, builds upon her basic understanding of a biblical narrative, but she, too, tweaks the story to reflect her sense of superiority. Thus, God's authority and agency give way to Lisa's own self-appointed leadership. This smug self-perception appears consistently when Lisa faces questions about Christianity. She usually provides the sole skeptical voice when religious questions emerge in her family or in Springfield. Her daydream thus provides a way to distort a biblical narrative that traditionally emphasizes God's liberating action. In place of God's authority, Lisa inserts her own vengeance against her brother as well as her leadership over her peers. These qualities require her to recognize the narrative's general trajectory, but at the same time she clearly alters in her own head how the story plays out. Her goal is not to understand the story as proving God's commitment to the Israelites. Instead, she wants to give voice to her already strong self-perception of herself as somehow better than others.

A concluding point about "Simpsons Bible Stories" reinforces the general argument about the Bible's role in American Christianity. The use of the Bible as punishment for some wrongdoing provides yet another example of how *The Simpsons* characterizes the Bible thematically in concert with the Old Testament emphasis on punishment. This particular example is striking because Easter should be the one day when Reverend Lovejoy speaks about Jesus's role of salvation in Christianity. Instead, Reverend Lovejoy diverts his focus from what Easter represents in order to represent the Bible as a punitive element of Christianity. In characterizing the Bible as such, *The Simpsons* summarizes the narrow understanding of the Bible that characterizes much of Christianity in American society. The Bible ought to provide a measure of spiritual guidance and comfort, as well as serve as an authoritative moral guide, but too often it becomes a source to be massaged in order to justify personally appointed positions of authority. Appealing to the Bible thus becomes a trap that diverts attention from what the Bible traditionally represents in Christianity.

The Bible can provide guidance to Christians, but a lack of awareness, or an unwillingness to adapt one's lifestyle based on what the Bible says, constitutes the heart of the problem that *The Simpsons* addresses. How a particular person interprets the Bible too often obscures the more important theological point. Throughout *The Simpsons*, different characters manipulate the Bible's authority in order to justify their own concerns. In "Co-Dependent's Day," Homer carries a copy of the Bible around, but not for any purpose related to his Christian faith. Instead, Homer hides a flask in the hollowed-out Bible. The image of the text as an authority is, quite literally, hollow. In its place rests something that pulls Homer away from a Christian lifestyle. The abuse is so overt that Homer refers to his alcohol-hiding Bible as "the Gospel according to Puke." Homer plays on this notion that the Bible justifies actions, but as this particular example illustrates, Homer's strategy merely alludes to the Bible in order to excuse his drinking problem. In justifying his individual actions or needs, Homer understands the Bible in a way that runs counter to what the Bible actually says. This diluted authority and active manipulation of what the Bible represents parallels the general state of Christianity in America's secular culture.

A final example of how *The Simpsons* portrays the Bible's role in contemporary culture summarizes the way in which American culture tends to respond to the notion of biblical authority. In "Homer and Ned's Hail Mary Pass," Ned Flanders partners with Homer to present a biblical narrative during the Superbowl halftime show. Homer and Ned tell the story of the flood[30] in hopes of conveying to a worldwide audience the importance of God. Society is at a point of "moral decay"[31] that is so pervasive God may bring about serious punishment.[32] The response to the halftime show is predictable; Homer and Ned are roundly booed. Subsequent fallout rejects the notion that a biblical message has relevance in American society. A follow-up television interviews asks a mother what she thought of the halftime show. She responds angrily that what she saw on television runs against the way she wants to raise her kids. She and her husband do not want Christian influences on their children. Such biblical messages interfere with the plan to raise her kids as "secular humanists."

A common thread runs through the different ways in which the Bible appears on *The Simpsons*. Christianity functions in a particular social context, which, in contemporary American culture, dismisses the notion that the Bible provides an objective moral presence in that culture. In place of a strong Christian ethic, one now finds the only thing that is truly "pure and good" is "candy."[33] This notion of Christian love, which is the bedrock of the New Testament's moral structure, no longer has currency in American culture. Rather, the desire to replace Christian love with candy reflects a desire for "information that is sweet and goes down easy, not something that is troubling and ethically difficult."[34] The Bible does not present guidelines that are always palatable. In the Garden of Eden story, humans must accept responsibility for their mistake. The general response to such dilemmas, however, plays out in the way that Marge imagines. Humans either make excuses for their moral failings, or they try to negotiate easy forgiveness. The irony, of course, is that the Bible is still present through this transition; it has just lost its traditional author-ity. Homer appeals to the notion of God as love in his efforts to get himself off the hook, but he fails to realize that his answer actually has theological currency. The Bible continues to be relevant in contemporary American culture, but in a form adapted to fit particular social needs rather than a sacred text to be interpreted with due diligence.

Chapter Five

A Bunch of Black Sheep: Reverend Lovejoy and Springfield's Congregation

"This is very sad news, and it would have never happened if the wedding would've been inside the church with God, instead of out here in the cheap showiness of nature."

—Reverend Lovejoy[1]

"Not that we are competent of ourselves to claim anything as coming from us; our competence is from God, who has made us competent to be ministers of a new covenant, not of letter but of spirit; for the letter kills, but the Spirit gives life."

—2 Corinthians 3:5–6

"And the very same goes for Ezekiel. Which brings us back to our starting point: the nine tenets of constancy."[2]

Reverend Lovejoy's sermon drones on. Homer, who has fallen asleep, leans forward and bangs his head on the pew. Snapped awake, he yells, "Damn it!"

Homer's sudden jolt causes commotion to spread throughout the First Church of Springfield. Even Reverend Lovejoy cannot ignore the interruption. Shuffling his papers, he says, with a touch of annoyance, that he has lost his place and now must start the sermon over.

Reverend Lovejoy's voice begins to drone again in the same monotone.

"Our sermon today is on constancy. . . ."

While watching Reverend Lovejoy ramble on about constancy, one cannot help but sympathize with the congregation. Before going to church that morning, Homer complains that the week is not long enough to sit through a boring sermon.[3] In America's consumer-driven culture, hours are precious. In this episode, Homer seems to be mildly prophetic in resisting Marge's imperatives to hurry up and get to church. Attending a service ought to inspire, or at the very least provide a meaningful experience amid the busy week. When the Simpson family arrives at church and Reverend Lovejoy tranquilizes them with his extended discussion of an obscure text, the only constancy present seems to be the bad quality of his sermons. He is consistent, to be sure, but only insofar as his pitch remains the same, his ability to bore his congregation never falters, and the central point to his sermon seems completely irrelevant to the congregants who, as Homer would say, are sacrificing an hour of their day off to come to church in the first place.

Any discussion of Christianity in Springfield will inevitably turn to the town's prominent minister, Reverend Lovejoy. He represents organized religion, and the way in which *The Simpsons* caricatures clergy through Reverend Lovejoy provides a revealing look at a particular element of American Christianity. People go to church, but their experiences, both with the pastor and the broader communal notion that the church represents, often unfold in a way that lacks the positive qualities associated with Christianity. The pastor represents Christianity's public face, which makes the pastor a kind of lightning rod whose job it is to absorb every possible congregational need. To understand how Christianity affects life in Springfield as an institution, an in-depth look at Reverend Lovejoy and his church thus becomes necessary. Given the show's tendency to present Christianity as detached from its traditional moorings, Reverend Lovejoy's leadership seems to invite criticism. After all, if Christians' journey of faith has gone off course, presumably the pastor should have done everything possible to help correct the error.

To understand how Reverend Lovejoy interacts with his congregation, it is helpful to look at the salient features that define his ministry. The most obvious quality that emerges consistently during Reverend Lovejoy's appearances on the show is burnout. Reverend Lovejoy tells Marge that he lost something essential to his vocation as his career in Springfield unfolded: "I arrived ready to roll up my sleeves and help my fellow man. There was just one fellow man I hadn't counted on."[4] As a young pastor, Reverend Lovejoy embraced a grand vision of exerting a lasting, positive influence on his new congregants' lives. He wanted to make a difference. This desire resonates with the Christian emphasis on hope, but as Reverend Lovejoy admits, when the time actually comes to put such dreams into practice, things play out differently. He finds that he does not have the patience or the empathy to provide the spiritual leadership that people in general, and Ned Flanders in particular, expect from their pastor. Over the course of his career, Ned breaks down Reverend Lovejoy's resolve until, as he confesses to Marge, he "just stopped caring."

Reverend Lovejoy may be honest with Marge in describing his ministry as hollow, but in doing so he betrays his shortcomings as well. The pastor, after all, will not be a very good spiritual leader if he simply does not care. This lack of sincerity constitutes the backbone of much criticism toward Reverend Lovejoy. Steve Tompkins, a former writer for the show, describes Reverend Lovejoy as a "pandenominational windbag."[5] Jim Trammell, from the University of Georgia, echoes this criticism of Reverend Lovejoy's impotent spiritual leadership in Springfield: "[He] is rarely depicted as helping to solve spiritual problems at all, another indicator of the inadequacy of the church."[6] In a word, Reverend Lovejoy is a failure. His job is to lead his congregation, but even he can recognize that he has become "a shepherd without a flock."[7] As denominational Christianity's representative on *The Simpsons*, Reverend Lovejoy seems to expose the ways in which Christianity is supposed to provide a positive influence in life but consistently fails to live up to this charge. Reverend Lovejoy very much goes through the motions associated with leadership, including sermons that use theologically rich language such as constancy, but he fails to provide any spiritually significant influence. In Springfield, the congregation suffers for this inadequacy. The show uses Reverend Lovejoy to convey the dire state of American Christianity vis-à-vis its leadership. What the church ought to provide to its members does not always flow out of its leaders as they minister to actual congregations.

In addition to Reverend Lovejoy's personal burnout, one also finds vague and irrelevant theology in the message he presents to his congregation. He routinely puts messages on the church's sign that "undermine what [he] is saying in the pulpit."[8] Such gimmicky messages include *No Shirt, No Shoes, No Salvation*;[9] *God: The Original Love Connection*;[10] and *There's Something about the Virgin Mary*.[11] Though each example suggests that the upcoming service will address a significant theological topic, the phrasing reveals a lamentable attempt to present such points in a culturally relevant manner. What the church should emphasize thus becomes distilled through shameless appeals to popular culture. Rather than speak directly about what his church can offer people, Reverend Lovejoy regresses into superficial theology, a shift that sacrifices the integrity of Christian beliefs to popular culture. If the church has lost its relevance in Springfield, then Reverend Lovejoy deserves much of the blame. Christianity's blunted authority in American culture is very much the result of leaders like Reverend Lovejoy bending their faith's fundamental beliefs to fit into a secular context.[12]

Reverend Lovejoy's poor spiritual leadership in Springfield manifests itself elsewhere. When Sideshow Bob frames Krusty the Clown for armed robbery, the entire town assumes that Krusty is guilty.[13] Reverend Lovejoy leads a mob bent on erasing Krusty's image from town. In a scene reminiscent of the post-Reformation struggle in England, as well as the Spanish Inquisition, Reverend Lovejoy ignites a pile of Krusty merchandise.[14] Reverend Lovejoy assumes that Krusty is guilty, a response that unfortunately suggests rash judgment can be a virtue. Reverend Lovejoy temporarily assumes a viable leadership role in Springfield, but only in response to a mob's desire to dispense quick punishment. Morality, or rather justice, is noticeably absent as a motivating factor in such projected piety. Reverend Lovejoy only assumes a self-inflated moral superiority when events in Springfield demand as much. However, leadership that sanctions immediate judgment without a reasonable inquiry into the facts surrounding the situation provides a poor example to those who follow. Reverend Lovejoy's actions run counter to basic notions of christianity. More troubling, even if Krusty were guilty, Reverend Lovejoy's rush to condemn him dismisses the relevancy of a foundational Christian belief: forgiveness.

The behavior is, unfortunately, a consistent pattern in Reverend Lovejoy's moral leadership. When Ned Flanders is stopped for drunken driving as a church bus passes by, Reverend Lovejoy is the first person on the bus to assert that Ned is guilty. Reverend Lovejoy's leadership subsequently fuels congregational assumptions about Ned's guilt.[15] The Sunday after publicly accusing Ned, Reverend Lovejoy adopts a hypocritical position as the church's leader. Reverend Lovejoy welcomes Ned to church as one would expect a pastor to do: "Oh, don't worry, Ned. This is a house of love and forgiveness." While he pays lip service to these Christian ideals, Reverend Lovejoy reverts to his judgment by titling his sermon, "What Ned Did." The superficial commitment to forgiveness quickly gives way to upholding the rush to judgment, a stance that clearly seeks to ingratiate Reverend Lovejoy to the mob. Ned does not experience a house of love and forgiveness, cared for by Reverend Lovejoy. Rather, voices in this house comment in a way that follows Reverend Lovejoy's example of assuming Ned's guilt. "There he is . . . the fallen one." *The Simpsons* drives the point home by redeeming Ned through Homer. Only when Homer comes to Ned's defense does Reverend Lovejoy retreat from his judgmental platform.

A willingness to judge often motivates Reverend Lovejoy's ability to lead a moral crusade. This tendency dovetails with Reverend Lovejoy's willingness to emphasize God's impending judgment. For example, Reverend Lovejoy uses the threat of damnation to coerce a confession from the Sunday school class.[16] He leads the children as they recite:

> If I withhold the truth, may I go straight to hell where I will eat naught but burning hot coals and drink naught but burning hot cola, [with Ralph Wiggum speaking clearly] where fiery demons will punch me in the back . . . [with Bart speaking loudly] where my soul will be chopped into confetti and be strewn upon a parade of murderers and single mothers . . . [with Milhouse speaking loudly] where my tongue will be torn out by ravenous birds.

While Reverend Lovejoy is right to seek out the child who disrupted the worship service, his tactics seem a bit out of line. He abuses his position of moral authority in order to scare children into submission. Severe pain defines each of the punishments the kids will supposedly face in hell. Asking them to envision such punishments reveals a clear bias toward judgment as encouraging morality. Moreover, Reverend Lovejoy acts in an inappropriate manner when he exposes children to overly violent images. He neither speaks to the Sunday school class about forgiveness, nor seeks to address the situation in a way that recognizes that just because people make mistakes does not mean they necessarily deserve eternal damnation. He reverts to the part of Christianity that uses the threat of punishment to ensure conformity with the leader's moral agenda. Thus, he fails to convey Christianity's fundamental beliefs in order to uphold a personal preference for judgment.

Whereas Reverend Lovejoy can play the part of a fire-and-brimstone preacher, when real spiritual challenges arise in Springfield, he often has little to say. For example, in "Bart's Comet," Springfield faces annihilation when a comet bears down. The town adopts a plan to destroy the comet with a missile. The Simpson family gathers on its roof to watch the missile save their town. When the missile launches, it soars into the sky, but then falls to the ground and destroys the only bridge out of town. The following conversation reveals the limits of Christian leadership in Springfield:

Lisa: It blew up the bridge! We're doomed!

Homer: It's times like this I wish I were a religious man.

Reverend   [running down the street]: It's all over, people! We
Lovejoy: don't have a prayer!

When Homer expresses a sincere desire for religion in the face of crisis, one knows the situation is serious. This is one of the few moments when Christianity truly could offer a sense of spiritual hope in the face of impending disaster. In this moment, one does not find Reverend Lovejoy's spiritual leadership; he runs down the street in fear. Whereas he should be a resource for comfort, he is actually the first person in Springfield to panic. Moreover, even if the comet were to destroy the town, presumably Reverend Lovejoy could find comfort offered in the Christian notion that salvation awaits believers. At a time when true spiritual leadership is possible, when Reverend Lovejoy could make the church relevant to the most disinterested Christian, he fails to offer spiritual guidance. He quite literally flees from the opportunity to positively affect the town's spiritual concerns.

In broad terms, and supported by multiple specific examples, Reverend Lovejoy embodies the way in which the church does not and seemingly cannot provide competent and legitimate leadership in contemporary American culture. Reverend Lovejoy's moral leadership reflects a mob-pleasing mentality. Moreover, in the face of real spiritual crises, he crumbles. These two qualities indicate a broader breakdown in America's Christian leadership. As a bulwark of a Christian nation, the Christian Church, its minister, and those who govern in the name of faith ought to uphold a corporate sense of morality, which should then filter into the private worlds of individual Christians. On *The Simpsons*, however, this paradigm is inverted. Public morality is nonexistent, and in moments of spiritual need, the minister has no comforting words to offer.[17]

The Simpsons offers many reasons to be critical of Reverend Lovejoy and thus of Christian leadership in general.[18] However, in Reverend Lovejoy's character, the show develops a more complex understanding of who the pastor is based on who the congregation expects the pastor to be. As Paul Cantor notes, when the show pokes fun at someone or the institution that person represents, the reason for doing so reflects a measure of "importance."[19] Thus, one should peel back Reverend Lovejoy's obvious faults to identify a deeper critical concern. While Reverend Lovejoy clearly has his flaws, an important question to ask is: what produced those problems? As mentioned earlier in this chapter, he tells Marge that he arrived at the First Church of Springfield with enthusiasm for his ministry. Moreover, despite his boring sermons he does not preach to an empty church. In Springfield, the pews are usually full on Sundays. The question of Reverend Lovejoy's abilities as a minister thus appears in a more nuanced portrait on *The Simpsons*. The dynamics between the minister and his congregation ultimately suggest that perhaps Reverend Lovejoy is not the only culprit in Springfield's sluggish spirituality.

When a group of people sees church as an obligation, the pastor is fighting an uphill battle. In *The Simpsons Movie*, church is quite literally the first thing on Homer's list of chores to do. In "In Marge We Trust," Homer and his kids can hardly stay awake in church, but once the service is over they enthusiastically head to the dump to sift through garbage. By comparing Reverend Lovejoy's ability to inspire with the entertainment offered by a bunch of trash, one can see the extent to which Reverend Lovejoy fails to reach his parishioners. *The Simpsons* uses hyperbole to indicate unreasonable attitudes on the part of the parishioners. When people literally find more intrigue in garbage than in church, a corollary critique must be made. This example conveys a set of expectations and preconceptions about church that Reverend Lovejoy can never satisfy. If Homer and his kids have dismissed completely the idea that church can be relevant to their lives, then Reverend Lovejoy truly faces a daunting weekly task.

Given that Reverend Lovejoy brought a vibrant leadership to Springfield, perhaps one cannot blame him solely for the boring tone that his sermons assume and more broadly the apathy he feels toward those under his spiritual care. Those who attend the First Church of Springfield bring attitudes to church that preempt the possibility of having a positive experience. Homer provides a good example of the way in which personal bias transfers blame for Springfield's stagnant spiritual life unfairly to Reverend Lovejoy. In "Homer the Heretic," Homer dreams that he talks to God about how he does not want to waste his time at church. God agrees with Homer that Reverend Lovejoy gives boring sermons, a fact that causes God to contemplate giving Reverend Lovejoy a canker sore. On the surface, Reverend Lovejoy is the reason behind Homer's problem, but the exchange is slightly more complex. Homer projects a particular understanding of God in his dream. Consequently, what God threatens to do ultimately reflects Homer's opinion about Reverend Lovejoy, which is probably not a reasonable indictment. In light of Homer's doubt about the church's ability to be valuable in his life, one should not be surprised that Homer subsequently blames Reverend Lovejoy for not meeting Homer's expectations. Reverend Lovejoy thus faces an impossible task: he must engender spirituality in Homer when Homer just wants to be entertained.

In many ways, Homer reflects a common attitude toward his pastor and the church in general that is present in many a contemporary American congregation. The residents of Springfield who attend the First Church of Springfield place unrealistic expectations on the minister. When Marge visits Reverend Lovejoy to encourage him to inject his sermons with some energy, Reverend Lovejoy responds in a telling manner.[20]

Marge: Sermons about constancy and provicitude are all very well and good, but the church could be doing so much more to reach out to people.

Lovejoy: Oh, I don't see you volunteering to make things better.

Marge: Well, okay, I will volunteer.

Lovejoy: I wasn't prepared for that.

In response to Marge's constructive criticism, Reverend Lovejoy identifies a problem with his congregation: apathy. Reading between the lines, one can see in Reverend Lovejoy's initial response an awareness of how people expect him to do everything without pulling any weight on their own. The unwillingness of his congregants to help out with life at the church is not a throwaway concern. Reverend Lovejoy is very much used to doing things without help. When Marge actually offers to volunteer, Reverend Lovejoy cannot hide his surprise. The exchange thus reveals a deeply rooted habit among Springfield's residents of expecting a lot while providing very little. Reverend Lovejoy can only do so much in his limited time with his limited resources, but Marge requests something that likely characterizes others' opinions about the pastor; there is always something more to be done for the congregation.

Unfortunately for those who have high expectations, Reverend Lovejoy has a lengthy list of duties in addition to his role as pastor. He is a father, a husband, a prison minister, a radio show participant, an author, and, perhaps most important, a pastor to Ned Flanders. While Ned Flanders may represent a positive side of Christianity, Reverend Lovejoy knows the other side of the story. Ned is not a model Christian as a member of a congregation insofar as he does more to problematize Reverend Lovejoy's ministry than anyone else in Springfield. Ned may attend church faithfully, but he also demands excessive attention from the pastor. Reverend Lovejoy says as much when he reveals to Marge

that Ned was the unexpected challenge he found when he arrived in
Springfield.[21] Reverend Lovejoy then reveals some of the problems Ned
has asked about over the years: he covets his own wife; he is meek but
could be meeker; and he swallowed a toothpick. The list of examples is
telling. It captures the way in which Ned has gradually become more
needy and thus intrusive in his relationship with Reverend Lovejoy. At
first, Ned calls with problems that, though perhaps extreme, are at the
very least spiritual in nature. When Ned worries about whether he could
be meeker, he has a biblically based concern.[22] The final example, however, reveals the extent to which Ned invades Reverend Lovejoy's life and
thus places excessive demands on Reverend Lovejoy's professional and
personal resources. When Ned calls to ask about the toothpick, he interrupts Reverend Lovejoy's vacation in Paris. Moreover, the concern has
nothing to do with Reverend Lovejoy's role as pastor.[23] If Ned is worried
that he swallowed a toothpick, he needs to call Dr. Hibbert, not Reverend
Lovejoy. Ned's willingness to call the pastor about such things illustrates
the unreasonable expectations that many people have of their pastors.
Congregants often expect the pastor to be on call at a moment's notice,
regardless of the problem. *The Simpsons* routinely shows Reverend
Lovejoy as dismissive in response to these calls, but such responses
invite criticism toward those who really do expect pastors to respond
at a moment's notice. The blame thus tends to fall on the pastor who
won't concern himself with Ned's toothpick problem when in fact Ned
deserves blame for thinking the pastor's responsibilities extend to such
trivial matters.

Perhaps, then, Reverend Lovejoy should not be expected to respond
in depth to concerns that infringe upon his privacy. A favorite point of
criticism about Reverend Lovejoy happens in "22 Short Films about
Springfield." When his dog needs to empty its bowels, Reverend Lovejoy
encourages it to do its "dirty, sinful business" on Ned's lawn. The act
might be petty, but the motivation is not. Reverend Lovejoy has good
reason to be fed up with Ned after all the phone calls. Thus, within his
role as minister Reverend Lovejoy manages to find a way to vent his
frustration. This is not to excuse Reverend Lovejoy's juvenile pleasure in
having his dog poop in Flanders's yard. The incident does, however, make
clear the rationale behind Reverend Lovejoy's actions. When he encourages his dog to do its business in Flanders' yard, Reverend Lovejoy comes
across in a way that rarely receives attention in discussing the minister's
role in society. In this vignette, *The Simpsons* conveys that Reverend
Lovejoy is a pastor, but he is also a person. His role as the former often
obscures that of the latter in the minds of the townspeople. It is easy to

criticize Reverend Lovejoy for his faults, but *The Simpsons* also includes in its characterization glimpses into Reverend Lovejoy's personal life that establish his humanity.[24] The critique of Christianity in Springfield is thus aimed not only at Reverend Lovejoy; his congregants also deserve scrutiny for their expectations and lack of commitment to their church. They deserve blame for holding Reverend Lovejoy to unreasonable expectations because he is a pastor, which ultimately denies him a more basic identity as just another Springfield resident.

A comparison between Reverend Lovejoy and Marge helps to clarify how a double standard exists with respect to what people expect from their pastor. In "Marge Be Not Proud," Bart wants the newest video game, Bonestorm, for Christmas. When Marge refuses his request, Bart decides to steal a copy. The store's security guard catches Bart and calls the Simpson house, but Bart manages to intercept the message and thus hide his actions from his parents. Unfortunately, the family then goes to the same store to take a holiday picture and the store security guard informs Marge what happened. At first, she denies that Bart would ever do such a thing. "My son may not be perfect, but I know in my heart he's not a shoplifter." Even after the security guard insists that Bart is guilty, Marge continues to support her son: "Fine. Play the tape. Then everyone can see you've got the wrong boy." When Marge sees the security tape that recorded the whole episode, she is crestfallen. As a mother, she cannot believe that her son would steal from a store. One cannot help but feel sympathy for her; Bart let her down, and she does not know what to do. The episode offers no indication that Marge is at fault for believing in her son, even though he may be a troublemaker. She responds initially to the accusation as many parents would in similar situations. *The Simpsons* portrays Marge's experience in a way that clearly invites and even encourages sympathy.

In a parallel example, however, Reverend Lovejoy does not elicit such sympathy. In "Bart's Girlfriend," Reverend Lovejoy finds himself in a similar position to Marge's. At the climactic point of Bart's relationship with Reverend Lovejoy's daughter, Jessica, one sees another example of how a parent responds to accusations that his or her child has stolen something. During the episode, Jessica steals money from the collection plate, an act so bad that even Bart knows what Jessica has done "is really wrong." When Mrs. Lovejoy notices that money is missing from the collection plate, almost everyone assumes Bart is to blame. It is only later, with Lisa's help, that Jessica's guilt is exposed. Upon learning that his daughter is the actual culprit, Reverend Lovejoy reacts in a way that is similar to what Marge does upon hearing similar accusations. He defends his child: "I guess it's obvious what's happened here. Bart Simpson has somehow managed to sneak his bedroom into my house. Well, come on! Use your imaginations!" Despite the parallel reaction of supporting his daughter in the face of serious allegations, somehow Reverend Lovejoy does not elicit sympathy. Rather, he comes across as hypocritical for asserting his daughter's innocence, a portrayal that rests on the expectations he must deal with as a pastor. As a parent, Reverend Lovejoy is no different from Marge. However, his job invites a double standard from his congregants, as they see his defense of Jessica as somehow inexcusable. The contrast points to a broader problem in the life of the minister: a sense of unappreciative hypocrisy in the minds of those who think that pastors should somehow be better than their parishioners. Though he deserves the same sympathy as a parent that Marge receives, Reverend Lovejoy tends to be understood only in the context of his role as a minister.

Money poses another challenge for Reverend Lovejoy. As the sole pastor of the First Church of Springfield, he must budget the church's resources appropriately. Just as Springfield's moral climate demands a certain response from him, so too does the town's financial support for the First Church of Springfield present a situation wherein Reverend Lovejoy seems almost predetermined to falter and thus to invite criticism. An acute example of an apparent flaw in his character arises during "Bart, the Mother." When Bart goes to the library to learn about birds, he sees Reverend Lovejoy engaged in a conversation.

> Librarian: You've checked this Bible out every weekend for the last nine years. Wouldn't it just be cheaper to buy one?
>
> Lovejoy: Perhaps. On a librarian's salary.

The obvious reaction is to condemn Reverend Lovejoy for being miserly, especially when the issue at hand relates to a fundamental part of his job. The Bible is the foundational tool that a minister needs to do his or her job. The exchange certainly raises questions about Reverend Lovejoy's commitment to his profession, but his response to the librarian contains an important truth. Pastors are notoriously underpaid, especially in light of the duties they are expected to perform. When people like Ned Flanders will seek help at any moment, a pastor is effectively on call all the time. Given the average salary a minister makes, the hourly wage breakdown would be appalling. Though Reverend Lovejoy comes across as overly cheap, he also calls attention to something that will jade many a person: not being paid enough for the work that they do, much less for the way in which people take advantage of the person who holds the job.

Reverend Lovejoy resents his low income, but this in only half the story. His barb toward the librarian does not make explicit another key point that affects his attitude toward money. A pastor's salary often comes in large part from what the congregation gives during collection. That is, a pastor's parishioners play an important role in determining how much their pastor makes.[25] In Reverend Lovejoy's case, there is reason to be resentful. Despite his apparent stinginess, several examples lend credence to the notion that the congregation shares responsibility for Reverend Lovejoy's need to be frugal. In "Viva Ned Flanders," one gets a glimpse of what Reverend Lovejoy has to work with when trying to ensure the church's and thus his own financial survival. He preaches about tithing and tells the congregation, "And once again, tithing is ten percent off the top. That's gross income, not net. Please, people, don't force us to audit. Now I'm going to pass this around a second time. Brother Ned, you'll do the honors." While the specifics that led to this comment remain hidden, one can assume safely that the congregation wants to give as little of their income as possible. Reverend Lovejoy's instructions suggest that once Springfield residents pay their taxes, they have little desire to part with any more of their income. When it comes to supporting the church's mission and the pastor who directs that charge, the congregation is thus culpable for its negligence. If the question were about taxes, perhaps one could sympathize with the congregation. However, trying to skimp on giving to the church constitutes a miserly quality that mirrors Reverend Lovejoy's unwillingness to buy a Bible.

More important, the congregation's attitude toward money is systemic. Reverend Lovejoy exhibits a constant awareness that he must make ends meet. In his essay inviting people to come visit Springfield, Reverend Lovejoy concludes by emphasizing the financial challenge he faces:

> A trip to Springfield can be informative, filling, and even fun as long as you plan in advance to pacify our vengeful God . . . by attending church at least once while you're here. And when the offering plate comes by, remember that most local churches honor traveler's checks, and several have installed pay-as-you-pray instant credit card kiosks for your convenience.[26]

While Reverend Lovejoy speaks hyperbolically to visitors, he reveals a reality that defines much of his work in Springfield. He must anticipate constantly that his congregation will not provide enough financial support for their church.[27] The problem is so pervasive that he must appeal to visitors to pick up some of the slack. His obsession with money not only indicts the congregation for its lack of financial support, it also prevents him from devoting more time to his other pastoral concerns.

The communal unwillingness to contribute to the First Church of Springfield comes into sharper focus in "The Joy of Sect." In this episode, a religious cult invades Springfield and convinces most of the town to give its money to the sect's leader. In return, they receive a promise that the leader will take them to Blisstonia. The advertisement and the town's subsequent acceptance of the promise cause Reverend Lovejoy to respond from the pulpit.

> Lovejoy: This so-called new religion is nothing but a pack of weird rituals and chants designed to take away the money of fools. Let us say the Lord's Prayer forty times, but first let's pass the collection plate. [The plate returns almost empty.]
>
> Lovejoy: Oh Lord, uh, try the emergency plate, Ned. [This also does not work, so he begins pouring gasoline on the church floor.]
>
> Lovejoy: Oh, I never thought I'd have to do this again.

Several key points emerge in Reverend Lovejoy's words. First, he identifies what most of Springfield cannot, that the Movementarians are scamming people out of their money. Of course, Reverend Lovejoy recognizes this to an extent because he is aware that, on average, most of those same people will not contribute their money to his church. At first, he tries a firmer hand to get people to contribute, but when this does not work, he faces a crisis. Again, the example of setting the church on fire to collect insurance money is extreme, but it brings into focus the extent to which Christians in Springfield fail to support their church. Reverend Lovejoy must resort to insurance fraud in order to keep the church soluble. In so doing, Reverend Lovejoy obviously invites criticism, but one cannot overlook the reason that forces him into this difficult position in the first place.

Reverend Lovejoy's personal stinginess meets the congregation's unwillingness to give head-on in "Simpsons Bible Stories." As the collection plate snakes its way through the pews, Reverend Lovejoy encourages his congregation to give generously: "And as we pass the collection plate, please give as if the person next to you was watching." Here, Reverend Lovejoy employs a slightly different tactic to generate financial support. He injects a biblical imperative into his exhortation,[28] but he does so by twisting the passage to support his financial goals. Quite simply, Reverend Lovejoy tries to shame his congregants into giving their money. Pastors should neither adapt the Bible for their own purposes, nor should they rely on shame to encourage giving. However, before labeling Reverend Lovejoy as a bad pastor, one should realize that much of his strategy stems from the fact that the congregation does not give money in the first place.

More important, Reverend Lovejoy implements this strategy on Easter, a day that often generates the highest collection totals. The message delivered on Easter Sunday is the one that should, more than any other, remind Christians what their faith represents, which should in turn encourage them to support their church. The fact that Reverend Lovejoy cannot count on this increased support shifts some of the blame for his money-focused attitude to the congregation. Again, Reverend Lovejoy is not faultless, as he uses Easter's sanctity to browbeat donations out of his congregation. He deserves criticism for his opportunistic fundraising approach. Still, his congregation generates the problem through their unwillingness to give their money on Christianity's holiest day.

The consistency with which this issue arises on *The Simpsons* ultimately points the critical focus at a very real tension in many Christian communities. Americans are quick to buy excessively large cars, or overly large houses, but they will also claim that they are too strapped financially to contribute to their church. When the minister's salary lags with respect to hours worked, as well as the hours she or he is expected to be on call, perhaps one can begin to find a reason to be sympathetic toward Reverend Lovejoy. Even Marge can afford a Canyonero,[29] but Reverend Lovejoy must drive the same Volkswagen-esque car that he has had since the beginning of his ministry.

Reverend Lovejoy may sound like a drone, and he may be cynical, but deep down, he still cares. When Marge volunteers at the church as the Listen Lady, people begin to seek her out for advice.[30] Reverend Lovejoy quickly recognizes what is at stake for his own identity as a minister. When he recognizes that he is becoming irrelevant as Springfield's spiritual guide, Reverend Lovejoy embarks on sincere self-reflection. In the quiet of the sanctuary, he is remarkably honest about what is happening. "I'm a shepherd without a flock. What have I done to lose them?" One of the saints in the stained-glass window responds, "What have you done to keep them?" The best Reverend Lovejoy can muster is to mention how he had the vestibule recarpeted. Unfortunately, this exchange cements the feeling of helplessness; Reverend Lovejoy becomes painfully aware that he has failed to provide a sincere spiritual leadership to his congregation. Consequently, Reverend Lovejoy retreats to his basement at home to play with his trains. His wife, Helen, becomes so worried that she calls Marge for advice. Even though she assumed some of Reverend Lovejoy's role as a spiritual counselor because of his apathy, Marge's advice focuses on the genuine spirit that lies buried beneath Reverend Lovejoy's detached ministerial duties. Marge tells Helen, "I'm sure he'll be back to his old, dynamic self." If one takes as genuine Marge's advice to others in this episode, then her words ought to soothe Helen. Marge can recognize that despite Reverend Lovejoy's struggle to recover meaning in his ministry, he still has something dynamic to offer.

By the end of the episode, Reverend Lovejoy gets a chance to prove that he can still provide spiritual leadership. When Ned calls about the teenagers who are loitering outside of his store, yet another non-church-related concern, Marge's advice to assert himself lands Ned in trouble. The teenagers run him out of town. Because of the Listen Lady's bad advice, Reverend Lovejoy must reassert his ability to lead. In the office, Marge frets, "Where do the helpers turn when they need help?" Peering out the window into a beam of light, punctuated when Marge sits on the piano, Reverend Lovejoy sees his opportunity to remember what it means to be a pastor. When someone needs help, the minister is called to provide that assistance, even if the person in question is more beloved that the minister.

Following Ned's clue about cheap gas, Reverend Lovejoy is able to find out where Ned went. He rushes in that direction to learn that Ned went into the zoo. After a brief search, Ned and the Simpson family find Ned in the baboon cage. He escaped the teenagers, but now the baboons want to devour him. The zookeeper offers little consolation about the situation. As he explains, it is bad for the baboons' social health not to kill an intruder into their space. Reverend Lovejoy seizes the moment and, using the zoo train that circles around the baboon cage, manages to rescue Ned. In gratitude, Ned exclaims, "You saved me, Reverend! You really went above and beyond. There's more to being a minister than not caring about people."

Ned's words make Reverend Lovejoy feel better in the moment, but their effect transcends this particular episode. Ned recognizes the extent to which Reverend Lovejoy commits himself to his congregants. The acclaim takes on more significance when one considers that Ned is, by Reverend Lovejoy's own account, the most difficult part of the job. When all is said and done, Ned appreciates Reverend Lovejoy, which ultimately validates Reverend Lovejoy's vocational identity. Ned may annoy

Reverend Lovejoy to no end, but when his most demanding congregant recognizes his efforts, and then offers sincere thanks, Reverend Lovejoy finds himself with a legitimate answer to questions about his ability to lead his flock. Marge, then, is right. Reverend Lovejoy still has a dynamic self buried beneath his burnout. He rarely rediscovers this quality, but he is also not entirely ineffectual as a minister.

The episode concludes with Reverend Lovejoy retelling the story of his harrowing experience during the following week's sermon. He tells the congregation how he sent baboons flying like "two hairy footballs," which is the turning point for Reverend Lovejoy. He subsequently becomes more animated and the congregation listens intently to what happened after Reverend Lovejoy "got mad." The concluding image thus contrasts with the sermon that Reverend Lovejoy gives at the beginning of the episode. Whereas a biblical explication bores the congregation, an animated, hyperbolic story about the minister's heroism captivates the congregation. The contrast reiterates the larger point about how the minister must operate within a specific set of congregational expectations. In this case, Reverend Lovejoy's sermon serves more to entertain than to instruct. Given the interest the shift in content generates in the pews, one can recognize the extent to which the congregation is complicit in Reverend Lovejoy's burnout. They care little about biblical lessons, or, through their faith, enabling spiritual growth in their lives. A minister who exerts spiritual leadership in this capacity will face the same apathy that Reverend Lovejoy battles week in and week out. However, if the minister appeals to the congregational desire for action, they will be all ears. Thus, such expectations draw critical attention away from Reverend Lovejoy by establishing the connection between the congregation's attitude toward their faith and church and the criticisms often leveled at Reverend Lovejoy. Considered in the abstract, the knocks against Reverend Lovejoy's ministry condemn him as a burned-out, disengaged pastor. However, when one remembers that his spiritual leadership adapts to fit the expectations of the congregation, one can see why Reverend Lovejoy deserves a measure of sympathy. Being the pastor at the First Church of Springfield is not just about spirituality leadership; it is also about competing with other cultural influences in order to keep distracted minds entertained.

Even though Reverend Lovejoy's sympathetic moments happen rarely, their presence on *The Simpsons* creates some breathing room for Reverend Lovejoy in the face of criticisms about what he represents. Despite the problems associated with Ned, or his constant financial concerns, Reverend Lovejoy will still embrace his parishioners, and he remains committed to the church. In "Pray Anything," after falling in the church parking lot, Homer sues the church and wins. The court announces a settlement, which, not surprisingly, the church cannot afford. Bankrupt, Reverend Lovejoy must hand Homer the deed to the church and leave town. Homer then desecrates the church in every possible way by throwing a house-warming party. Watching the action from afar, Ned notes that eventually the partygoers violate all Ten Commandments. By the end of the episode, God apparently exacts revenge on the crowd, as a heavy rainstorm floods the town and threatens to drown the partygoers who have gathered on the church's roof. As the floodwaters rise, Reverend Lovejoy appears overhead in a helicopter to rescue those who desecrated the church.

Just as Reverend Lovejoy comes to the rescue when Ned needs him, so, too, will he come back to the town that forsook him. His willingness to return to those who quite literally ruined what he stands for captures the extent to which the townspeople can rely on Reverend Lovejoy to stand by them. The moment echoes Jesus's advice to Christians: they must seek out the black sheep, regardless of conditions.[31] Even when things are so dire that Reverend Lovejoy must risk his own safety, he will do so to help his flock. Moments like this characterize Reverend Lovejoy's true Christian leadership. He accomplishes more than simply recarpeting the vestibule. He is inconsistent and cynical, to be sure, but he shows that he is capable of making himself and the church he represents relevant to a town that will turn its back on its faith. Springfield's parishioners will fall away, neglect the demands their faith places upon them, do their best to avoid their fiduciary obligation to the church, but their pastor will trudge along, even at a low hourly wage.

Chapter Six

Who Is My Neighbor? Ned Flanders and Evangelical Christianity

"Bless the grocer for this wonderful meat, the middle-
man who jacked up the price, and let's not forget
the humane but determined boys at the slaughter-
house."

—Ned Flanders[1]

"In everything do to others as you would have them
do to you."

—Matthew 7:12

When exploring the texture of Springfield's Christianity, the Flanders
family presents a necessary point for discussion. As the embodiment of
Evangelical Christianity in Springfield, Ned, Maude, Rod, and Todd
represent a large slice of the American Christian population.[2] Amid the
show's constant satire and social critique, Ned in particular attracts
sympathetic voices; he is one of the few characters who posits and upholds Christian values. How others react to Ned, and not Ned's character
itself, often provides the departure point for the show's social critiques.
According to Gerry Bowler, Ned Flanders is "television's most effective
exponent of a Christian life well-lived."[3] He provides a sense of spiritual
stability in a town whose Christians often skew or ignore altogether their
faith. Because he is a composite of stereotyped Evangelical characteristics,
many rush to defend Ned against the show's caricature.[4] He upholds a
Christian ethic perhaps better than anyone. For example, even though
he has numerous excuses to condemn Homer, Ned constantly treats

Homer with respect; Ned seriously embraces the call to love his neighbor.[5] However, the Flanderses' presence in Springfield, and Ned's in particular, invites a bit more scrutiny before they are declared to be immune to the show's critical purpose, especially with respect to Christianity. While Ned is a generally positive influence on the town's Christian culture, he, too, reveals a quality in his Evangelical Christianity that deserves the same critical exploration that defines other aspects of Springfield's broader Christian character.

In "Weekend at Burnsie's," *The Simpsons* offers a symptomatic look at Ned's supposedly exemplary faith and how other Springfield residents interact with that faith. When genetically modified vegetables threaten the Simpson family's plan to become vegetarians, Marge decides that she will grow her own vegetables in the backyard. Her plan goes awry when a flock of crows continue to eat whatever she plants. Fed up, she tells Lisa, "I've tried heckling them, I've tried jeckling them, it's time I made myself a scarecrow." The solution is a good one, and Marge goes about implementing it with due diligence. First, she places two sticks in the shape of a cross to hold up the scarecrow. She then goes inside to construct the actual scarecrow. When Marge goes back outside, once against she must brandish her broom to fend off a pest in her garden.

One can see the joke coming. This time, the crows are not swooping in to eat Marge's vegetable seeds. Rather, Ned and his two sons are kneeling before the cruciform scarecrow support, praying earnestly. "Go away! Go away!" she shouts as she waves her broom menacingly. Ned does not hear her at first and he continues his prayer. "God, the Father Almighty, Creator of heaven and earth." Frustrated, Marge says again, "Shoo, shoo!" Their concentration broken, Ned and the boys run away. Satisfied, Marge disappears back into the house; not a moment later, Ned and the boys return to continue praying. "Heaven and earth . . . where are we now? Now I'm lost," Ned says. Before he can get back on track, Marge once again emerges to shoo him out of her garden.

This vignette offers several constructive points concerning the role of Christianity in contemporary American culture. Ned acts in a way that could be understood in positive terms. His personal faith extends beyond the church experience on Sunday. In contrast to Homer, who concludes that God should have made the week an hour longer if God wanted people to go to church,[6] Ned enjoys his faith and does not view it as a chore to address once a week.[7] When Marge shoos him away, Ned exhibits a commitment that is clearly lacking in most of Springfield; he returns to continue his prayers. Rather than rejoice in an excuse not to pray, he calmly resumes what he is doing, unfazed by Marge's forceful, dismissive interruption.

While this moment certainly affirms Ned's commitment to his faith, it also clearly critiques his devotional practices. The very presence of something cruciform, even if it is the support for a scarecrow, is enough to attract his attention. The fact that he brings his kids along speaks to an overzealousness that the episode, and the show in general, satirizes. The object that grabs Ned's attention is a secular (and ultimately inconsequential) thing, decidedly not something that he should worship. Ned's faith thus comes across as undiscerning. His devotion and persistence are extreme in such a way that invites criticism. The stereotypical Evangelical Christian may be respectable in terms of a willingness to embrace what a devoted personal faith implies, but he or she often does so without questioning whether such acts can truly be understood as faithful.[8]

Marge's reaction to Ned's devotion sharpens this critique. She does not kindly ask Ned not to pray in her yard. More tellingly, she does not engage Flanders in discussion to point out the extreme nature of his actions. She responds as one would to any kind of pest. Frustrated that Ned is interrupting her task, she quite literally wants to sweep the problem away so she can finish what she is doing. His persistence only aggravates her annoyance. That Marge is the one who responds to Ned in this way constitutes an important component in the critique in question. In the Simpson family, Marge is often the one who evinces a moderate kind of faith. If anyone were going to be sympathetic to Ned in this situation, it should be her. However, she recognizes that Ned is clearly crossing a line. Her reaction thus characterizes a common critique leveled against the Evangelism that Ned represents. His caricatured personal faith clearly oversteps some reasonable boundaries. He demeans himself (and his children) through the eager application of faith. He ceases to be a neighbor who is the model Christian and he becomes the pest whose actions infringe on others' personal lives in such a way that prevents them from going about their daily business.

This tension between the Evangelical community and mainstream American culture, as that mainstream culture perceives the Evangelical community, illustrates the extent to which *The Simpsons* is conscious of a significant schism in the American Christian landscape. The way in which the above examples critiques both sides of the equation gives reason to explore the complex texture that defines Ned's identity in the show as well as how Springfield's other, decidedly non-Evangelical, residents interact with Ned and his family.

Ned Flanders offers a foil to the apathetic Christianity that otherwise defines most of Springfield. In his book *The Gospel According to* The Simpsons, Mark Pinsky understands the portrayal to be sympathetic in a way that buttresses Christianity's role on the show. In the face of "the chief sin of Christian character . . . hypocrisy . . . Ned Flanders is exemplary; his Christianity is unassailable."[9] In broad strokes, Pinsky's summary is accurate; Ned does warrant sympathy insofar as he embraces thoroughly that which he believes. However, at the outset it is important to recognize that Ned is far from perfect. Just as Ned often serves as a foil to expose the flaws in others' relationships to Christianity, their Christian faith provides a similar critical dynamic that enables one to address Ned's own flaws.[10] Though Marge is not blameless in shooing away Ned and his boys as nothing more than pests, the fact that his actions elicit this reaction makes clear that Ned's character is more complex than many acknowledge. In Ned Flanders, the Evangelical community faces a caricature of itself that demands self-examination.

"Homer and Ned's Hail Mary Pass" captures the complex relationship between Ned and other Springfield residents, especially Homer. In response to Comic Book Guy's Web site, http://www.dorks-gone-wild.com, Ned decides to film biblical scenes with his home camera. With Rod and Todd as actors, Ned records a rendition of the Cain and Abel story that portrays the murder as excessively bloody.[11] The contrast between what Ned is doing with his kids and what he understands himself to be doing is striking. Ned portrays the scene in a way that clearly embraces violence. He is so caught up in conveying a biblical lesson to the town that he is unable to recognize that he exposes his boys to experience something he otherwise prohibits them from seeing.[12] For Ned, a biblical foundation for his home movies excuses the questionable material in his projects. Ned accepts that the biblical content behind his film permit his boys to experience. More troubling, Rod and Todd do not seem to be bothered by their gruesome roles in the film. If the Bible demands that Rod and Todd perform violent acts on film, and they also become desensitized to that violence, then so be it. At stake in this episode is Ned's inability to recognize that he is hypocritical in choosing to what he will expose to his children.

Given that Ned actively campaigns against exposing children to violence because they might imitate what they experience in the media,[13] his willingness to allow the very thing he condemns outside of a biblical context is problematic. Frank G. Sterle, Jr., suggests, however, that such examples ridicule Ned unfairly: "For many viewers, the show goes too far in a few of its jabs at Christianity that appear more ideological than humourous, perhaps overly philosophical enough to be construed as naught but political *Simpsons* script-writing."[14] Those who criticize how *The Simpsons* portrays Ned miss the show's broader point if they sympathize with Sterle's comments. In these examples involving the Flanders family, ideology and its negative effects stem from the person who condemns and seeks to correct American culture's spiritual apathy. The critique here focuses on how the Evangelical community often adopts a clearly hypocritical attitude when using its belief system to condemn culture.[15] Put simply, the Evangelical community often endorses the very things it so adamantly denounces. If violence truly has a harmful effect on children, then presumably one should protest all ways in which American culture exposes children to violence. Evangelicals participate in this culture equally and thus they, too, expose their children to questionable influences. There is little difference between a mouse hitting a cat with a mallet and one brother stabbing the other brother with a sword. The act itself, inflicting harm on another, does not change; only the context in which the act occurs is different. Thus, in condemning violence and other negative influences in American culture, Ned exhibits a problematic hypocrisy. He determines the basis for disapproving one thing and endorsing another based solely on whether the thing in question upholds his beliefs. He accepts this biblical framework and a stereotypical political agenda held by some Evangelicals as unassailable and thus does not question the actual content of his own actions.

If Flanders exhibited this double standard only with respect to his children, one might dismiss the effects of his faith as a father's protective quirk. In "Home Sweet Homediddily-Dum-Doodily," one finds such a sympathetic portrayal of Flanders with respect to the question of violence. While watching *Itchy & Scratchy* with the Simpson children as well as Rod and Todd, Ned faces a parenting challenge. After Itchy stabs Scratchy with a broken bottle, Rod asks, "Daddy, what's the red stuff coming out of the kitty's ears?" Flanders offers an answer that avoids the question; the blood, he says, is just "raspberry jam." When Todd asks if he "should poke Rod with a sharp thing like the mouse did," Ned provides the appropriate response: "No, son. No sirree Bob." This effective parental response to violence on television, and the way it invites mimicry, only magnifies the way that Ned exhibits hypocrisy in permitting the same thing he is quick to denounce. Flanders is willing to jettison his good sense when his faith becomes a factor. Flanders rightfully dismisses *Itchy & Scratchy* as a bad influence; his answer assumes no disconnected notions of reality based on faith. It is only when his faith presents the same dilemma that Flanders is unable to be reasonable as a parent.

The Simpsons offers such examples of Ned's critical nature toward most of Springfield as an obvious contradiction in the moral example that Ned supposedly represents. Tellingly, Ned seems to be oblivious to the problems posed by his self-understood moral superiority.[16] In the show's four-hundredth episode, "You Kent Always Say What You Want," one finds just how narrowly Ned sometimes understands his role in a culture that does not necessarily uphold his personal values. In this episode, Homer appears on Kent Brockman's show, *Smartline*, to discuss his newest accomplishment: purchasing the one-millionth cone at a local ice cream parlor. As he does so often, Homer acts in a way that enables controversy in Springfield. Specifically, Homer spills coffee on Brockman's lap. As one might expect in response to such a painful situation, Brockman swears out of frustration. Unfortunately, the scenario unfolds on-air, which soon leads to serious repercussions. Later in the episode, Ned is sitting in his living room in order to review tapes of all recent television programming. As he watches various recordings, Ned decides whether they should go in the "Nice" pile or the "Naughty" pile. The allusion to Santa Claus sketches a portrait of Ned as an arbitrary though unrealistic voice on the moral character of what he evaluates. Of course, he bases his criteria for evaluating shows solely on the standards that his beliefs impose. Such evaluative criteria doom almost every show, including a program where Superdog "licks himself."[17] As an animal, Superdog should neither face moral judgment nor be condemned for acting as any animal would. That Ned deems Superdog to be "naughty" for being a dog illustrates how Ned's narrow moral standards necessarily dismiss everything that does not square with his particular religious biases.

Eventually, Ned finds the tape of Homer's appearance on Kent Brockman's show. When Flanders sees that Brockman swore on television, his moral alarm bells start to ring. He responds immediately with astonishment: "God's least favorite word uttered on the public airwaves!" Given his willingness to condemn Superdog, one should not be surprised at how Ned reacts to Brockman's slip. Still, an important critical point emerges. To assume that God even has a favorite word reveals that Ned understands God in a way that is expedient to his self-assumed moral policing. To suggest that God would be interested in such minutiae demeans the notion of God as wholly other from humanity.[18]

Convinced that Kent Brockman's words are blasphemous, Ned races to alert other Evangelicals, who presumably support his moral crusade. He logs in to a Christian chat room to post a message about a "televised super-swear." As he types his complaint, Rod and Todd enter. The conversation that follows reveals further how *The Simpsons* critiques the Evangelicals' perception that they serve the role of moral guardians in American culture.

Rod: Daddy, what are you doing?

Ned: Imploring people I never met to pressure government with better things to do to punish a man who meant no harm for something nobody ever saw.

Rod: [touching his dad tenderly]: Daddy, we think you need a new mommy.

Ned's assumed moral authority ignores just how absurd he is in judging Brockman. Aside from the fact that he does not even know what word Brockman said (it had been bleeped out), Ned admits tacitly that his errand smacks of self-righteousness. What Ned finds offensive depends on doing something that he probably should not have been doing in the first place. Surely Ned has better things to do besides critiqueing television programming for his own satisfaction. Even Rod can identify that his father's actions cause more harm than good. Rather than concern himself with his own loneliness, Ned seeks to punish an act that is, by reasonable standards, understandable. Brockman clearly did not have malicious intent. Rather, he responded in the moment to what was likely a painful experience.[19]

The extent to which Ned involves himself in policing the culture in which he lives is troubling, as it reflects an assumed moral superiority that ultimately reveals Christian hypocrisy. The clear critique that the show offers revolves around the hypocrisy that Flanders is supposed to avoid as the show's paragon of the religious life. Specifically, Flanders fails to live up to a clear biblical imperative against judging others. Jesus famously states, "Judge not, lest ye be judged."[20] The command is clear enough, but Ned often understands himself as exempt from the injunction. In "Home Sweet Homediddily-Dum-Doodily,"Maude Flanders makes this disconnect obvious. In response to Homer and Marge's parenting, Maude refuses to say anything about the people involved. Rather, she says succinctly, "I don't judge Homer and Marge. That's for a vengeful God to do." If she were sincere, Maude would very much embody Jesus's moral injunction. However, she clearly disapproves of Homer and Marge and thus she reveals yet again the moral hypocrisy that the Evangelical community often exhibits. In such cases, *The Simpsons* echoes the simple biblical idea in order to reveal just how far from fulfilling that moral humility the moral Flanders family is. In failing to uphold the idea that they should not judge others, Maude invites viewers to remember a corollary biblical command: "Why do you see the speck in your neighbor's eye, but do not notice the log in your own eye? Or how can you say to your neighbor, Let me take the speck out of your eye, while the log is in your own eye? You hypocrite, first take the log out of your own eye, and then you will see clearly to take the speck out of your neighbor's eye."[21]

Though the social role that Flanders's Evangelical Christianity plays in Springfield is clearly inconsistent with his claimed beliefs, the extent to which he embodies a stereotypical Evangelical hypocrisy appears most forcefully at a different point in "Home Sweet Homediddily-Dum-Doodily." When Homer and Marge must attend a parenting class to reclaim their children, Bart, Lisa, and Maggie face the extent to which Flanders and his family will thrust their faith upon others. When he finds out that the Simpson children have never been baptized, Ned frantically calls Reverend Lovejoy: "Reverend. Emergency! It's the Simpson kids. Eedily. I, uh, baptism. Oodily. Uh, doodily doodily!" Lovejoy, who is otherwise enjoying his free time with his trains, gives an exasperated response: "Ned, have you thought about one of the other major religions? They're all pretty much the same." Though Lovejoy dismisses Ned's concern with a theologically flippant remark, the response's tenor conveys the extent to which Ned is meddling. Reverend Lovejoy rightfully dismisses Ned's concern as irrelevant.[22] The notion of forcibly baptizing another person's children does not warrant a response because Christianity does not endorse this action.[23] Still, Ned ignores Reverend Lovejoy and decides to baptize the Simpson children by himself.

From Ned's own perspective, the notion of the Simpson children as unbaptized constitutes a spiritual crisis, but theologically speaking that is not anything that can or should concern him. According to Calvin, "Baptism serves as our confession before men. Indeed, it is the mark by which we publicly profess that we wish to be reckoned with God's people; by which we testify that we agree in worshipping the same God . . . by which we finally affirm our faith."[24] At the heart of baptism, then, lies a need for the baptized to understand his or her receiving the baptism as an outward confession of faith. This implies clearly that the individual must exercise agency in accepting the baptism.[25] Ned, however, understands baptism in a way that reflects his skewed personal beliefs. Thus, in taking the matter into his own hands, Ned ignores a defining characteristic in the notion of baptism. He should realize that when he asks, "Who wants to be the first to enter into God's good graces?" Bart and Lisa point at one another, an act that indicates clearly they do not assent to being baptized. Ned, then, acts yet again in a way that imposes his personal beliefs on others. As with previous examples, this vignette illustrates that while he believes himself to be acting in accordance with good faith, he fails to recognize that his personal faith does not and indeed cannot necessarily apply to others.[26]

The self-righteousness and the lack of self-awareness with which Evangelical Christianity often conducts itself lies at the heart of these critiques. When Ned disapproves of something, he quickly assumes the role of moral, or worse, spiritual, policeman. In "Father, Son, and Holy Guest-Star," Ned initiates a kind of crusade against the notion that someone might not adhere to his personal understanding of Christianity. When Bart and Homer decide to convert to Catholicism, Ned enlists Reverend Lovejoy to force them out of the church. When he sees Bart and Homer in First Communion 101, Ned exclaims, "Oh, we've got to stop them now! Once they seal the deal, there's no turning back!" While the Catholic Church and Protestant denominations certainly understand Communion's theological and ecclesiastical points in different capacities, to suggest that participating in a specific denominational practice of Communion places an irrevocable divide between the two runs against the grain of the act as symbolizing unity and forgiveness. Ned echoes this militant response when Bart threatens to pick Judaism instead of Catholicism. In fact, Ned pulls out a bottle of chloroform. The situation in his mind is so critical that he must assault Bart to enforce his participation in Christianity in a way that Ned deems acceptable.[27] Thankfully, Reverend Lovejoy waves his hand to encourage Ned to put the bottle away.

Bart's speech at the end of the episode addresses precisely this point. He says, "It's all Christianity, people. The little, stupid differences are nothing next to the big, stupid similarities." Ned recognizes the value of these words, though why they are valuable reinforces his problematic moral agenda. He responds, "He's right! Can't we all get together and concentrate on our real enemies like monogamous gays and stem cells?" Even though he acknowledges Bart's call for unity, Ned fails to grasp what that unity entails. He can reconcile himself to the Catholic Church only if doing so means he can campaign against another issue.[28] Not surprisingly, by the end of the episode Bart's reconciling words become a later source of conflict between denominations. Once again, the way in which people dissect issues of faith enables conflict that can easily escalate into violence. It is this risk that underlies the critique of Ned's desire to impose his faith on others.

While there is much to criticize in the Evangelical faith that Ned represents, it is important to note that others recognize the positive aspects of his committed spirituality. In "A Star Is Born Again," Ned meets Sarah Sloane, a movie star whose religious and moral character falls closer to Homer's than Ned's. Still, Ned's naïveté and morals appeal to Sarah, who enjoys a relationship where she is not solely an object of lust. They begin to date and, as their bond strengthens, Sarah begins to pressure Ned to have sex. Importantly, Ned agrees to do so, but the following morning he alerts Sarah that the condition for his participation is that they now discuss marriage. Shocked, Sarah decides to terminate the relationship.

Ned's brief encounter with Sarah Sloane points toward several qualities that define Ned as something other than a pestlike presence in Springfield. He treats Sarah with respect at the outset, an outgrowth of his general moral approach to anyone on the show. As an outsider, Sarah gravitates toward this type of character when she has been used to relationships with men who presumably lack moral grounding. Sarah thus provides a contrasting foil to Ned in relation to other Springfield residents. The consistent spiritual and moral character that Ned exudes, and that often elicits criticism from characters like Homer, is a highly desirable quality. It is significant that, when relating to Sarah, Ned does not represent a faith that demands he repress all desire.[29] He allows himself to indulge his desires; the only condition is that such an indulgence translates into a committed relationship. In a media-driven culture where treating sexual relationships with a strong moral elements carries negative connotations, Ned's willingness to uphold his morals warrants praise. Moreover, he refuses to compromise what he believes in, even at the cost of a continued romantic relationship with a desirable partner.

The notion that Ned Flanders constitutes a role model, complete with qualities that can be desirable even within the critiques that *The Simpsons* levels against Evangelical Christianity, appears strongly in *The Simpsons Movie*. When Homer lavishes his fatherly affection on a pig, Bart sits outside on a tree and watches the pig receive the attentions he desires. Bart then looks into the Flanders household and observes Ned tucking Rod and Todd into bed. Noticing that something is bothering Bart, Ned offers a cup of hot cocoa, which Bart rejects. Ned makes a cup to leave on the windowsill, complete with whipped cream, a graham cracker, and a marshmallow. The drink is too much to resist and Bart finally takes the cocoa. After his first sip, Bart exclaims, "Oh my God."

On the surface, Bart's words appear to be a delighted response only to the cocoa. However, his words add an important layer to the dynamic that develops between Bart and Ned throughout the movie. As Homer consistently proves himself to be an inept father, Ned continues to provide the attention that Bart craves. Once the Simpson family has escaped Springfield, Bart makes several revealing comments that convey a clear awareness of Ned's genuine affection. Hidden away in a hotel and drunk on whiskey, Bart exclaims, "I miss Flanders. There, I said it." Though one could easily dismiss Bart's comment as a result of the alcohol he is drinking, the words constitute an honest confession. Bart means it; the alcohol, far from distorting his reasoning, allows him to be honest. He recognizes that Ned provides more as a father figure than Homer does. Bart makes this point clear when the family is in Alaska and the following exchange occurs.

Bart: I wish Flanders was my father.

Homer: You don't mean that.

Bart: Yes I do.

To prove his sincerity, Bart pulls out a picture of Homer to show what Bart has realized during the family's adventure. Bart has literally drawn Ned's face over Homer's. He makes explicit his realization that, as a father, Ned provides everything that Homer does not.

As the movie nears its conclusion, Bart makes a striking decision. During the town's last minutes before its destruction, Bart shuns Homer and seeks out Ned, who is sitting in church with Rod and Todd. Bart asks Ned if he can join the Flanders family. His reason for doing so ties back to Bart's initial comment about the hot cocoa. Bart wants to be a Flanders before he dies because he wants a "father who cares about him." Bart's words have a distinct layer that transcends his mere desire to experience fatherly affection. He desires comfort in a way that exhibits clearly theological overtones. Bart's words refer directly to Ned, but the underlying desires recall how the Bible characterizes God.[30] The fact that he confesses this desire in church illustrates that Bart is becoming aware of how a sincere Christian faith, as embodied in Ned, can provide meaning in his life. Ned thus symbolizes the positive changes that one traditionally experiences in ascribing to a Christian faith. Bart's initial comments in response to Ned's kindness thus generate a desire for a more involved relationship with God. Coming from Bart, this is no small request. Bart's small sip of cocoa generates a symbolic affirmation of the positive way that Ned and the faith he represents can improve everyone's life. Ned embodies the qualities that Christianity traditionally associates with God.

In this face of crisis, Bart seeks comfort. Given the extreme nature of this moment, only comfort from a true "father" can satisfy Bart's longing.

If Bart can recognize the positive qualities of Ned's faith, then Ned's flaws cannot be overly problematic. Bart's admiration of Ned is telling, but perhaps the best endorsement of Ned's role on *The Simpsons* comes from Homer. "Diatribe of a Mad Housewife" captures the positive influence that Ned brings to Springfield in general and the Simpson family in particular. Marge pursues her new dream to write a romance novel, *The Harpooned Heart*, which eventually becomes a best seller. The episode switches between the story that Marge envisions as it unfolds in her head and her real life as her work develops. The events in her real experience clearly provide the basis for the story that happens in her head. The novel's antagonist, Temperance, is married to a rather boorish fisherman, who clearly embodies all of Homer's negative spousal and moral qualities. While her husband is out drinking, Temperance meets Cyrus Manly, who Marge imagines as a sexually attractive and morally grounded gentleman. In a word, Temperance meets Ned Flanders.

Marge waits to publish the novel, with its unflattering portrayal of Homer, until Homer says that he read it and expresses that he is comfortable with its content. Of course, Homer falls asleep in his hammock before he can finish the first sentence. When Marge asks him what he thinks, he lies and affirms the story. Once published, the novel ignites gossip all over town, as no one can mistake what the story in the novel represents. Once Homer does decide to read the novel, which he accomplishes by listening to it on tape, he discovers how Marge has characterized his flaws. Moreover, he recognizes that Marge's heroine sees an escape from those flaws in the character based on Flanders. The world of the novel and the Simpsons' real life converge at the end of the episode. Temperance's husband pursues Cyrus to the edge of a cliff to exact his revenge, while Homer pursues Ned to a cliff somewhere on the outskirts of Springfield. In the novel, Temperance's husband kills Cyrus by stabbing him with a harpoon. When Marge arrives on the scene that is unfolding in actual life, she gasps when she sees that Homer has cornered Ned. What happens next is completely unexpected. Homer drops to his knees and says to Ned, "Can you help me be a better husband?"

Homer's plea is telling. The person who serves constantly as a foil for Ned recognizes that, in the end, Ned is the one who is happy. Ned's Evangelical Christianity, for all its shortcomings, ultimately enhances his life and, more important, can do the same for others. Even Homer can recognize the positive parts of Ned's character. Generally, Ned escapes scrutiny of the show without inviting serious criticism. Still, he does have serious flaws, which adds an important component to the way in which *The Simpsons* characterizes and critiques religious life in Springfield. However, when Homer can recognize that Ned is a good person, and that such goodness can bring value to his own marriage, Homer reveals that, despite his shortcomings, Ned Flanders provides a more optimistic take on how Christianity can have a positive effect on the lives of contemporary American Christians, even in Springfield.

Chapter Seven

The Only Gate Out of Town: Springfield's Spiritual Wanderers

"I will pass the surly bounds of gravity and punch the face of God!"

—Homer Simpson[1]

"He has told you, O mortal, what is good; and what does the Lord require of you but to do justice, and to love kindness, and to walk humbly with your God?"

—Micah 6:8

When Krusty the Clown gives away his trampoline, Homer jumps at the chance to get something for free.[2] Springfield's residents soon stop by Homer's house to try out the trampoline. A string of injuries and accidents ensues, but this does nothing to deter Rod and Todd Flanders from taking their turn. While jumping, they make clear how they interpret their experience:

Todd: Each leap brings us closer to God.

Rod: Catch me, Lord, catch me!

[They jump into each other and fall to the ground.]

Rod: What have we done to make God angry?

Todd: You did it!

At first, this conversation reveals little more than the typical Flanders family spiritual hyperbole. Rod and Todd use the best reference point they know to convey how excited they are about jumping on the tram-poline. Moreover, understanding their experience as a way to jump closer to God falls within their parents' expectations that recreation somehow relate to their Christian faith.[3] The Christian influence on their upbring-ing drives the interpretation of both what they are doing and the result they expect, which lasts until reality interrupts their fun. As soon as they tumble to the ground, their joy evaporates. Somehow they have done something wrong, which causes Todd to play a different kind of game. If God is angry, then Todd wants to make sure Rod takes the blame.

The Flanders kids offer a helpful window into the way that people's faith affects how they interpret their experiences. Rod and Todd are chil-dren, but they understand their world in a way that adopts almost wholly their parents' Christian influence. They exhibit clearly the values that Ned and Maude Flanders have instilled in their young lives.[4] The extent to which this upbringing emerges when they appear on *The Simpsons* points to a deeper issue concerning Christianity in Springfield. Having explored the general spiritual pulse of *The Simpsons*, as well as specific concerns contained in how *The Simpsons* portrays central elements of Christianity, this chapter will look more deeply into the unique characteristics that define Springfield's relationship to the Christian faith as distinctly Amer-ican. As Rod and Todd make clear, one's faith can have tangible effects on how one interprets everyday experiences.

Robert Wuthnow provides a helpful framework with which to pur-sue this task. In *After Heaven: Spirituality in America Since the 1950s*, Wuthnow describes spirituality in useful terms. "At its core, spirituality consists of all the beliefs and activities by which individuals attempt to relate their lives to God. . . . [S]pirituality is not just the creation of in-dividuals; it is shaped by larger social circumstances and by the beliefs and values present in the wider culture."[5] To explore the broader cultural elements that define Christian spirituality, one needs to cast one's net widely. A critical exploration of American Christianity must, then, bal-ance an individual's experiences with the wider cultural influences that affect the individual's life. For example, Rod and Todd embody their personal experiences with respect to Christianity. Based on their con-versation, there is little doubt that they are products of the Flanders family. However, what they discuss after they bump into each other is slightly more varied. Rod still speaks in the naïve terms that his parents would likely appreciate. Rod recalls immediately the appropriate frame-work through which he should evaluate what just happened. Somehow he and Todd have incurred God's punishment.[6]

Todd, on the other hand, skews that framework slightly. Thus, he reflects at least a measure of individual spirituality that is, importantly, distinct from the sanctity and sanctuary of the Flanders house. Ned would never try to dodge responsibility for his own actions when dealing with God. Todd still understands the situation within the framework that his upbringing constructed, but he is not going to sit idly by and wait for God's punishment. He acts in a way that he most likely learned from Homer; he deflects blame. This is not a lesson he learned from his parents. Todd very much reflects a spiritual residue that is indicative of broader social influences, even if those influences come from the next-door neighbor. Wuthnow's point thus comes into focus in a seemingly innocuous example. Rod and Todd are spiritually undeveloped. For the most part, they have yet to carry their faith into their social world. However, even they exhibit the comprehensive and complex nature of spirituality in American culture. The example that Rod and Todd provide establishes a precedent that is developed more clearly in the spirituality of the show's major characters.

In contemporary American culture, Wuthnow recognizes broad patterns in how Christians understand and practice their faith. The days when the town hall and church were quite literally the same building are gone. Christianity in America is displaced. It has become "a vastly complex quest in which each person seeks in his or her own way."[7] Importantly, this journey occurs on the individual's own terms. Organized religion, especially as embodied in traditional Christian churches, plays a reduced role in developing an individual's spirituality.[8] This represents a shift away from the established spiritual centers that constitute what Wuthnow calls "[a] spirituality of dwelling [which] emphasizes *habituation*: God occupies a definite place in the universe and creates a sacred space in which humans too can dwell."[9] Traditionally, Christianity emphasizes practices that fit squarely within Wuthnow's notion of a spirituality of dwelling. It believes the church to be the center of the spiritual and communal life of the Christian body. God dwells in the church, which provides a place for the community to nurture its faith. When Jesus first articulated the notion of community as foundational for the church's role in people's lives, he made clear that one could not nurture a life of faith in solitude.[10]

In Christianity's Reformed churches, the presence of the community gathered in the church lies at the heart of a person's spiritual life. According to John Calvin:

Nothing fosters mutual love more fittingly than for men to be bound together with this bond: one is appointed pastor to teach the rest, and those bidden to be pupils receive the common teaching from one mouth. For if anyone were sufficient to himself and needed no one else's help (such is the pride of human nature), each man would despise the rest and be despised by them.[11]

Calvin adopts Paul's metaphor of the church as a body[12] to emphasize that God utilizes corporate worship to "govern the church, [which] is the chief sinew by which believers are held together in one body."[13] Consequently, spiritual development and a rewarding personal faith must grow out of a collective center. Calvin thus describes clearly the notion of habituation. For example, spiritual leadership often resembles a caretaker as opposed to someone who provides spiritual influence.[14] In order for Christians to participate in what God offers, they must participate in the church's communal life that occurs in this space. Part of this life is to accept the authority of a particular person whose job is to teach. Regardless of how one understands one's own spiritual tradition, Christianity emphasizes that people should participate in what Wuthnow calls habituated spirituality.

In "Brother's Little Helper," Reverend Lovejoy speaks of the church in a way that echoes Wuthnow's notion of spiritual dwelling. To address his newly diagnosed attention deficit disorder, Bart begins to take Focusyn. His academic performance improves, but eventually doctors decide that he should stop taking the drug. The results approach disaster. Without the drugs, Bart's behavior becomes unpredictable. He eventually sneaks into a military base and then steals a tank. His mind rattled, Bart drives the tank through town and threatens to shoot at various Springfield institutions. With each swing of the turret, another building is threatened. When the tank zeroes in on the First Church of Springfield, Reverend Lovejoy cries out, "Not the church! Jesus lives there!" In this plea, one can see a traditional notion that the church provides a physical dwelling space for the holy. Reverend Lovejoy conceptualizes Jesus's (and thus God's) presence as a physical reality. Thus, the church building represents a traditional place for spiritual dwelling. If Bart shoots the church with the tank, then he will destroy not just a symbol, but a literal space needed for the Christian community's spiritual development.

Despite Reverend Lovejoy's concern for his church, Christianity in Springfield reacts strongly to the traditional dwelling spirituality that Wuthnow describes. For most of Springfield's Christians, faith resembles

> [a] spirituality of seeking, [which] emphasizes *negotiation*: in-
> dividuals search for sacred moments that reinforce their con-
> viction that the divine exists, but these moments are fleeting;
> rather than knowing the territory, people explore new spiritual
> vistas, and they may have to negotiate among complex and
> confusing meanings of spirituality.[15]

This spirituality, which replaces commitment to a specific physical place of worship and thus a more traditional form of worship, defines the majority of Christian spiritual practice in Springfield. Ned Flanders is the only one who can probably claim to embrace consistently a Christian faith that one could call a spirituality of dwelling. Whereas the spirituality of dwelling emphasizes a consistent approach to one's faith in the context of one's spiritual peers, the spirituality of seeking turns away from such corporate notions of Christianity. God does not set up shop in the church building and others do not help to nurture one's own faith. Rather, spirituality is an individual concern, a journey that one must navigate on one's own terms. God still exists in this conception, but God does so in a way that can more easily be adapted to one's own experiential and spiritual framework. God becomes "fluid, portable, and spirituality must be pursued with a sense of God's people having been dispersed."[16] Spiritual seekers do not reject the divine; they merely recast the divine in terms that are flexible enough to adapt to particular situations.

In "El Viaje Misterioso de Nuestro Jomer," *The Simpsons* captures the way that American spirituality has gravitated toward Wuthnow's model of the spiritual seeker. In its first few minutes, the episode presents Homer as an unlikely candidate for a spiritual journey. As he reads the paper, Homer discards sections that do not interest him. He throws away significant sections from the paper with disdain in his voice: "The world. The arts. Religion." Homer manifests his distaste for the religion section in particular by drawing out the word, a delay that he matches with a look of displeasure. Only when he finds the "Kickin' Back" section does Homer feel at ease. His willingness to do nothing at the expense of involving himself in other more significant aspects of his culture quite literally rejects religion as relevant. The point is punctuated when Homer becomes agitated. He realizes that Marge has been trying to keep the annual Chili Cook-off a secret so that Homer will not repeat the previous year's performance: he got drunk and spun around in the cotton candy machine, without any clothes on. At the outset, then, one sees Homer not only as disinterested in religion, but also as someone whose appetitive desires demand significant personal resources.[17]

Once at the cook-off, Homer aggravates the marital discord that his devotion to the event already generated. Marge does not want him to go because she knows Homer is likely to get inebriated and embarrass her. She relents, however, when Homer promises not to drink. Homer still manages to anger Marge, though not because he decides to drink beer. Rather, he eats far too many Guatemalan insanity peppers from Chief Wiggum's chili. Subsequently, Homer begins to hallucinate. He suddenly finds himself on a desert road as he travels toward an endless horizon.[18] His apparently antireligious hobby has planted him firmly in a hallucinogenic spiritual journey. Instead of heading in the direction of a fixed spiritual point, Homer presses on toward the unknown. In line with Wuthnow's paradigm of the spiritual seeker, Homer is alone.

Initially, Homer has no idea what he is supposed to do in the desert, so he spells out a giant "Help" with a bunch of rocks. The corner rock begins to walk away and Homer finds the first guide to help him on his quest. The rock is actually a turtle that writes out in the dust that Homer should "follow ... the ... turtle." As far as turtles go, the message appears quickly, but Homer's frustration boils over. Having already waited for the turtle to spell out the message, Homer is not interested in plodding along as the turtle ambles through the desert. He begins to prod it with his foot and says, "When I'm kicking you that means hurry up." To vent his building frustration, Homer kicks the turtle over the horizon, and then runs to where the turtle lands. The brief exchange reveals an emotionally rich quality to Homer's spiritual quest. True to his character, he understands personal satisfaction in the American way: immediate gratification. Thus, he feels legitimate frustration, which thus clarifies something that he needs to learn: he lacks patience. As someone who demands immediate satisfaction, Homer will face significant challenges in his spiritual journey.

When Homer eventually finds the turtle, the turtle nods to indicate that Homer must climb a pyramid that is only three steps high. Homer cannot believe how small the pyramid is, a reaction that reveals his expectations. If he has to wait, he wants something grander than an easily scalable destination. Of course, Homer is about to pay for his earlier frustration. The pyramid grows exponentially and Homer now faces an exhaustive climb to the top. Significantly, Homer recognizes the consequences of his actions: "This is because I kicked you, isn't it?" The turtle nods in agreement, and Homer, contrary to his earlier desire for an expedient journey, resigns himself to the task. He begins to haul himself up the pyramid; his spiritual quest is already producing results.

When Homer reaches the top of the pyramid, he sees an outline of Marge, who is turned away from him. He is sincerely glad to see her, but when he races to see her face, the figure rotates in such a way that Homer can never see Marge's face. The source of the day's trouble, his marital problems with Marge, thus provides the impetus for Homer's spiritual quest. The figure eventually blows away. Only a pile of dust remains, and Homer once again finds himself alone. Fortunately, this time around he does not have to wait for company. A spiritual guide in the form of a coyote appears to Homer and dictates the terms of Homer's upcoming spiritual journey. In response, Homer becomes self-reflective and says, "You know, I have been meaning to take a spiritual quest." Happy to see that Homer assents to the task, the coyote tells Homer to find his soul mate. At first, he resists what the guide says and attempts to fulfill the quest as quickly as possible. Homer says without hesitation that Marge is his soul mate. Only when the coyote asks Homer if he is sure that Marge is his soul mate does Homer pause. At this point, Homer begins to recognize what Wuthnow calls a "spiritual homelessness."[19] This void causes spiritual seekers to "negotiate their own understandings and experiences of the sacred."[20] For Homer, the epiphany does not include God. He sees in his quest the source of what bothers him. He needs to recalibrate his spirituality because he is not getting along with Marge. Thus, what is sacred for Homer is not the God he hears about in church but rather his relationship with his wife.

The rest of Homer's spiritual journey responds to the search for his soul mate. When he arrives at home after his experience with the coyote, he assumes Marge will simply excuse his actions:

Homer: Oh-ho. I guess you're cranky 'cause I didn't come home last night.

Marge: I'm "cranky" because my husband got drunk and humiliated me in front of the entire town. You broke your promise, Homer.

Homer: Oh, honey, I didn't get drunk, I just went to a strange fantasy world.

In response, Marge merely grits her teeth as she seethes in response to yet another fantastic explanation. Homer fails to realize her anger, as he says hopefully, "Marge. Soul mate." Marge explodes in response: "Don't soul mate me!" Shocked, Homer retreats anxiously, then spends the rest of the night pacing in his living room as doubt sets in; he interprets

Marge's anger as proof that they are not soul mates. Homer's assumption proves to be inaccurate, which aggravates his spiritual discomfort. Doubt seeps into his mind, and Homer begins to wander around Springfield in search of a new soul mate. He asks everyone and everyone denies a special, spiritual connection with him. Homer slips into a melancholic state as he wanders the streets of Springfield looking for a soul mate.

Eventually, Homer returns to the point of departure; Marge finds Homer at the lighthouse and reassures him that just because they had a fight, they still share a "profound mystical understanding." Their conversation shores up Homer's awareness of the sacred:

Homer: But how did you find me?

Marge: Well, I was sure you'd be on foot, because you always say public transportation is for losers. And I was sure you'd head west, because Springfield slopes down that way. And then, I saw the lighthouse, and I remembered how you love blinking lights. Like the one on the waffle iron.

Homer: Or that little guy on the Don't Walk sign. Wow, Marge, you really do understand me.

For a brief moment, then, Homer experiences a sense of peace in his marriage with Marge. Thus, the root of the spiritual crisis, his marital tension, fades as he reaches a state of spiritual awareness. This renewed sense of the sacred, however, does not include an element that one can associate with traditional Christianity. He understands his completed spiritual quest in the context of his daily life. Thus, Homer does not find God per se. Rather, he experiences something like God in his relationship with Marge.

The entire episode exhibits a literal and spiritual sense of fluidity that Wuthnow emphasizes as definitive in the seeker's spirituality.[21] The landscape constantly shifts, which reflects Homer's unstable spiritual identity. Perhaps it is just the insanity peppers talking to Homer, but the underlying narrative point is that what initiates and encourages Homer's journey is anything but the spirituality embodied in the traditional, physical church. Only through a hallucination can Homer consider, much less accept, a spiritual quest.[22] Whereas a spirituality of dwelling finds answers in the church, a fixed location with a defined spiritual framework, the spiritual seeker necessarily travels into the unknown. The result likewise does not clarify a conception of the divine. Rather, as Wuthnow points out, the result of the spiritual seeker's quest usually produces "pragmatic"[23] effects. In Homer's case, he rediscovers that he and Marge are soul mates, which, at least in the context of the episode, rekindles his appreciation for the sacred. The effect is ultimately fleeting in their marriage, as Homer will soon be back to his self-absorbed ways. Thus, his experience points again to his epiphany's transitory nature, which, as a spiritual seeker is characterized by "dabbling rather than by depth."[24]

Such individualism is a consequence that defines a spirituality of seeking, which thus characterizes America's postmodern Christian tendencies. The "private"[25] emphasis in American spirituality emerges consistently on *The Simpsons*. One strong example of this dynamic emerges from the idea that moral education occurs in the home and, therefore, not in the church. This emphasis on the home constitutes a large part of the show's moral foundation. However, this shift produces a tangled relationship between traditional spirituality, as embodied in the Christian Church, and the tendency to seek the spiritual on an individual's own terms. For example, in "Homer the Heretic," Homer uses this distinction to support his decision to stop going to church: "Hey, what's the big deal about going to church every Sunday? I mean, isn't God everywhere?" For Homer, spirituality does not necessarily exist within the parameters that define Wuthnow's notion of a spirituality of dwelling. In Homer's mind, spiritual nourishment is available from the comfort of his own couch. His decision, then, shows that part of the spiritual seeker's journey includes the need to distance oneself from the influence that traditional guardians of spirituality exert on the individual's spiritual experiences.[26]

Wuthnow is quick to point out that a spirituality of dwelling remains "appealing;"[27] it just fails to elicit a commitment to the life of the institution. Thus, Homer does not reject the notion of God—he simply rejects the requirement that he experience the divine in a traditional church setting. At the heart of this tension between dwelling and seeking spirituality, then, is a notion that is common in American culture and Christian theology: self-centered, self-directed, and self-defined approaches to spirituality. Wuthnow cites the interest in one's own welfare as the primary roadblock to the sense of communal identity that defines traditional Christianity.[28] When the individual assumes responsibility for his or her own spiritual direction, the consequent spiritual quest can jettison responsibility toward others. Loyalty may exist to one's past, but only insofar as that past remains complicit with one's immediate, individually chosen spiritual needs.

When the traditional guardian of spirituality is perceived as infringing on one's spiritual journey, a divorce from that past seems inevitable.

In one of the classic episodes that explores Christianity, "Homer the Heretic" characterizes this process. A more thorough analysis of this episode will therefore prove helpful. Homer's frustration with church begins before he can even leave his house. He struggles to get his pants on; when they rip, he decides to skip church.[29] Marge cannot convince him to change his mind, so she takes the kids to church while Homer stays in bed. At this point, the separated family experiences very different kinds of spiritual nourishment. Homer revels in his freedom. He pees with the door open and "loves it," he dances in his underwear after turning the thermostat all the way up, and makes his patented moon waffles, a glutton's dream. Meanwhile, Marge and the kids are freezing as they listen to Reverend Lovejoy drone on about Jeremiah's lamentations. After watching an amazing football game, Homer finds a penny on the floor. He has a new favorite day, which he owes "to skipping church."

When Homer sets out to practice his own religion, he does so only after a dream in which he tells God why he has given up on church. In the dream, God offers tacit approval for the plan, so Homer sets out on his new spiritual journey. Now he does not have to attend church and listen to Reverend Lovejoy's "boring sermons." Despite Marge's later entreaties, Homer seems to be taking his new spiritual path seriously. He dons a monk's robe and walks around in his yard. He goes to Moe's in order to skip work for his religion's first holiday, the Feast of Maximum Occupancy. His religion, however, eventually imperils his safety. While resting on his couch one Sunday, Homer lights a cigar and stretches out to read some *Playdude* magazines. He falls asleep and the cigar ignites the magazines. Suddenly, Homer is about to "fry like the proverbial pancake [he] is." The volunteer fire department rushes to the rescue, and Ned Flanders, who embodies the traditional spirituality of dwelling, pulls Homer out of the burning house to safety.

While literally at home, Homer could not be farther away from something one could legitimately call spiritual nurturing. He skips out on church to indulge his appetite and laziness, and then justifies the move in spiritual terms. Though he thinks he is on a different spiritual path, Homer actually converges on the traditional church that he neglects in the first place. Ned pulls him away from the burning house, an act that symbolizes how Homer's personal religion does more harm than good. Moreover, Ned represents that which can save Homer's life, literally and spiritually, despite Homer's decision to reject Christianity. Homer ultimately learns his lesson, but only in a way that grows out of his own chosen way of endorsing spirituality. Homer promises Reverend Lovejoy that he will be in church the next week, but once there, Homer is asleep.

The lesson's efficacy, of course, turns out to be short-lived, which reinforces the notion that no matter how clear the story's moral may be, the effect is fleeting. For Homer, spirituality always drifts away from the established church to a hackneyed notion of spirituality that endorses his lifestyle.

The desire to feel at home when exploring one's spirituality points to the root of a key problem with American Christianity: people do not feel as though they belong to the Christian community as individuals. Ironically, membership in a group approaches a more traditional notion of Christianity, but membership must not demand that the individual sacrifice her or his own personal spiritual interests. "Homer the Great" provides an excellent example of this point. In this episode, Homer notices that something is amiss with Lenny and Carl. After prowling around, Homer realizes that they belong to a secret society called the Stonecutters, and he desperately wants to join. Lenny and Carl inform him that one can only gain admission either by saving the life of a Stonecutter or if one is the son of a Stonecutter. Apparently excluded, Homer tries to take the issue of membership into his own hands. He attempts to manufacture circumstances wherein he can save the life of a Stonecutter and thus be eligible for membership. When this strategy fails, he complains bitterly at the dinner table about his willingness to join, despite his ignorance about what he would be joining:

Homer:	I'd give anything to get into the Stonecutters.
Lisa:	What do they do there, Dad?
Grandpa:	I'm a member.
Homer:	What do they do? What don't they do? Oh, they do so many things they never stop. Oh, the things they do there, my stars.
Lisa:	You don't know what they do there, do you?
Homer:	Not as such, no.
Grandpa:	I'm a Stonecutter.
	[A conversation ensues about the importance of ignoring Grandpa, who continues to address the problem.]
Grandpa:	I'm a member.
Homer:	Huh?

Grandpa:	What?
Homer:	What?
Grandpa:	Huh?
Lisa:	You're a member of the Stonecutters, Grandpa?
Grandpa:	[as he looks through his wallet to find his membership card]: Oh, sure.
Homer:	This is it! My ticket in: they have to let me in if I'm the son of a member.

The notion of membership in an exclusive community will satisfy Homer's needs. Importantly, this need is so pervasive that Homer blindly accepts whatever membership might entail. Homer is so focused, both in the moment and more broadly with respect to ignoring Grandpa, that he fails to see that he can join immediately. This narrow-mindedness anticipates that Homer will experience little actual contentment in the group, but his self-manufactured desire sustains his interest.

Once Homer joins and participates in the Stonecutters, he does enjoy himself, so much so that he unknowingly blasphemes by using the Stonecutters' sacred parchment as a napkin. The mere availability of the parchment at the dinner table points to the ultimately shallow spiritual depth that defines the club. This fact becomes more apparent when, after disciplining Homer by stripping him of his robes, the Stonecutters realize that he has the birthmark identifying him as "the Chosen One." Homer consequently assumes leadership over the entire group, which leads him to abuse his power. Homer's willingness to indulge himself at the expense of the other Stonecutters quickly grates on the group. By the end of the episode, the Stonecutters tire of his governing style and start a new club. The traditions and parchments apparently do not carry enough weight to ingratiate the club to their prophetically appointed leader. Thus, they form the No Homers Club, which leaves Homer back at square one. He looks into the windows of the No Homers Club and expresses another desire to join. The quickness with which the Stonecutters jettison the very tradition they value so strongly at the beginning of the episode reiterates the point that American spirituality values personal contentment over personal commitment. Exclusivity is more important than tradition. The Stonecutters would rather deny the very tradition they upheld in order to keep Homer out of the group than accept him as their Chosen One.

Several salient features characterize the Stonecutters in terms that Wuthnow recognizes as salient in contemporary American spirituality.

First, despite the club's identity as a sacred secret society, it quickly becomes clear that their meetings produce little spiritual nourishment. Their focus seems to be on drinking beer. Moreover, they lack a true leader. Homer's ascension betrays their baseless claim to be a group of spiritual consequence. True belief in a Chosen One ought to embrace that person, even if that person proves to be rather boorish. Most tellingly, the Stonecutters themselves lack an anchored sense of the divine. They feel let down with their Chosen One, so much so that they will jettison him and define their new group in terms that explicitly reject who they previously held to be sacred. Their willingness to distance themselves from Homer, despite his authority vis-à-vis the club's prophetic tradition, betrays their desire for a comfortable and self-satisfying source of spiritual nourishment. The Stonecutters thus define the sacred in terms that are ultimately pragmatic. They subsume a robust sense of the divine in the service of a social stable environment. This fulfills a need of all involved, and it may elicit longing in Homer's thoughts, but the Stonecutters embody the way in which a good part of Springfield's population will redraw their spiritual fault lines when doing so is personally convenient.

A final footnote about the Stonecutters captures the extent to which Wuthnow's understanding of American spirituality resonates with the spirituality that *The Simpsons* portrays in Springfield. Most of Springfield's male population belongs to the Stonecutters. Reverend Lovejoy, however, is nowhere to be seen. Though not explicit, his absence reinforces the notion that the Stonecutters constitute a nourishing environment that does not incorporate elements of many of its members' Christian faith as seen in their weekly church attendance. The Stonecutters, then, offer a distinct experience in relation to Christianity. Wuthnow emphasizes that, for churches and their ministers to be relevant to contemporary society, they must serve as "facilitators"[30] during individualized spiritual journeys. Pastors should furnish resources to help along the way, but they should not be seen as intrusive on the journey itself. Reverend Lovejoy's conspicuous absence here, as well as in other significant spiritual journeys on *The Simpsons*, hints at his irrelevancy or inconvenience to Springfield's spiritual seekers.

While other characters on *The Simpsons* undergo spiritual journeys that exhibit similar tendencies,[31] Homer exemplifies Wuthnow's paradigm of the spiritual seeker. Lisle Dalton, Eric Michael Mazur, and Monica Siems summarize well how Homer personifies precisely the tendencies that define postmodern American spirituality:

Homer fulfills the role of the American spiritual wanderer;
though linked culturally (if unsteadily and unenthusiastically)
to biblical tradition, he regularly engages a mosaic of other traditions, mythologies, and moral codes. In the face of these ever
shifting layers of meaning, he stumbles along, making the most
of his limited understanding of their complexities.[32]

Homer is very much a product of his past. Consequently, he must deal
personally and corporately with his Christian heritage. Homer thus provides *The Simpsons* with a stereotyped but accurate example of how
American spirituality exhibits tension between a spirituality of seeking
and its heritage as a Christian culture defined by a spirituality of dwelling.
Dalton et al. are right in claiming that Homer cannot escape the traditional Christian spiritual influences that are a part of his familial and
cultural identity. At best, he can seek to dilute them or replace them
temporarily from any number of sources. Whatever tack he takes, the
point remains that Homer does so alone in pursuit of his own spiritual
desires. He remains naïve or rejects altogether the idea that organized
religion can help him on his journey. Homer's spirituality remains in
flux, and when he just might need help from Christianity, the reality
remains that his spiritual framework does not admit a companion, much
less a guide. Unfortunately for Homer, the Christian tradition has little
to say about hallucinogenic meetings with coyotes.
   A final tendency in Wuthnow's work proves to be important with
respect to understanding how *The Simpsons* portrays American spirituality. By embracing a fluid notion of spirituality, American Christianity
faces a dilemma. While it often rejects its roots, or approaches traditional
churches with suspicion, American Christianity also struggles to replace
the spiritual resources that such institutions furnish. This tension manifests itself strongly when a community of spiritual seekers encounters a
miraculous event. That is, when individual-defined spirituality cannot
make sense of a situation, trying to understand phenomena that lie
outside of a normal range of spiritual experiences can be overwhelming.
When Homer hallucinates and embarks upon his spiritual journey,
if becomes clear rather quickly that he ultimately lacks the spiritual
resources to understand his experiences. At one point, Homer realizes
that when he walks toward the horizon, the sun rises; when he retreats,
the sun sinks. He goes back and forth a couple of times in order to enjoy
the effect. The result, however, is not worth the trouble. The sun eventually hits the ground and shatters. Suddenly wary, and in the dark,
Homer tells himself quietly, "Note to self: stop doing anything." The

situation's novelty has worn off and Homer realizes that he is in a peril-
ous situation. His experience transcends his available spiritual resources.
After he breaks the sun and decides to stop doing anything, Homer begins
to spell out "Help" with rocks. Homer's need for help is obvious. On his
own, he has no idea what to do in this strange spiritual world. His self-
defined spirituality reveals its inability to "make sense of a world that is
increasingly dangerous and chaotic."[33]

Despite the spiritual uncertainty that Homer exhibits in his hallucination, Wuthnow argues that miraculous situations ultimately appeal
to spiritual seekers because the paranormal affirms that something
greater exists in the universe.[34] Wuthnow takes up the example of angels
to clarify his point. When encountering something that does not fit neatly
within one's personal spiritual matrix, a spirituality of seeking often affirms angels to address "the growing uncertainty . . . about the existence
and presence of God."[35] Angels provide an "intermediary"[36] that in con-
junction with their cultural and spiritual heritage[37] produces an "appeal
of universalistic, nonjudgmental beings in a society that has difficulty
convincing itself that absolute truth can be known."[38] Angels, then,
provide a kind of half-god that can fit more easily within individualized
notions of the sacred.[39]

In "Lisa the Skeptic," an angel visits Springfield, or at least what nearly
the entire town of Springfield thinks is an angel. A new mall construction
project threatens an area that is a known fossil bed. Lisa leads a charge to
halt construction, which results in Springfield Elementary School going
to the site for an archeological dig. While participating, Lisa uncovers
what appears to be a human skeleton. The find is unique, however, because the skeleton also has wings. Consensus arrives quickly. The entire
town, except for Lisa, buys into the notion that the skeleton must be an
angel. The receptiveness toward the hypothesis, coupled with the severe
reaction against scientific institutions elsewhere in town, characterizes
openness to spiritual beings like angels that Wuthnow describes. Something does not make sense, so the town almost unanimously embraces
the angel. Thus, when the town is uncertain about the skeleton because
it does not fit within their spiritual frameworks, they opt to accept an
idea that reduces their spiritual uncertainty because something divine
has visited Springfield. The angel solidifies the town's otherwise fluid
spirituality because it offers something tangible to believe in, but without requiring anyone to commit all of his or her spiritual resources. The
town accepts that this paranormal situation must affirm something
spiritual in part because doing so will not constitute any kind of binding
commitment.[40]

Overt references to God are significantly absent as the town processes the skeleton's spiritual significance. Collectively, Springfield is not ready to connect the spiritual dots. They will, however, assent to a spiritual idea that keeps God distant in two ways. First, the angel exemplifies Wuthnow's characteristic that the phenomenon must unfold in a manner that is nonjudgmental and, more important, exhibits broad enough appeal to accommodate the multitude of individual spiritualities that interpret the angel. Second, the skeleton gains spiritual currency because it remains a physical object. The angel's "truth" is more palatable because it can be seen, unlike God, who remains distant and undefined in contemporary American society.

Broadly speaking, the skeleton produces individual and communal responses that summarize well the general texture of American Christianity. Americans are spiritually confused. A spirituality of dwelling still exists in contemporary American society, but the committed, consistent quality that defines traditional Christianity has splintered in response to cultural dynamics. For example, spiritual leadership often resembles a caretaker as opposed to someone who provides spiritual influence.[41] Moreover, the doctrinal restrictions that come with traditional Christianity prohibit significantly or disallow altogether an individually constructed and understood spirituality. Ned Flanders, then, is a bit of a dying breed, while Homer Simpson personifies the contemporary American Christian. The former adheres to a restrictive and somewhat naïve commitment to his church, while the latter ascribes little, if any, value to church to begin with. These spiritual trajectories manifest themselves differently on *The Simpsons*, but both represent competing spiritual tendencies in American Christianity that create an individual and communal void. Both sides long for spiritual satisfaction, but neither seems to be content with its approach to spirituality. The challenge, then, becomes the need to identify and lift out the source of the spiritual anxiety that afflicts so much of American Christianity. *The Simpsons* makes clear what it thinks the answer is, and the show presents a strikingly consistent indictment of how a fundamental component of American culture has stained the doors of America's homes and churches.

Chapter Eight

Decreasing Returns: Economics and Faith in *The Simpsons*

"Don't worry, Homer. Nine out of ten religions fail in their first year."

—God[1]

"No one can serve two masters; for a slave will either hate the one and love the other, or be devoted to the one and despise the other. You cannot serve God and wealth."

—Matthew 6:24

When a hurricane is bearing down, praying may not seem like a bad idea. When the hurricane actually hits, praying would seem to become second nature. Marge Simpson, the most committed Christian in the Simpson family, can only turn to God when, amazingly, a hurricane threatens Springfield.[2]

Marge: Dear God, this is Marge Simpson. If you stop this hurricane and save our family, we will be forever grateful. And recommend you to all our friends! So, if you could find it in your infinite wisdom to . . .

Lisa: Wait! Listen, everybody.
        [Sunlight shines into the shelter and the family hears birds chirping.]

Lisa: The hurricane's over.

Homer: He fell for it! Way to go, Marge!

This exchange reveals much about how Christian faith often plays out practically and not because it suggests the efficacy of Marge's prayers. Rather, in Marge's language one finds a tendency in how she understands her faith that is pervasive in Springfield. She does not pray to so much as negotiate with God. Marge asks God for help in terms that reflect something closer to a business deal. She introduces herself, first and last name, and then presents her request. In return for the favor, she promises to advertise God to others, though this is contingent on God holding up God's end of the bargain. Marge could very well be buying salvation on eBay. So long as God follows through with God's end of the deal, Marge will have nothing but positive things to say about the transaction.

If the scene stopped at this point, one could see clearly a quality in American Christianity that is widespread in Springfield: understanding one's spirituality in economic terms. The intersection and consequent entangling of religion and economics in American Christianity gives rise to much satirical emphasis on *The Simpsons*. Marge's prayer hits home precisely because this is the kind of approach so many Christians take with their own prayers. People approach God not as a loving, redeeming deity to worship but rather as a potential partner with whom one can negotiate a good deal. The relationship is thus understood through an economic prism. Moreover, the praying party usually defines the conditions of the exchange. Such an approach to prayer, which is an important part of Christian life, strips God of God's authority as traditionally understood in Christianity. God thus becomes a client more than a creator, who, incidentally, should be taken advantage of whenever possible. Homer reacts not in a way that exhibits the gratitude Marge suggests but rather as one who has pulled the proverbial economic wool over God's eyes. Apparently, God is a sucker, which, ironically, might be reason enough to recommend God to others. After all, Christians in Springfield, as representative of American Christianity in general, are on the lookout for the best spiritual deal possible.

Leaving aside the theological question of whether God answers these kinds of prayers, the tenor in Marge's prayer is unmistakable.[3] She clearly understands God as part of an economic paradigm. She still stands as one of the more positive portraits of Christianity in Springfield, but in acquiescing to a general cultural trend, she brings into sharp focus the way in which American Christianity sacrifices part of itself within the economic framework that defines American culture. The effects can be far-reaching. For example, Bart clearly accepts the idea that God is somehow involved in financial matters. In "Two Cars in Every Garage and Three Eyes on Every Fish," Mr. Burns makes a mayoral campaign stop at the Simpson home to have dinner with the family. When he sits down at the table, Bart gets the honor of praying over the meal: "Dear God, we paid for all this stuff ourselves, so thanks for nothing." Bart's prayer assumes that God not only relates to humans in economic terms, but also that those terms provide a reason to reject God's authority if God does not provide. When Christian practice exhibits this kind of economic language, its theological integrity suffers. In this case, Bart approaches God with economic assumptions, which leads him to conceptualize God in terms that deny God's power. Instead of understanding God as an all-powerful creator, Bart points out that, as far as he understands the situation, God had nothing to do with the particular moment. If God does not pay, then God deserves no thanks.

Marge and Bart both pray in a way that reflects a broad trend in American Christianity. Viewing God through an economic prism produces two defining characteristics of contemporary American Christianity: convenience and expediency. Robert Wuthnow describes the role of Christianity in America as necessarily sacrificing theological or spiritual integrity in service of economic ends. Church experiences "function as a supplier of spiritual goods and services."[4] This consumer-driven model produces two results. First, Christianity loses spiritual authority on its own terms. If the social attitude dictates that the church provide rather than guide, then to fulfill its perceived role the church must be willing to bend its doctrinal standards in order to accommodate such expectations. Second, Christianity can quickly become irrelevant if its demands are too great. Contemporary Christianity thrives only when it offers "spiritual comfort without making demands on people's time or commitments."[5] In "Lisa the Greek," *The Simpsons* illustrates this point. Reverend Lovejoy stands in the pulpit to give his sermon, but the pews are empty save for a few people. It is also Super Bowl Sunday. Lovejoy says sardonically, "Well, I'm glad some people could resist the lures of the big game." A man near the back then stands up quickly, exclaims, "Oh, my God! I forgot the game!" and runs out of the church. In Springfield, as in America, people are willing to attend church, but as soon as something else comes up, church goes by the wayside. In this particular case, what comes up is, spiritually speaking, irrelevant. The Super Bowl may be an event to see, but when compared to one's spirituality, it really should not matter. The willingness to leave church in order to watch the game on television thus illustrates Wuthnow's point about American Christianity. In a culture of competing influences and events, Christianity will appeal only so long as people can participate in it without sacrificing their schedules, hobbies, and other interests.

In Springfield, expediency and convenience dovetail to generate a broad tendency to economize the sacred. As Wuthnow points out, such approaches to spirituality create ample space for economics to replace Christianity as a point of concern: seeking one's own spiritual experiences outside of the church "has become big business, and big business finds many of its best markets by putting things in small, easy-to-consume packages."[6] In "Lisa the Skeptic," one finds a clear example of this dynamic. A mysterious skeleton that resembles an angel produces just such an economic opportunity in the name of the sacred. Homer quickly realizes that he can turn a profit by tapping into a demanding public's desire for a spiritual boost. He not only charges admission to see the supposed angel in his garage, he also develops a more sustained marketing campaign. The possibility that the skeleton really is an angel produces the need for gimmicky souvenirs, such as the ashtrays with an angel logo that Homer orders. When the angel disappears, Homer is frustrated, but not because his faith has been challenged. Rather, he has both lost a source of income and suddenly found himself stuck with thousands of angel ashtrays. The episode's conclusion emphasizes the connection between packaging spirituality with the sacred when the town finds out that the angel skeleton was an advertising stunt. Tellingly, the town's disbelief about the cynical manipulation of its spiritual identity lasts only briefly. The angel's prophecy, that "The End Is Near," proves effective. The entire town affirms the message, but only when the end of the episode describes what will happen to high prices at the Heavenly Hills Mall. Springfield's Christian community may not give readily to their church, but they will flock to a mall that offers them a good deal. When economics and spirituality converge in Springfield, everyone will readily believe in what the advertising angel has to say because they stand to save some money.

The tension between Christianity as a spiritual commitment in one's life and the realities that contemporary American culture present often produces a religious climate wherein the most appealing product wins out. That is, when secular interests make Christianity untenable for an individual, that individual will often shop around for a better way to address her or his spiritual desires. This dynamic receives direct critical attention in "The Joy of Sect." A mysterious but idyllic group of people called the Movementarians moves into Springfield. The group brainwashes its new converts into accepting the sect's practices, which ask that people work difficult agricultural jobs like picking lima beans. The group eventually captures the spiritual imagination of most of Springfield by promising an edenic trip to Blisstonia in exchange for their spiritual and financial commitments to the mysterious Leader. Homer eventually imperils the group's trip to paradise when he opens the Forbidden Barn and sees "one hell of a giant spaceship." Having doubted the Leader, Homer and the rest of Springfield now stand to experience a life outside of paradise.[7] To punctuate the point, the spaceship sets off, which leaves even Marge and Reverend Lovejoy wishing that they had not doubted the Leader's message. However, the spaceship turns out to be poorly built. As it flies off, it falls apart and everyone can see that the Movementarian leader is just a con man who is trying to get away with everyone's money.

This visual image underscores how the town's commitment to the Movementarians demanded financial resources. However, this spiritual investment failed miserably because, of course, the Movementarians offered nothing that one could consider spiritually substantive. Given the amount of money that the Leader had with him as he flew away, one can assume safely that Springfield residents embraced fully the edenic program that the Movementarians offered. In turn, this reveals the extent to which Springfield's residents are open to the paradisiacal promises, so long as the price is right. The Movementarians captivate Springfield to the point that even Reverend Lovejoy will reject Christianity in favor of a more visible path to eternal paradise. When he sees the Leader fly away, Reverend Lovejoy throws his clerical collar to the ground and stomps on it. His actions embody Springfield's general attitude toward its Christian faith that reveals a deeper spiritual problem in American culture. People in Springfield understand the sacred in terms that produce a certain kind of result. If one can lock in admission to eternal paradise by participating in the Movementarian program, then one is more than willing to follow the Leader. The dynamic echoes strongly the presence of indulgences that drew Martin Luther's ire. Christianity is not about buying one's way to heaven, which is exactly the spiritual dynamic that emerges in "The Joy of Sect." The speed and depth with which most people commit to the Movementarians underscores the extent to which people are open to spirituality, but also reveals the degree to which people will take the most convenient path to salvation. Ultimately, this episode exposes the lack of commitment to Christian faith. When a more expedient and more promising spiritual path appears in Springfield, people are more than willing to reject Christianity.

By recalling the general postmodern texture of *The Simpsons*, one can recognize the crux of the problem between Christianity and America's capitalistic culture, which "The Joy of Sect" characterizes so well. Homer succumbs to the Movementarian phenomenon for two key reasons. First, like many Americans he desires a religion that pays dividends. The First Church of Springfield clearly fails in this regard, so Homer seeks spiritual refuge in a religious cult that guarantees more tangible results.[8] Homer's self-affirming, appetitive spirituality recognizes a better deal, so to speak, in the exchange that the Movementarians offer. Importantly, Homer and others must commit financially in order to participate in the Movementarian payout. As the saying goes, one has to spend money to make money. Of course, the end of the episode exposes the Movementarians for what they are: a pyramid scheme built on an appeal to Springfield's desire for spiritual satisfaction.

The town's willingness to buy into the promised trip to Blisstonia indicates the shallow nature of its Christian faith. Wuthnow argues that these kinds of circumstances precisely characterize Christianity's faltering influence in contemporary American spirituality: "Current spiritual interest is more consistent with consumer culture than with theology."[9] Thus, the second key point from Homer's involvement with the Movementarians focuses on the broader postmodern texture that emerges so forcefully in this episode. As he does elsewhere, Homer provides a touchstone to recognize the way in which America's secularized culture chips away at the integrity of its individual and communal commitment to its Christian roots. Brian L. Ott argues that, because Homer's "whole identity, then, resides in his endless consumer practices,"[10] he ultimately has "no base to return to."[11] Without a way to anchor his spiritual identity, Homer seems destined to drift from religion to religion without ever realizing any kind of substantive spiritual experience. A lack of definitive personal formation lies at the root Homer's willingness to embrace the Movementarians. What becomes clear in "The Joy of Sect" is the extent to which an economic model of faith fuels this spiritual crisis. Homer will affirm someone or something so long as the object of his devotion appeals to his personalized version of what constitutes the sacred.

One of the more important questions to ask in response to "The Joy of Sect" is what about the Christian Church fails to appeal to Homer's consumer-driven spirituality. The obvious criticism to level is that Homer's traditional Christian Church fails to offer him what he desires in terms he will accept. Granted, such desires may be misplaced, but the First Church of Springfield ought not to exclude Homer as a person worthy of spiritual resources. If anything, a strong biblical imperative exists to seek out people like Homer, whose spirituality twists to the whims of the latest spiritual fad. Jesus makes clear that the lost sheep demands priority.[12] The question is thus: why has Reverend Lovejoy failed to speak to Homer's spiritual needs? The easy response is to claim that Reverend Lovejoy is a bad pastor. However, a closer look at the church's place in a consumer-driven climate reveals a more complex answer.

While Homer is free to jump from one religious group to another, Reverend Lovejoy finds himself constrained by the realities of his job. As a part of America's capitalistic society, Reverend Lovejoy's church also functions within an economic model. The contemporary American pastor not only has to provide for his or her congregational needs but must also function as a kind of corporate manager. Reverend Lovejoy clearly struggles to keep his church running in a financial sense. Even on Easter, Reverend Lovejoy must cajole his parishioners to give to support the church.[13] With fickle congregants, the pastor must be aware of the ways in which the economic realities of American culture affect individuals' level of commitment to Christianity. For example, in "The Monkey Suit," Reverend Lovejoy decides to take up the politically sensitive issue of whether to teach creationism alongside the theory of evolution at Springfield Elementary School. Helen Lovejoy encourages her husband to take up the cause not for theological reasons but rather because doing so will put "more meat in the seats." Convinced, Reverend Lovejoy agrees to campaign for creationism because unlike the new, wealthy Episcopalian Church, his church is struggling to stay financially afloat. Because American culture permits individuals or entire groups to disassociate themselves from their churches at a moment's notice, the pastors of such churches must organize their role as minister around economic factors. This necessarily shifts attention away from the basic theological tenets that made Christianity a staple of American culture in the first place. Economics is a reality for contemporary Christian churches, but this fact often leads the church to sacrifice its own integrity and thus its ability to significantly influence American culture.

This difficult relationship between Christianity and the economic realities that intersect with the lives of its churches is not a new thing. However, when the tension between economics and religion is aggravated, the consequences that follow often bruise the church's integrity. At critical moments in the church's history, the relationship between money and theology is often deep and complex. For example, the Medici family ruled Renaissance Florence with power built upon their bank's economic influence. Such wealth allowed the family to lean upon the church in order to bring about politically and economically expedient decisions.[14] This example points to a broader pattern in the church's history. Constant economic interference and influence often proved to be beneficial to members of the church's leadership, which then placed them in powerful social positions. The corollary effect was often that such people failed to uphold the integrity of their faith tradition or bend their beliefs to accommodate economic interests. The results could be disastrous, as Martin Luther's critique and subsequent move to reform shows so clearly.[15]

The Protestant Reformation ultimately produced a new paradigm for Christianity. In responding to the church's economic abuses, Luther initiated a movement that sought to restore the church's positive influence over secular matters such as economic activity. In his seminal work, *The Protestant Ethic and the Spirit of Capitalism*,[16] first published in 1904, Max Weber credits this shift with the emergence of the cozy but tangled relationship between faith and economics. With the breakdown of ecclesial authority and a renewed emphasis on God's grace as the sole provider of salvation, several elements of everyday life were recast in religious terms. The "positive valuation of routine activity in the world . . . the valuation of the fulfillment of duty in worldly affairs" produced an understanding of the Christian life wherein "[t]he only way of living acceptably to God was not to surpass worldly morality in monastic asceticism, but solely through the fulfillment of the obligations imposed upon the individual by his position in the world. That was his calling."[17] This new framework wherein economic activity could legitimately be a part of one's spiritual identity trickled through American Christianity.[18]

The Simpsons captures this idea clearly in "El Viaje Misterioso de Nuestro Jomer." Having met his spiritual guide and recognized that he must undergo a spiritual journey, Homer immediately assumes that his task involves getting rid of material possessions. Thus, he echoes a point that Jesus makes[19] about the importance of rejecting worldly wealth on the way to salvation:

Coyote: Clarity is the path to inner peace.

Homer: Well, what should I do? Should I meditate? Should I get rid of all my possessions?

Coyote: [laughing]: Are you kidding? If anything, you should get more possessions.

In contrast to a standard usually presented in Christian thought, the coyote introduces a new standard that fits nicely within Weber's economic paradigm. Traditionally, Christianity is understood to shun materialism, much less endorse purposefully increasing one's wealth as a kind of spirituality. Homer, however, hears different advice. In America, one nourishes one's spirituality by seeking more things.

By combining moral guidelines and the acquisition of wealth, Weber produces a classic phrase in American Christianity: the Protestant work ethic. Though developed more than a century ago, Weber's phrase characterizes much of Christianity in contemporary American culture. In the abstract, the idea focuses on the positives that making money can produce in society. So long as one stays within certain ethical guidelines, the result can be understood in terms that Christianity will find palatable. As Weber states, "The earning of money within the modern economic order is, so long as it is done legally, the result and expression of virtue and proficiency in calling."[20] Economics defines the modern world, so if Christianity wants to remain relevant in that world, it ought to adapt its beliefs to the social realities it encounters. So long as this unfolds in a way that is consonant with Christian values, then one's spirituality can provide guidance in America's economic culture. For example, given some of the unethical actions in corporate America, this would seem to be a good thing. The problem, of course, comes when one is unable to distinguish Christianity from the economy. Inevitably, the former is subsumed into the latter. As a result, Christianity sacrifices or is stripped of its identity. When Christian beliefs and practices become cogs in the corporate wheel, its relevance takes on a troubling character.

"Bart Sells His Soul" presents a penetrating look at how economics can affect the spiritual domain. At the beginning of a church service, Bart substitutes "In the Garden of Eden," by "I. Ron Butterfly" in place of a more traditional opening hymn. For once, the congregation at the First Church of Springfield seems alive, as everyone sings the hymn enthusiastically. Even Homer resonates with the new spiritual direction; he asks Marge, "Remember when we used to make out to this hymn?" However, once Reverend Lovejoy realizes that the church is singing "rock and/or roll," he seeks the guilty culprit in the after-church Sunday school class. When Milhouse rats out Bart, they both have to clean the church's organ pipes as punishment. Milhouse explains his actions to Bart as resulting from his desire not to have birds pecking at his soul for eternity. Bart cannot believe his ears; in his mind, the soul does not exist. The two argue whether not there is a soul. Milhouse insists that everyone has a soul, while Bart wonders "how someone with glasses that thick can be so stupid?" He then exclaims, "I don't have a soul. You don't have a soul. There's no such thing as a soul." Milhouse does not waver. Instead, he offers to buy Bart's soul for five dollars, a deal Bart is all too willing to accept. He writes out "Bart Simpson's Soul" on a piece of paper and exchanges it for Milhouse's five dollars. As the scene closes, Bart says, "It's a pleasure doing business with you, chuuu-umpp." On a piece of church stationery, Bart has transformed his soul into a spiritual commodity that can be exchanged.

Gradually, Bart realizes that he might have made a bad decision. When Lisa learns what Bart did, she can hardly believe it. She asks in disbelief, "Bart, how could you do that? Your soul is the most valuable part of you. It's the symbol of everything fine inside of us." Bart still does not understand what he has done, a fact evident when he tries to sell Lisa his sense of decency. Despite Bart's spiritual naïveté, Lisa's words express a fundamental Christian belief: the soul is the fundamental part of one's spiritual identity. Even though Lisa does not embrace Christianity, she articulates a conception of the soul that resonates strongly with traditional and popular Christian thought. Thus, she is rightly disturbed that Bart was so quick to part with his soul.[21] Weird things begin to happen, from Santa's Little Helper's unprecedented growling at Bart to Bart's inability to fog up the ice cream counter at the Kwik-E-Mart with his breath.[22] Bart gradually realizes that Lisa may be right, and he spends the rest of the episode trying to recover what he lost. When the trail goes cold, Bart kneels at his bedside and prays, sincerely,[23] that God will help get his soul back. After a moment of silence, the piece of paper that says "Bart Simpson's Soul" floats down to his bed. Shocked, he turns around to see Lisa, who bought the soul with money from her piggybank. She begins to lecture Bart on the idea that some believe the soul must be earned, but Bart is only half listening. His primary concern is to eat the piece of paper so that he cannot lose his soul again.

Several troubling issues arise in this episode. Foremost among these is Bart's willingness to part with his soul so easily. He steadfastly resists the idea that the soul exists, while popular conceptions of the soul understand it as the fundamental basis for reaching the afterlife. Bart, however, recognizes the soul's relevancy only insofar as it is a thing to be exchanged. Any spiritual value is absent in Bart's conception of the soul. Moreover, given Bart's age, the recognition of how easily Bart recasts his soul in economic terms should give one pause. Robert Sloane argues that capitalism is so ingrained in American culture that Bart's actions are precisely what one should expect.[24] Moreover, As Kurt M. Koenigsberger summarizes this episode, "Bart's self-commodification, then, shows how easily use value can convert to exchange value in the marketplace . . . [and] how the spiritual can manifest itself in the material."[25] In this case, the use value becomes clear to Bart only after he has sold his soul. During a nightmare, Bart realizes that, without his soul, he is unable to row his boat out to a paradisiacal island. Without his soul, Bart simply spins in a circle in the middle of the sea. Though the island does not exhibit any definitively Christian ideas commonly associated with heaven, it clearly represents a desirable location to be. Bart's inability to reach the island reflects what he lacks: a metaphysically necessary element to transfer himself to a spiritual destination. The point is punctuated when Milhouse, who now has two souls, does not have to do any work to row himself out to the island. He can relax while his own soul and Bart's soul do all the work. The soul's spiritual value in Bart's dream reveals what a bad deal he made. The soul's use extends beyond the physical world and certainly beyond the five dollars Bart received. For a five-dollar gain, Bart parts with his most valuable spiritual asset.

As a postmodern show, *The Simpsons* reflects an obvious social reality that has, for better or worse, infiltrated Christianity's cultural identity. Bart's willingness to commodify his soul thus points to a second more problematic and endemic issue that results from an economized Christianity. Insofar as he reflects the characteristics of the Christian culture that raised him, Bart demonstrates the results that emerge when spirituality becomes an economic reality, as it has in American culture. According to Vincent Brook, "Postmodern theorists such as Fredric Jameson regarded the relentless commodification of everyday life by the culture industry of late capitalism as one of the defining characteristics of postmodernism."[26] In so doing Bart invites criticism of the Christian culture that has failed to teach him the reason that such decisions are so problematic. He lacks the intellectual and spiritual resources to understand fully what his actions signify. As a member of a Christian community, and more importantly as a child, Bart should receive appropriate guidance with respect to such issues. His church, therefore, is complicit in the mistake he makes. Reverend Lovejoy only addresses concerns about the soul in order to smoke out who was behind the hymn prank. He does not adequately teach the students why their souls are so valuable.

"Bart Sells His Soul" thus establishes clearly what is at stake when Christianity fails to provide responsible spiritual guidance, especially when children are the ones who need such positive influences. Behind this failure lies a faith tradition that ultimately moves in step with America's emphasis on economic activity. At the beginning of the episode, the church's bulletin board reads: *No Shirt, No Shoes, No Salvation*. Though catchy, this phrase aligns the church with the same corporate mentality. Faith exhibits its spiritual value in terms that find an analogue in the fast-food industry. This suggests not only a willingness on the church's part to sacrifice the theological integrity of its belief system, but also an attitude within Springfield that faith attracts peoples' attention only when presented in terms that produce quick, palatable results. Even if Marge and Homer are complicit with this cultural reality, then one would expect the Christian structure around Bart to correct the commodification of his faith. The failure to teach Bart why he should consider his soul to be an invaluable part of who he is proves to be socially comprehensive, which illustrates the extent to which Christian culture has lost its authority in America's consumer-driven culture. When the only voice of reason is Bart's younger sister, the Christian community ought to stop and ask if its cultural identity is no longer upholding the values it asserts.

Perhaps the most revealing element of this episode's criticism comes in its final moments. Having prayed sincerely and received his soul, Bart would seemingly have learned a valuable spiritual lesson. He recognizes the value of his soul, a fact evident when he eats his soul to protect it. One the one hand, his actions argue that he exhibits more awareness that, despite his foray into commodifying his spirituality, he ultimately comes to appreciate that his soul should not be considered in capitalistic terms. Thus, when he eats the paper symbolizing his soul, Bart acts in a way that reinforces the consumptive cycle he struggles against throughout the episode.[27] He protects his spiritual core in a way that cannot completely escape the influences that caused the problem in the first place. Moreover, one can argue that in consuming his soul Bart recognizes its value, but he is also aware that someone else could, in theory, reacquire his soul. Even if Bart has a legitimate personal epiphany, he cannot protect himself completely from his surrounding culture. The piece of paper is merely symbolic, but, like a stock certificate, it can be sold to anyone who is willing to pay.[28]

Bart's willingness to sell his soul may invite criticism, but it also reflects an inevitable development in a society with such deep religious roots. A moral shift best characterizes the commodification of faith in America. People with religious motivations founded the colonies,[29] but Christianity eventually had to adapt itself to capitalism's spreading economic influence or lose its cultural relevancy.[30] In Weber's words, the "spirit of capitalism" constituted the "motive force" behind economic expansion.[31] Sheer resources were not the ultimate catalyst. Rather, a desire to increase one's net worth, coupled with the need for a morally intact reputation,[32] generated within American society a close bond between Christianity and economic activity. By upholding Christianity's stringent moral guidelines, one could benefit because such morality offered collateral within an economic framework that was ultimately more important than how much money one had. Given the tension between Christian doctrine about such activity and the world's new economic paradigm, the eventual divorce between America's capitalistic cultural and its Christian heritage became inevitable. Christianity provided the foundation for America's founding and eventual independence, but in contemporary society, "[t]he people filled with the spirit of capitalism . . . tend to be indifferent, if not hostile, to the Church."[33]

The relationship between economics and Christianity manifests itself clearly in Springfield. Even the town's most obviously Christian residents embrace on one level or another economic pursuits. Marge embraces the spirit of capitalism in "The Twisted World of Marge Simpson." After having second thoughts about participating in the local investment club's latest venture, which gets her kicked out, Marge decides to invest in a pretzel-making franchise. Ned Flanders likewise engages in capitalistic opportunities. He currently makes his living by operating the Leftorium at the Springfield Mall. Ned shuns alcohol and insurance, which he considers a form of gambling, but he is more than willing to work in jobs that underscore America's capitalistic culture. Finally, even Reverend Lovejoy will wade into profit-generating hobbies. He has written a cookbook called *Someone's Been in the Kitchen with Jesus*.[34] Such a gimmicky publication may offer good recipes, but the marketing angle betrays the project's capitalistic intent. The theme appeals to a consumer base with incredible purchasing power, a bent that reveals an obviously profit-driven motivation on Reverend Lovejoy's part to write such a book.

If residents who uphold Springfield's Christian heritage involve themselves in capitalistic pursuits, and also manage to maintain the integrity of their faith commitments,[35] then one might dismiss the claim that the church and capitalism are necessarily at odds in American society. However, Springfield's true capitalist, Mr. Burns, makes clear the extent to which Christianity should concede that it has lost its cultural relevancy. Mr. Burns may be one of the least invested people in Springfield, spiritually speaking. So thorough is his commitment to the town's economic life that he ceases to find any value in religion. For Mr. Burns, Christianity threatens one's ability to succeed in the world. In "The Old Man and the Lisa," Mr. Burns makes his feelings about Christianity clear:

> I'll keep it short and sweet. Family, religion, friendship. These are the three demons you must slay if you wish to succeed in business. When opportunity knocks, you don't want to be driving to a maternity hospital or sitting in some phony-baloney church.

In Mr. Burns's view, the church is a distraction, something that prevents people from embracing economic opportunity. Of course, Mr. Burns understands opportunity in purely economic terms, which helps to explain why religion is a demon. He is far from scrupulous, a quality that has generated a fortune worth more than one hundred million dollars. For Mr. Burns, religion in general, and Christianity in particular, represent a constraint that, with its moral core, disallows action that he understands to be necessary to succeed in business. In a consumer-driven society such as contemporary America, Mr. Burns's words constitute an authoritative take on Christianity. Mr. Burns may not be Springfield's most popular resident, but he represents wealth, and most of the people in Springfield desire the same thing. After all, they are willing to work for Mr. Burns.[36]

Though one can easily conceive of the Christian Church as prohibiting economic activity, the relationship between the two is ultimately more complex. Weber suggests that despite the apparently mutual exclusivity between economics and religion, "an intimate relationship"[37] may actually exist between the two. Specifically, Weber cites the notion of "a duty of the individual toward the increase of his capital"[38] as a consequence of the relationship between religion and economics. Just as Christianity demands a firm and lasting commitment from its adherents, so, too, does success within the capitalistic framework require sustained effort. Weber thus argues that if one engages in capitalism with sincere motives and upholds a distinct morality within one's pursuits, then capitalism need not sacrifice the integrity of one's spiritual identity. Jesus suggests as much in the parable of the talents.[39] After the master provides his slaves with different amounts of money, he encourages them to go out and "do business"[40] to increase their talents. Those who embrace the imperative and double their money receive praise, while the one who fears losing his money and thus does nothing receives the master's rebuke. The parable's tenor lends credibility to Weber's claim that so long as one pursues economic goals with appropriate behavior, the "result and the expression of virtue"[41] upholds a biblical precedent. As Weber quotes from the Book of Proverbs, "Seest thou a man diligent in his business? He shall stand before kings."[42] In response to Mr. Burns, then, one can point to that businessman's own unhappiness as characteristic of the real problem between religion and economics. Because he fails to uphold certain principles in his business, Mr. Burns ultimately finds himself unsatisfied.[43] Within Weber's paradigm, Mr. Burns's opposition to Christianity may increase his net worth, but if he were to incorporate

Christianity's moral structure into his business, he might find that Springfield would embrace him.[44]

The other extreme possibility would be that Mr. Burns's economic agenda would consume the church. That is, Mr. Burns is not only adverse to what religion represents vis-à-vis his own economic interests; he is also ambivalent about what religion represents to other people. This actually occurs in "She of Little Faith." When Homer's plans go awry and a model rocket destroys a good part of the First Church of Springfield, Mr. Burns offers the church his financial resources to rebuild. Problematically, even before he speaks, one can realize that he represents complete opposition to the church. Quite simply, Mr. Burns represents the devil. When he walks up to the church, Mr. Burns casts a shadow on the wall. The silhouette is not of a decrepit old man but rather of a person with devil's horns. Only when the shot pans back does it reveal that Mr. Burns's hair is sticking up. He smoothes back his hair and resumes his normal silhouette. The image, however, leaves no doubt that Mr. Burns will prove to be a negative influence on the church's integrity. The image conveys the notion that capitalism is quite literally Christianity's enemy. Mr. Burns's offer of financial help represents an invasion that will require the First Church of Springfield to sacrifice its moral and spiritual integrity.

Given the conditions that govern Mr. Burns's donation, one can see why the image is apt. He commercializes the church to the point that one has trouble finding anything sacred. Advertisements flash across Reverend Lovejoy's pulpit, which seems mild when one sees the church's stadium-like television screen, the jumbotron that broadcasts information to the crowd in action. Despite her general distrust of Christianity, Lisa exhibits skepticism toward Mr. Burns's corporate influence on the church. Whoever is working the jumbotron does not miss the point. During a church service, a shot of Lisa sulking in her chair appears on the jumbotron, complete with the caption "Pouting Thomas."[45] Though one can paint Thomas as lacking faith, his doubt is entirely reasonable. Fantastic claims should by no means be accepted without doubt. Accordingly, Lisa expresses reasonable and understandable doubt about what she witnesses in church. Though everyone else seems to buy into the change, Lisa recognizes that Mr. Burns's money has smeared the very heart of what the church represents. To prove the point, *The Simpsons* includes a shot of a banner that now hangs in the church. Jesus is dressed in an American-flag-themed jacket and pants. He grins, as though he has reversed his condemnation of treating the temple as a den of robbers.[46]

As it does so often and so well, *The Simpsons* bends its social critique back onto the American culture that provides the narrative point of criticism. Throughout the show, Springfield's residents blatantly contort their Christianity into an idea that fits nicely within America's capitalistic culture. Perhaps the most telling examples occur when the family completely buys into the commercialism that surrounds Christian holidays. In "Miracle on Evergreen Terrace," Bart gets up early to play with his Christmas presents, one of which is a fire truck. Unfortunately, as Bart drives the fire truck around the living room, it ignites the Christmas tree, which destroys the family's presents. Bart manages to bury the charred evidence of his mistake beneath the snow, but his family takes the missing presents to indicate that somehow Christmas is not complete. To deflect attention away from the presents he has ruined, Bart offers words of wisdom about Christmas's true meaning: "Hey, since when is Christmas just about presents? Aren't we forgetting the true meaning of this day: the birth of Santa?" Bart tries to condemn the consumerism that obscures why Christians celebrate Christmas. He gets the basic framework right; Christmas does celebrate a birthday and this is Christmas' true meaning. However, Bart does not mention anything that is actually related to Christianity. Santa replaces Jesus as the holiday's focal point. Instead of proclaiming the arrival of the world's savior, Bart reminds his family that Christmas celebrates a fictitious person who satisfies a person's material wishes at no cost. Thus, atonement becomes the property of a person who embodies consumerism in American culture. Whereas Christianity understands the person of Jesus to enable salvation for all, Bart trumpets Santa's material provision. The show's larger point is unmistakable in Bart's plea: a hallmark of contemporary American Christianity is that consumption masks or overrides altogether Christianity's doctrinal beliefs.

Chapter Nine

Reason's Revenge: Science Confronts Christianity in Springfield

"Your theory of a donut-shaped universe is intriguing,
Homer. I may have to steal it."
                                   —Stephen Hawking[1]

"By faith we understand that the worlds were prepared
by the word of God, so that what is seen was made from
things that are not visible."
                                   —Hebrews 11:3

Television has a way of creating problems in Springfield.[2] For example,
in "She of Little Faith," Bart sees a commercial for a model rocket kit,
which he promptly orders with Homer's credit card number. When
the rocket arrives, Bart enlists Homer to help put it together and, not
surprisingly, Homer's construction skills fail to live up to the task.
Meanwhile, Ned Flanders helps his own kids build their model rocket,
which performs admirably well. Jealous of Ned's success, Homer asks
some old college roommates[3] to help him build a rocket that is better
than Ned's. They oblige and produce a technologically superior rocket.
When Homer launches the rocket, it goes awry and crashes into the
church. The result is a disaster; the ensuing fire ruins the church.

The scene offers a rich image of how science and the church can be
at odds with each other in contemporary society. Ned's hard work and
technical know-how produce an excellent model rocket, but when
Homer turns to scientists, he emerges with a vastly superior device. The
intellectual ability between the two camps produces similar things, but

the abilities of their respective devices bring about vastly different con-clusions. When it comes time to perform, science's rocket leaves a lasting effect on the church. Science's ability quite literally guts the church. Symbolically, then, science wins the competition. Not only does it pro-duce a better rocket, it also affects the community in a significant manner. Religion's rocket, on the other hand, launches well, but it ultimately flutters harmlessly to the ground. Science wins this round.

Because his actions often produce disasters, Homer Simpson has come to embody stupidity, but it turns out that his limited intellectual ability is not actually his fault. In "HOMR," *The Simpsons* presents the real story behind Homer's faulty intelligence. After losing the family sav-ings chasing a hot stock, Homer must find a way to earn back the money. He settles on offering himself as a medical testing guinea pig. During one of the tests, researchers find that a crayon is stuck in Homer's brain. A flashback reveals that, as a child, Homer pushed the crayon up his nose, which, once lodged in his brain, causes his notoriously subpar IQ. Once the doctors remove the crayon, Homer exhibits remarkable intellectual breadth. In fact, while doing a routine task, Homer discovers a proof that God does not exist, which he is more than happy to share with his Christian neighbor:

Homer: I was working on a flat tax proposal and I accidentally
         proved there's no God.

Ned: We'll just see about that. Oh, maybe he made a mistake?
         Nope. It's air-tight.
         [As Homer walks away, Ned pulls out a lighter and
         ignites the piece of paper.]

Ned: Can't let this little doozy get out.

Homer's proof accomplishes many a scientist's dream. He finds definitive proof, contained in a mathematical equation, that God does not exist.[4] Though Ned quickly destroys the evidence, the implication is clear. The incident underscores that science and religion are not only perceived to be intellectually opposed to each other but also that, when the two collide, science usually triumphs. Reason is able to undermine the very founda-tion of Christianity's belief system. Ned knows this, which explains why he quickly burns up the piece of paper. Of course, Homer is one step ahead of him. As the original proof burns and Ned exhales a sigh of relief, Homer is placing copies of the proof on the windshields of every car in the neighborhood.

Homer's intelligence, however short-lived, characterizes one of the chief cultural challenges that Christianity faces in Springfield. Scientific reason consistently undermines the town's spiritual foundations. When Homer, or as is more often the case, Lisa, brings reason to bear on Christian questions or concerns, the culturally driven dichotomy of science versus religion unfolds. Those Springfield residents who stand on science's side usually understand their position as intellectually superior and they often dismiss Christianity as intellectually vapid mysticism. In privileging science as more authoritative in Springfield's culture identity, *The Simpsons* mirrors not only the perceived conflict between the two schools of thought in contemporary American culture, it also captures a general intellectual bias against religion. Thus, the show implies that when it comes to rockets or cultural reputation, Christianity is fighting a losing battle.

Despite the cultural authority that intellectuals often assume when discussing religion, the idea that science can invade religion's turf is shortsighted. In order to assert its influence over Christianity, scientific thought must alter the parameters that define Christian beliefs in the first place. To relate science and religion on the same intellectual plane requires that they address similar topics. Historically, the move to do so produces the theory that God exists only insofar as the concept of God can fill a gap that science has not explained. This approach implies that God is a temporary explanation that science will remove as soon as it finds the actual explanation. Despite this paradigm's cultural currency, the idea proves to be flawed. Diogenes Allen makes clear that such theories skew how Christianity defines God in the first place:

> God is inserted in the gaps that could not be occupied by members of the universe. This is theologically improper because God, as creator of the universe, is not a member of the universe. God can never properly be used in scientific accounts, which are formulated in terms of the relations between the members of the universe, because that would reduce God to the status of a creature.[5]

The Simpsons presents in "HOMR," then, the intellectual flaw that Allen describes. To disprove God during a mathematical task requires that God be understandable wholly within mathematical terms. However, such standards are precisely the limits of scientific reason that Allen discusses. In God, Christianity posits a belief that is, by definition, ontologically different than any field of scientific inquiry. The Christian doctrine of God usually holds that God exists outside of space and time, which means that mathematics cannot account for God's existence or nonexistence.[6]

Another example of the God-in-the-gaps approach occurs in "Treehouse of Horror XVI." In this episode, Kang and Kodos face a significant problem: they want the World Series to speed up so it will not be so boring to watch. Using an accelerator device, they spin the earth to achieve the desired effect, but an unforeseen consequence occurs. The earth spins so quickly that everything in the universe begins to disappear as time rewinds. God is the final thing to vanish, which implies that God is part of the physical universe. Allen's argument rejects this notion of God as theologically imprecise. Any criticisms of Christian thought based on understanding God as part of the universe are not intellectually consistent with Christianity's basic beliefs. Science can argue about God's existence in mathematical terms, just as Homer does in "HOMR," but such arguments rely on science's definition of the parameters involved. Christian theology would thus reject the idea that God could vanish with the rest of the universe[7] because God exists outside of universe.[8]

Conflict between science and religion often emerges when scientific discovery threatens established religious beliefs. Galileo provides a striking historical example of how Christianity's leaders can react to advances that bump up against church doctrine.[9] For his discoveries about the solar system's structure, Galileo faced excommunication. Such stories from history only cement the idea that "Christianity has long been discredited on the grounds that it has been injurious to the development of science because of its restrictive and oppressive attitudes toward the discoveries of classical science."[10] However, this false dichotomy ignores the fact that "Christianity was a major factor, perhaps an essential ingredient in the rise of science."[11] The relationship between science and religion, both academically and culturally, often suggests that the opposite is true. As Homer's rocket implies, the two are not only at odds, but the conflict will inevitably produce harmful consequences for one of the two intellectual traditions. Thus, the two sides square off in a kind of zero-sum game. If Homer's intelligence somehow calculates God's nonexistence correctly, then Ned's entire belief system crumbles. The only reasonable solution is to erase all traces of Homer's accomplishments rather than explore the proof in more depth.

During "The Monkey Suit," the conflict between science and religion explodes in Springfield. The episode begins innocently enough. The Simpson family heads to the Springfield Museum to see a weaving exhibit. As luck would have it, the exhibit changes suddenly. Instead of learning about weaving, the Simpsons will experience the "History of Weapons." The Springfield populace has flocked to the museum, and the line stretches out the door. Oddly enough, Ned Flanders and his boys are at the head of the line. After Homer cuts in line, the rest of the crowd does likewise, which leaves the Flanderses with a long wait to learn about weapons. Just as Ned and his boys reach the front of the line, the weapons exhibit closes for the day. Ned then takes Rod and Todd to an alternative exhibit on evolution. Ned is overwhelmed by what he finds: the idea that humans evolved from apes and the notion that the Bible is a mythical set of documents. All Ned can do as he leaves in a huff is cover his kids' eyes so they cannot see what science has to say about Christian beliefs.

Appalled by his experience, Ned approaches Reverend Lovejoy to help with a new agenda: pushing the public schools to teach creationism. Reverend Lovejoy agrees to help, and the two blackmail Principle Skinner. If he does not introduce creationism into the curriculum, they will burn up the lease for his car, which has an unbeatable interest rate. The town gets caught up in the movement and votes to replace Darwin's theory of evolution with creationism. Lisa, of course, cannot believe her eyes when her teacher, Ms. Hoover, writes creationism on the chalkboard. As Lisa says succinctly, creationism is "not science." She rebels against the new law and organizes a secret meeting to discuss the theory of evolution. She is caught and sent to trial for "the teaching of non-biblical science." Thus, the lines have been drawn and the tables have been turned. Religion has usurped science's intellectual domain.

The subsequent trial pits Lisa's scientifically oriented intellect against Ned's biblically based beliefs, or, as the media says, "Lisa versus God." At first, the trial seems to go Ned's way, as the notion of the missing link threatens the legitimacy of Darwin's theory. Luckily, Marge decides to read Darwin's *On the Origin of Species*, which convinces her that Darwin has a point. She then orchestrates a scene in the courtroom to support Lisa's case. When Ned takes the stand to testify that he has no evidence that humans could have descended from apes, Marge offers Homer a beer, which he gladly accepts. However, Homer is unable to get the bottle open. He becomes more animated as he struggles with the bottle cap and he eventually mimics a monkey's posture and noises. Frustrated, Ned eventually calls Homer "a big monkey-faced gorilla." His language leaves no room for doubt: Homer is several kinds of primate rolled into one human. Ned undercuts his own beliefs, and Lisa prevails.

Of course, legitimate science need not be understood as Christianity's enemy. In fact, Darwin's theory of evolution can enhance Ned's Christian understanding of the world. Rational thought can help Christians to understand their world better (and in this case with the added benefit of understanding Homer better). As Allen writes, "Reason is used, not only to examine the grounds for Christian claims but also to understand them better . . . [W]e are to relate Christian claims to our best estimate of what we believe to be true of the events of history and to the workings of nature and the human mind."[12] Marge demonstrates how science can coexist with Christian faith. Marge begins the episode much like Ned: she rejects the idea that evolutionary processes exist in the world. However, her convictions rest on her Christian beliefs alone. When she actually reads Darwin's work, she recognizes that her stringent faith actually represents closed-mindedness. Importantly, Marge shifts her position to one that can support Lisa's rationalistic bent without compromising her religious beliefs. Though Ned does not create intellectual space for science to enhance his Christian faith, at the very least Ned can agree to respect Lisa's beliefs. Given his extreme version of Christianity, Ned's softened position points to the possibility that faith can seek intellectual clarity without compromising its foundational beliefs.

In rejecting the theory of evolution, Ned characterizes a common but misguided understanding of how science and religion relate. Though concerned with a distinct sphere of inquiry, Christianity can turn toward science for help in better understanding the physical world. Allen calls Christians who welcome science on an intellectual level people "with faith seeking understanding."[13] For example, Christians who believe in the traditional Christian doctrine of creation can incorporate science into their faith because their world operates on physical principles. If one assumes that God made the world, then science can interact with Christian thought insofar as science seeks to understand this particular world. Springfield's Christian populace, however, tends not to understand or embrace its own theological beliefs, so to expect the same people to engage science responsibly seems unreasonable. Most characters on The Simpsons lack reliable intellectual skills. Moreover, those who do stand among the town's intelligent population tend to have at best a lukewarm relationship with Christianity. Without a reasonable voice to mediate between closed-minded Christians and skeptical scientists, it is not surprising that Springfield continually finds a place for the two intellectual traditions to clash.

Ned stands at the extreme end of narrow-minded faith. However, the culture he represents tells only half the story. Just as Ned's personal faith contorts the way in which he views his world, those who believe scientific thought to be above reproach also view their surroundings through a particular lens, which ultimately proves to be equally problematic.

Within Springfield's cultural makeup, science acts as a kind of intellectual club with which one can wield significant influence. Those who are not well versed in science can easily succumb to the cultural authority that it represents. One can see this dynamic clearly in "Two Cars in Every Garage and Three Eyes on Every Fish." When Bart catches a three-eyed fish at Lake Springfield, an uproar ensues concerning Mr. Burns's polluting business practices. Rather than adopt environmentally appropriate policies, Mr. Burns decides to run for governor so he can change the laws to accommodate business as is. To win, he has to explain the three-eyed fish in a positive light. To accomplish the seemingly impossible task, Mr. Burns runs a commercial in which an actor playing Charles Darwin explains the fish's scientific significance:

Darwin: Hello, Mr. Burns.

Mr. Burns: Oh, hello, Charles. Be a good fellow and tell our viewers about your theory of natural selection.

Darwin: Glad to, Mr. Burns. You see, every so often, Mother Nature changes our animals, giving them bigger teeth, sharper claws, longer legs or, in this case, a third eye. And if the variations turn out to be an improvement, the new animals thrive and multiply, and spread across the face of the earth.

Mr. Burns: So you're saying this fish might actually have an advantage over other fish? It might actually be a kind of "Super Fish"?

Darwin: I wouldn't mind having a third eye, would you?

Mr. Burns: [laughing]: No.

Backed by the scientific authority that Darwin represents, Mr. Burns can recast his environmental irresponsibility as something that science affirms. By invoking science's cultural authority, Mr. Burns presents his mistakes not only as part of a natural process but also as something that is ahead of the evolutionary curve, so to speak. The fish has something that everyone, even Darwin, would want. Mr. Burns, then, manages to manipulate a cultural image of science's authority, Darwin, to distance himself from what legitimate science would otherwise say: the fish clearly represents a scientific mutation that resulted directly from Mr. Burns's pollution. The implication is clear; anyone who doubts Mr. Burns's scientific evidence comes across as ignorant.

Mr. Burns's commercial message suggests on the surface that Darwin's theory not only explains aberrant evolutionary behavior, but it also does so without rejecting completely the common notion that science and religion are opposites. This example points to the way in which general cultural ignorance fails to recognize faulty science. Mr. Burns's commercial initiates a strong climb in the polls. The initial boost is small, but it provides enough momentum to produce eventually an electorate that sees Mr. Burns as "imperial and godlike." The first quality probably exists in public perception well before Mr. Burns runs for office. However, understanding him as a divine figure points to his strategy's effectiveness. Bad science produces good political results. Thus, Mr. Burns manages to collapse two spheres of inquiry in a way that does justice to neither, which ultimately produces his desired result. This vignette suggests that misunderstood Christian theology may not be the only intellectually troubled area in Springfield. The public readily accepts Mr. Burns's faulty science, which ignores the obvious inaccuracies that actual science would otherwise point out.[14] By relying on science's perceived cultural authority, Mr. Burns can achieve his political ends by harnessing science's cultural authority.

In contrast to Mr. Burns's skewed scientific standards, Professor John Frink offers a more nuanced look at how science and religion intersect in Springfield. Professor Frink is the town's most visible scientist. He is an oddball whose interests incline toward the fantastic. In addition to being an eventual Nobel Prize recipient,[15] Professor Frink also seems to have a religious streak to his personality. On Easter Sunday, he sits in the second row of pews.[16] More important, in "Treehouse of Horror VII," Professor Frink reveals that for all science's accomplishments in society, in the face of God it has little to say. When Lisa's created world shrinks her in order to have her visit, the plan has one flaw. The machine they use to bring Lisa into their world cannot reverse the process and allow Lisa to depart. A Professor Frink look-alike is responsible for building the machine, so he stands to face punishment when Lisa expresses frustration that she is stuck in her shrunken state. Professor Frink becomes nervous and babbles, "Unshrink you? Well, that would require some sort of a re-bigulator, which is a concept so ridiculous it makes me want to laugh out loud and chortle, and . . ." When Lisa looks sternly at him, Professor Frink continues, "But not at you, O holiest of gods, with the wrathfulness and the vengeance and the blood rain and the hey-hey-hey-it-hurts-me."

Professor Frink's rapid speech conveys clearly the notion that, should science ever have to answer to God, science would be in trouble. For all its positive contributions to society, science cannot override God's authority. Frink initially scorns the idea that he could develop a re-bigulator. However, when faced with the divine wrath of Lisa, he quickly becomes penitent. Though Professor Frink represents true scientific exploration and achievement, he does not reject entirely the possibility that something else could trump his genius. Ironically, on *The Simpsons* Professor Frink embodies perhaps most clearly the notion that one should truly fear God. In other episodes, Professor Frink also shows a willingness to consider the sacred. In "Lisa the Skeptic," he comes to Homer's garage to view the skeleton of a supposed angel. His scientific mind should reject the notion outright, but he remains pointedly silent when science and religion clash.

Whereas Professor Frink mostly stays out of the science versus religion conflict, either remaining within his area of expertise or staying silent when he enters Christianity's space, Lisa exhibits a more involved and thus instructive look at how science and religion intersect in Springfield. She must navigate a complex relationship between her mom's strong Christian beliefs, her father's inabilities in the domains of both science and religion, as well as her own intellectual biases against faith. In "Lisa the Skeptic," *The Simpsons* directly addresses the conflict between science and religion, as well as the ways in which Lisa must navigate between competing influences. After finding a skeleton that resembles an angel, Lisa must balance her intellectualism with the possibility that things she would otherwise dismiss might be real. When Ned Flanders asks Lisa if the skeleton is an angel, she responds, "Obviously that's impossible." This initial interaction between Lisa and Ned sets the stage for another tug-of-war between his faith and her reason.

Strictly speaking, an angelic skeleton is impossible, if nothing else because angels could not have skeletons if they existed. In order to fly, an angel could not have a human's skeletal structure because the bones would make the body too heavy to lift off the ground. Thus, an angel would need to be a metaphysical hybrid, which would not produce a completely physical skeleton. These obvious points, however, never appear on Ned's or the rest of the crowd's radar. They immediately embrace the idea that the skeleton must be an angel. When Moe asks Lisa how she can be so sure what the angel is not, but cannot explain precisely what it is, Lisa loses traction. She posits that perhaps the skeleton was a Neanderthal and the wings are the remains of two fish that bit his arms. The subsequent dream sequence makes clear that this thesis is highly unlikely. As her hypothesis hangs in the air, Lisa begins to look sheepish. As if on cue, Ned leans down and says, "Lisa, it sounds like you're straining to do some explaining." Chief Wiggum joins the argument with another revealing comment: "Everyone's heard of angels. Who's ever heard of a Neanderthal?" Wiggum's comments reveal yet again the relative ignorance that defines Springfield, as well as the way in which Christianity provides an alternative explanation. Science cannot answer the obvious question, so the religious explanation takes hold.

Hysteria soon grips Springfield. People begin stopping by the Simpson house to see the angel. Everyone's motivation is spiritual. Ned wants his family to share a prayerful moment with the angel, while Agnes Skinner wants a kind of blessing before her surgery the following day. As an increasing spiritual hysteria develops in response to the skeleton, Lisa remains the lone holdout. She tells Homer that he should not be charging people to see something without knowing what that thing is. "Dad, it's not fair to call this thing an angel. There's no proof of that." Lisa reveals a classic scientific argument against faith claims. She demands proof in a scientific sense, which, by virtue of the thing discussed, she has already established has no definitive scientific explanation.[17] She necessarily excludes the possibility of the skeleton actually being an angel. According to the standards Lisa brings to the table when trying to determine what the thing is, her rational approach disallows the possibility for a metaphysical explanation. Whereas some Christian thinkers have opened the door to possibility that science and religion can coexist, Lisa steadfastly upholds a division between the two. Thus, she reflects a common attitude in American society. Religion and science cannot coexist.

When Homer refuses to allow Lisa to take the skeleton to the museum for tests, she has to break off a piece of the skeleton's foot in secret in order to test whether the skeleton could be an angel. She sneaks a bone from the skeleton's toe and takes it to the Museum of Natural History, where Stephen J. Gould works.[18] When he hears of her errand, he exhibits a similar skepticism, which makes Lisa feel better:

Gould: [looking suspiciously at the bag with the bone]: Oh yeah, the so-called angel. The whole thing's preposterous, of course.

Lisa: Quite preposterous. But no one will believe me until I can prove what it really is. Can't you do a DNA test or something?

Gould: Certainly. I'll have the results by tomorrow.

Lisa: Oh, thank you so much![19]

Despite her steadfast insistence that the skeleton is not an angel, Lisa reveals that her own way of understanding the world is not entirely reliable. She, too, trusts completely that her understanding of the skeleton will resolve the issue once and for all. The point parallels Lisa's own criticism of Christians' supposedly shortsighted approach to the skeleton. The religious camp must embrace a thesis, which cannot be disproved, to accept the skeleton as an angel. In a similar capacity science must perform certain basic tasks in order to establish its own position. In this case, Gould has to do the test, which he never actually gets around to, if Lisa wants to have definitive scientific proof that the skeleton cannot be an angel. Science, then, may understand itself as a definitive, factual, and thus unassailable authority, but it cannot compensate for basic lapses in its intellectual processes. When Gould fails to follow up on Lisa's request, her position assumes the same character as the beliefs of her Christian counterparts. No one can know for sure whether the skeleton is real.

The precipitous position that Lisa adopts becomes apparent when she tells everyone that she took a piece of the angel to the museum for analysis. She assures everyone that they will soon have the "facts." Homer is the first to respond: "Facts are meaningless. You can use facts to prove anything that's even remotely true." Even Homer buys into the religious possibility that the angel presents and in so doing jettisons common sense. Despite admitting his ignorance, and revealing an absurd bias against facts that Christianity often exhibits, Homer stands by the Christian position.[20] This, in turn, suggests that science loses its appeal when the possibility of the sacred presents itself. If the angel convinces Homer, then science faces a foe it is helpless against. The truly unreasonable person will not even acknowledge science's legitimacy as a cultural authority. When Gould arrives a moment later and says that the tests were inconclusive, even though he never actually tested anything Reverend Lovejoy joins the antiscientific chorus. In a satisfied tone, he says, "Well, it appears science has faltered again in the face of overwhelming religious evidence." Like Homer, Reverend Lovejoy regresses into nonsense. Using scientific language to make his point, Reverend Lovejoy utilizes a religious equivalent to science's flawed God-in-the-gaps strategy. By positing the notion of religious evidence, Reverend Lovejoy commandeers an intellectual pursuit that belongs to science. The defense against science's incursions into religious territory rests on the ontological distinction between the world that God created and God the creator. Thus, Christians ought not to suggest that when the roles are reversed, religion can produce the same kind of results to prove its point. The very notion of evidence is scientific. Thus, Reverend Lovejoy adopts the very thing that he dismisses. His mixed-up arguments reiterate the town's willingness to jettison common sense when the possibility of the sacred appears. The point here is similar to the problem that defines Christianity elsewhere on *The Simpsons*. American culture shifts its intellectual and spiritual allegiances so frequently that it clearly lacks the kind of depth that both fields traditionally value.

Lisa begins to realize the implications of her dismissive attitude when she complains to Marge about the town's "morons" who believe in angels. Her conversation reveals the crux of the problem between science and religion:

Marge: Maybe so, but I'd appreciate it if you didn't call them morons.

Lisa: But they are morons! What grown person could believe in angels?

Marge: Well, your mother for one.

Lisa: You? But you're an intelligent person, Mom.

Marge: There has to be more to life than just what we see, Lisa. Everyone needs something to believe in.

Lisa: It's not that I don't have a spiritual side. I just find it hard to believe there's a dead angel hanging in our garage.

Marge: Oh, my poor Lisa, if you can't make a leap of faith now and then, well, I feel sorry for you.

Lisa: Don't feel sorry for me, Mom. I feel sorry for you.

Marge does not judge Lisa as Lisa has been judging others. Rather, she offers sincere sympathy because Lisa cannot stretch her mind beyond its preconceptions. Lisa assumes that to be a reasonable person one must dismiss the possibility that something outside of reason's boundaries might be possible. Marge cuts to the heart of the issue. The content of one's beliefs does not matter; reason and belief are not exclusive. What is important is remaining open to possibilities from a way of thinking that differs from one's own. Just as Marge shows a willingness to read Darwin, Lisa should show a willingness to consider the possibility that the angel might be real. For Marge, verifiable truth is secondary. Lisa, however, cannot absorb the advice. She remains intellectually closed to the notion of belief.

Lisa takes her crusade to the airwaves. She goes on Kent Brockman's talk show, *Smartline*, to make her case. Once again, she spars verbally with someone who has accepted the angel as real.

> Kent: Miss Simpson, how can you maintain your skepticism despite the fact that this thing really, really looks like an angel?
>
> Lisa: I just think it's a fantasy, if you believe in angels, then why not unicorns, sea monsters, and leprechauns!
>
> Kent: That's a bunch of baloney, Lisa. Everyone knows that leprechauns are extinct!
>
> Lisa: Look, you can either accept science and face reality, or you can believe in angels and live in a childish dreamworld.

As the conflict intensifies, Lisa's unreasonable stubbornness emerges more forcefully. Brockman presents the very thing Lisa uses to support her stance: supposed facts. Unlike Lisa's trust in DNA testing, which produces nothing definitive because Gould never does his job, Brockman's empirical data is verifiable. The skeleton does look like an angel; Lisa cannot deny this. Just as Reverend Lovejoy confuses scientific paradigms with his religious claims, so, too, does Brockman collapse science and something that is wholly unscientific. Leprechauns cannot be extinct, mostly because according to science they do not exist.[21]

After Lisa's appearance on television, the town's opposition to science reaches a fever pitch. A few examples show the extent to which Christians can become unreasonable in defending their faith against science's influence. Ned exclaims, "Science is like a blabbermouth who ruins a movie by telling you how it ends. Well, I say that there are some things we don't want to know. Important things!" Ned's call for intentional ignorance suggests that he not only understands that science can provide answers, but also that those answers will undercut his faith in the unknown. He would rather remain ignorant of what science has to say about the world. Of course, the rest of the town agrees, which leads them to arrest Lisa for supporting science. When she goes on trial, Judge Snyder exerts a measure of reason: "I find the defendant not guilty. As for science versus religion, I'm issuing a restraining order. Religion should stay five hundred yards away from science at all times." Whereas Judge Snyder finally shows restraint in the conflict by not imprisoning Lisa for her scientific understanding, he does conclude in a way that captures the broader point about science and religion. The two are incompatible in American culture. Thus, they must uphold a distance that echoes the historical division that is, despite its erroneous nature, so set in America's cultural consciousness.

Despite what science might say about the possibility of angels, which Lisa embodies so clearly, popular conception embraces the idea that angelic beings participate in Americans' spiritual lives. The fact that science seems to have no answer for the possibility of an angel makes that same possibility more attractive to the nonscientifically inclined. When science and religion are culturally understood as oppositional, the spiritual camp relishes the fact that the supposed scientific experts cannot exert their authority over a matter of popular interest.[22] Thus, one should understand part of the conflict between science and religion not as contained wholly within authoritative arguments but also within the public consciousness. Marge and the rest of Springfield embrace the angel not to flaunt science, but because it offers a tangible way to exercise belief. Thus, Wuthnow argues, one should recognize that "the relationship that needs to be understood is that between the supernatural and everyday life, more so than between the supernatural and science."[23] The mystery that defines the supernatural in the public consciousness appeals precisely because it is "not something that is revealed in an authoritative text or institution."[24]

Ironically, it turns out that Lisa was right all along, though this truth comes to light only after Lisa almost yields to the possibility that the angel is real. The angel is just an advertising stunt for the new mall that caused Lisa to look for fossils in the first place. Thus, the ending reinforces the economic realities of contemporary American culture discussed elsewhere. In American culture, both science and religion ultimately compete with, and usually lose to, economic interests. The conflict in "Lisa the Skeptic" thus clarifies not only the specific friction between science and religion as intellectual traditions, but also the broader problem that affects American society. Like religion, science struggles with a crisis of authority. According to Diogenes Allen, "What is dismissed as incompatible with rational inquiry is not Christian faith but faith understood as a blind submission to authority. . . . Christian faith, however, involves the use of reason and without reason it is not Christian faith."[25] Depending on which character one identifies with in Springfield, science or religion will struggle to offer a cultural voice that maintains its intellectual and historical integrity. The larger point, then, is that science certainly offers a different way of looking at the world, but it also need not be understood as necessarily excluding religion as a relevant cultural voice. Both science and religion are cultural realities, and both must understand their respective spheres of influence in a way that does not ask the other to sacrifice its integrity. Merely rejecting faith in the name of science creates a world in which people can be duped by those who, like Mr. Burns, can and will manipulate science's cultural authority. Likewise, a Christian faith that rejects science's legitimacy risks an equally troubling abuse of authority. Ignoring the other side exposes a narrow-minded belief in one's own superiority, a fact evident when either scientists or theologians claim to know definitive answers.

A Concluding Trumpet Blast: Taking Christianity Seriously, At Least in Springfield

> "It seems liberals want to give NASA the right to abort space missions whenever they feel like it!"
> —Birch Barlow, Springfield's conservative television commentator[1]

> "Give therefore to the emperor the things that are the emperor's, and to God the things that are God's."
> —Matthew 22:21

The Simpsons Movie begins with Homer at the center of an environmental crisis. Lake Springfield has been polluted seemingly beyond repair. The situation is so precipitous that even a single act of additional pollution will have dire consequences. Always ready to completely disregard such warnings, Homer tosses a silo full of his spiderpig's poop into the lake. Just as the warnings predicted, the lake reaches a tipping point. The water begins to bubble as a deadly reaction spreads through its waters. Then weird things begin to happen. Mr. Burns's pollution may produce a fish with three eyes, but Homer's actions spawn a multieyed squirrel that is far more grotesque.

When Ned Flanders is out hiking with Bart, he encounters this new creature. Shocked by the squirrel's appearance, Ned cannot help but exclaim, "That's some mighty fine intelligent design!" It seems as though Ned has forgotten what happened when the theory of evolution last visited Springfield.[2] The squirrel is not a picture of God's creative beauty. Rather, it points harshly to the idea that humans can enable disastrous environmental consequences through their careless actions.

Ned, however, retreats to his scientifically naïve but spiritually sound way of understanding his world. Faced with a creature that is completely out of place in the world, Ned can only praise what he takes to be God's creative ability to produce such an animal.

Ned's comment might seem like a throwaway line that reveals nothing more than the tunnel vision he uses to understand the world around him. However, when the EPA traps the squirrel and takes it back to Washington, D.C., a significant political issue overlaps Ned's innocent label. When EPA chief Russ Cargill shows President Schwarzenegger the monstrosity, a dangerous convergence begins. Cargill tells the president:

> You know, sir, when you made me head of the EPA, you were applauded for appointing one of the most successful men in America to the least successful agency in government. And why did I take the job? Because I'm a rich man who wanted to give something back. Not the money, but something.

Money, politics, and misconstruing the squirrel as part of some divine plan come together in a dangerous marriage. The combination of these factors, which echo a similar convergence in contemporary American culture vis-à-vis the rise of neoconservative politics, produces a horrible fate for Springfield and a financial boon for Cargill's company, which makes the glass dome that eventually covers Springfield. Cargill thus embodies a political and business admixture that echoes a Republican administration that advances its own interests by plugging into Evangelical Christian concerns. In order to make money for his company, Cargill encourages a plan that disregards completely Springfield's interests. The president proves to be ignorantly complicit in the scheme. When Cargill presents several options to deal with Springfield, President Schwarzenegger tells him, "I was elected to lead, not to read." The entire sequence takes a clear jab at America's current political power structure. An obviously Republican administration yields to financial interests to solve a problem that a constituent misidentifies as God-given. Given Ned's Evangelical belief system, the political commentary is clear: neoconservative politicians will disregard resonable inquiry in order to appeal to their Evangelical constituents. Thus, a religious interpretation obscures what is really at stake, which leads to a political decision. The result proves to be disastrous for everyone. Whereas Cargill and the Republican government trumpet their decision's positive social influence, all in God's name, it cannot escape ready contradictions. Ned believes erroneously that Homer's mistake is actually God's creative power at work. This produces a response from a government grounded in an Evangelical Christian base that serves its own interests while, like Ned, remaining ignorant of, or actively ignoring, the larger parameters of their decisions.

The social, political, and religious critiques that weave their way into *The Simpsons Movie* identify clearly the extent to which Christianity's problems emerge in contemporary American society. Religion and power are a potent mix, especially when both institutions lose sight of their heritage and subsequently move forward without addressing their shortcomings. Pervasive ignorance of alternative possibilities and a self-appointed (and self-assured) monopoly and power warrant suspicion. *The Simpsons* makes clear that a marriage between political power and America's Christian heritage has marched on without critical pause in recent years. When political powers harness Christianity's traditional cultural authority, the integrity of all institutions involved tends to suffer. For example, in "You Kent Always Say What You Want," Kent Brockman incurs the Republican Party's moral policing wrath when he swears on television. When Ned Flanders complains about Brockman's profane slip on television, the FCC hands down a ten-million-dollar fine against his employer, Channel Six. Ned's self-appointed role of moral watchdog attracts the Republican government's attention in a way that not only exerts control over the media, but also does so in a manner that is financially beneficial to the government. Thus, the Evangelical community's moral agenda, as embodied in Ned, dovetails with its political agenda. The result costs Brockman his job because of the hefty fine that his employer must pay. Faith and government thus work together in order to bring about a conclusion that satisfies a moral agenda, but in a way that makes clear how those who pursue the agenda often abuse their power.

The fine is excessive and the result alone captures the strong link between Christianity and government, but the episode pushes the point. Whereas Brockman's accidental and understandable slip produces disastrous results, the conservative media's response does not elicit a single sanction from the same governmental officials. Birch Barlow, Springfield's conservative television commentator, takes up the issue on his program. Because of Brockman's "shameful swear-nami," Channel Six's mascot, Newshound, will not have surgery to correct his lazy eye. Barlow alludes to a true tragedy, the 2004 Indian Ocean tsunami that killed hundreds of thousands of people, to smear a reporter. Again, the impetus for doing so is an Evangelical's moral objection to an accidental and understandable slip of the tongue. Cynical though he may be,

Brockman is not a moral degenerate. Still, Ned's moral sensibilities set off a chain of events that ultimately elicit a heavy-handed and self-serving response from Republican politicians and media personalities. The implication is clear: the marriage of Evangelism and neoconservative politics presents a real danger to anyone who runs against the grain that their converging interests produce.

Admirably, Brockman makes a stand against the abuse of authority, at least for a while. He calls out the Republican officials for their hypocrisy. He urges viewers to reject the skewed values that result from the coalition of political and Evangelical social forces in order to return to their Christian roots. Brockman says, "Reject your corporate masters. Hug your children. Love the one you're with." The message is simple; it recalls Christian values that lie at the heart of American culture. Brockman calls on the town to turn away from the consumer-driven culture that has sacrificed genuine values. For a brief moment, so much of what has sacrificed the integrity of Springfield's Christian identity is exposed for what it is: a constant and shameless drive for power at the cost of what made the political and religious institutions important in the first place.

Of course, at Springfield's Republican Headquarters, the message causes those who implement and nurture such power-seeking social structures to bristle, but not because they will be honest as they look into the mirror of Brockman's words. Rather, they understand the message rightly as undercutting what they are doing, but not in a way that will produce positive change. Mr. Burns grumbles, "Look at that rabble-rouser." Exposing the shortcomings of those with cultural influence in Springfield is then seen as rebellion against the established authority. Brockman states publicly the ways in which the social, political, economic, and religious elites, embodied in their ruling political party, have hijacked their institutional integrity in order to serve their own interests. *The Simpsons* drives the point home when, at the episode's conclusion, the Republican leadership silences the rebel not by reforming their practices, but rather through bribery. In order to bring Brockman back into their fold, Republican interests simply offer him more money than he can refuse to uphold their and their constituents' cause. After hesitating for a moment, Brockman accepts the money. The threat seems to have passed, but not before someone reveals the problems that are so pervasive in Springfield. The episode does not include change within Springfield, but the implication for the viewer is clear. This interaction captures the cultural climate in contemporary America, and it is up to the viewers to assume the socially critical mantle that Brockman has dropped.

The Simpsons thus makes apparent the negative effects that grow out of the combination of Christianity and other social institutions, especially political ones. Dangerous consequences await a culture that sanctions such unions. Young Americans are one significant victim. Throughout the show, Springfield's children demonstrate how religion misrepresents a key part of their cultural identity. In "Team Homer," Bart and Milhouse reveal the extent to which Christian leaders have deceived their young minds. When the two boys buy a *MAD* magazine, they find a puzzle that asks, "What is it that television evangelists worship the most?" Bart answers, "God," while Milhouse answers, "Jesus." Both turn out to be wrong. When they fold the page together to check their answers, they see a dollar sign. Once again, economic influences on Christianity prove to be problematic. Under a banner of spiritual purity and moral motives, Christianity's leaders often pursue economic interests. *The Simpsons* makes the point explicit by identifying a primary victim of this kind of religious climate. When children affirm Christianity's belief system, and then find out they have been misled, Christians ought to take notice.

Such blind spots demand the attention of Christians as well as broader American culture. *The Simpsons* thus accomplishes an important social task by making visible how religion has lost direction in the midst of competing cultural influences. Despite the caricatured nature that defines how the show portrays religion, the message emerges clearly. Robert Knight, the former director of the conservative Family Research Council, recognizes the show's value: "The Simpsons do function in a moral universe, and, while the show seems to make fun of moral standards, it often upholds those same standards in a back-handed way."[3] Even though politically conservative groups have received a significant share of the show's satire, Knight can still see how the show does not completely undercut the values that Evangelical Christianity upholds. Rather, he recognizes *The Simpsons* for what it is: a critical voice that, through satire, identifies the ways in which elements of American culture can address its own problems. Robert Short, author of *The Gospel According to Peanuts*, echoes this point: "The arts get under our skin far more effectively than direct discourse, far more effectively than a sermon. . . . It's a form of indirect communication."[4] The show thus presents "great values"[5] by exaggerating stereotypical tendencies in Christian culture. While it may generate criticism as an offensive cartoon, *The Simpsons* pinpoints elements of Christianity that have failed to live up to their name.

When Christianity loses its integrity, one can understand how individuals who adhere to the faith in name do not always uphold its values in practice. Worse, some will accept a distorted version of Christianity as legitimate and thus repeat the same problematic behavior that exists institutionally. For example, in "Two Bad Neighbors," former President George H. W. Bush moves to Springfield.[6] Everyone is excited to have a famous neighbor and they welcome him accordingly. Homer, of course, is the exception. When President Bush spanks Bart for ruining his memoirs, Homer takes matters into his own hands. With Bart's help, he undertakes a campaign of pranks to let President Bush know how upset he truly is.

One prank is particularly revealing of the problematic nature that characterizes so many moments when Christianity and politics meet. Homer and Bart are walking through the sewer to President Bush's house to enact their next prank and Bart is carrying a box of locusts. Their conversation captures the way in which political feuds can turn to Christianity with malicious intent:

Homer:	So I thought to myself, "What would God do in this situation?"
Bart:	[laughing]: Locusts! They'll drive him nuts!
Homer:	It's all in the Bible, son. The prankster's Bible.

This brief exchange raises several key points. The first is Homer's belief that the Bible justifies his actions. Whereas Homer should understand the story of the locusts as a call to uphold God's commands,[7] a vastly different interpretation emerges. In Homer's mind, the Bible sanctions his upcoming actions, even though in reality they will only aggravate an already senseless conflict defined by several peoples' stubborn pride. Moreover, the political overtones are hard to miss. President Bush Sr.'s presence very much alludes to the neoconservative shift in Republican politics that occurred during this time in American culture. The notion that he, like Pharaoh, deserves the invasion of a swarm of locusts casts the political party that he represents in the role of a tyrannical leader who enslaved God's people. Finally, Homer understands the entire act to be somehow bearing the mark of God's approval. Just as God permitted the locusts to ravage Pharaoh's Egypt, so, too, is Homer permitted to release a swarm of locusts on a political leader who exerts a heavy-handed influence on his surroundings.

The entire sequence is thus problematic in several ways, all of which point to the effect that Christianity can have when invited into political contests. Biblical authority is massaged to support a vindictive agenda.

Moreover, the political target comes across as somehow deserving what is coming insofar as within the allusion he symbolizes the proud, abusive political leader. More important still, the conflict exhibits a clear Christian influence, despite the fact that neither side upholds true Christian values. In addition to Homer's problematic appeal to the Bible, President Bush's suspicion grows out of the advice he receives from the Evangelical Flanders family:

Maude:	What brings you to Springfield?
Barbara Bush:	Well, George and I just wanted to be private citizens again, go where nobody cared about politics. So we found the town with the lowest voter turnout in America.
President Bush:	Just happy to be here among good, average people with no particular hopes or dreams.
Rod:	But, Mr. President, we're not all good people.
Todd:	There's one little boy you should watch out for. He's a bad, bad little boy.
Ned:	[laughing uncomfortably]: Now, Todd, don't scare the president.

The Flanderses very clearly measure Bart against their Christian standards. The conversation not only casts doubt on the sincerity of a faith that will so quickly judge others, it also betrays that Ned and Maude are well aware that they are slandering Bart in the eyes of President Bush. Ned does not denounce the description that Rod gives. Rather, he seems to recognize implicitly that it is true, so he does his best to move the conversation forward.

The underlying texture of the conflict between the Simpsons and President Bush Sr. provides another example of how *The Simpsons* critiques religion in American culture. As Paul Cantor points out, "When *The Simpsons* satirizes something, it is usually acknowledging its importance."[8] By virtue of its medium, *The Simpsons* suspends a measure of reality; what matters is their critical point. American Christianity is highly secularized and, while it is a strong presence, that presence is viewed through any number of prisms that distort or erase altogether the theological core of Christianity. When it comes time for religion to be a factor in the lives of Springfield's individual residents or the larger community, this lack of grounding becomes apparent. The town will embrace a spiritual fad or view church as an obligation because as a whole it fails to recognize, or remember, why Christianity matters in the first place. Springfield's residents, like many American Christians, desire a spiritual "home,"[9] but the church, its leadership, and its community fails to create a safe space. When Christianity fails on its own to fill this void with its own content, other institutions, especially politics and economics, highjack what Christianity stands for in order to enforce their own agendas. The results, as have been discussed above, can be devastating on many levels.

When it fails to live up to its own principles, Christianity creates cultural space for someone or something else to influence American culture in its name. In Springfield, as in America, the result has been a political push to harness Christianity's traditional authority, a move that requires Christian churches, and individuals, to be complicit in stripping their faith of its integrity. Neoconservative politics is only too happy to fill the void that Christianity creates when it becomes unhinged in the face of secular cultural influences. The result is a kind of social club that can be used to beat back criticisms that identify exactly what neoconservative politicians and constituents are doing in the first place. Christianity needs to recover its social identity in American culture quickly, or it could become the banner under which the neoconservative movement in America passes a tipping point. On the small and large screen, *The Simpsons* makes the risk clear. Its goal is, in part, to elicit a response from its viewers to address Christianity's problems before they lose the chance to do so.

In many ways, reconciliation defines Christianity. Its ability to bring together disparate people or ideas offers a tangible and viable reason to recognize that, for all of its problems, Christianity can have a positive social influence. In Springfield, this hopeful note sounds softly; a palpably spiritual sense pervades the lives of Springfield's Christians, even if they frequently sacrifice the integrity of their beliefs. Money, power, and politics threaten Christianity's ability to positively influence its surrounding culture, but this is not a new problem. Roman imperial policy did likewise during Christianity's infancy. A spiritual civil war unfolded in the wake of the Protestant Reformation, but the faith tradition survived. In many ways, Christianity on *The Simpsons* recalls this ability to overcome adversity. Granted, Christianity finds itself at a crossroads in America's postmodern, consumer-driven culture. However, *The Simpsons* never loses sight of the power of love and reconciliation. M. S. Mason recognizes this baseline as critical for the way in which *The Simpsons* levels its criticism against Christianity's flaws. Homer may be a consummate sinner and Lisa may reject the notion of belief in her hyperintellectualism, but in the end, "the Simpsons love each other."[10] Steve Tompkins, a former writer for the show, echoes the point: "Somehow there is goodness at the end."[11]

While the extent to which *The Simpsons* is critical of American Christianity suggests that the faith tradition has lost its ability to be relevant in American culture, one can see in the show's inevitable emphasis on coming together that *The Simpsons* does not give up on Christianity. Cantor may argue that "*The Simpsons* is not pro-religion—it is too cynical for that,"[12] but Christianity's pervasiveness in Springfield suggests otherwise. Christianity's general character comes across as something that can address and then correct its problems. The point is not to dismiss Christianity as a dinosaur buried beneath America's postmodern culture. Rather, *The Simpsons* "merely puts forth the idea that blind obedience to dogma and lack of awareness towards the self are undesirable qualities in modern western society."[13] What Christianity represents is not the problem. How those undesirable qualities manifest themselves in a distorted fashion invite the critiques that *The Simpsons* happily level. Through such criticism, the show creates a safe space for its viewers to recognize clearly the ways in which a significant element of their culture has come loose from its moorings. Moreover, *The Simpsons* makes clear that cultural forces, especially neoconservative political groups, are more than willing to recalibrate Christianity's role in American culture, but the results are quite troubling.

Just as Martin Luther had to nail a list of criticisms to the door of the Wittenberg Church to get the attention of Christian authorities and those who called themselves Christians, so, too, does *The Simpsons* present for public viewing the ways in which American Christianity has veered off course. Such criticism need not be a disservice. If Christians can see themselves in the mirror that *The Simpsons* provides, then needed change is possible. When Christianity has become the property of the social and political elite, then reform will have to emerge from those who recognize in American culture what Christianity's role has become. If viewers fail to see the truth behind the joke, then change may come anyway. Luther did not envision a reform movement that would fundamentally alter the church, much less give rise to a nation on the other side of the Atlantic Ocean. Still, those things happened because Christianity had started to serve ends other than its God. What *The Simpsons* makes apparent is that a tendency is unfolding in contemporary American society, which, if Springfield is any indication, is indeed something that American Christians should be watching.

Notes

Introduction

1. "Bart Gets an F."
2. All biblical passages cited in this book come from: *HarperCollins Study Bible*, New Revised Standard Version, ed. Wayne A. Meeks (New York: HarperCollins Publishers, 1993).
3. "Treehouse of Horror VII."
4. According to Alister McGrath, a foundational point in this doctrine is that "[a] distinction must be drawn between God and the creation. A major theme of Christian theology from the earliest of times has been to resist the temptation to merge the creator and the creation" (270). Alister McGrath, *Christian Theology: An Introduction* (Oxford: Blackwell Publishers, 1997). Christianity, then, understands itself as somehow related to but distinct from God. God remains outside of the created world and God retains authority over that world. See Genesis 1, Romans 1:25.
5. For more on the events that preceded the Protestant Reformation, see McGrath, 37–42.
6. The Treehouse of Horror episodes are usually considered paranormal with respect to the normal narrative fabric on *The Simpsons*. Though "The Genesis Tub" is not real per se, it provides an example that is thematically consistent with other "real" episodes of *The Simpsons*.
7. See Mark I. Pinsky, *The Gospel According to* The Simpsons: *The Spiritual Life of the World's Most Animated Family* (Louisville, KY: Westminster John Knox Press, 2001).
8. Pinsky, *The Gospel According to* The Simpsons, 8.
9. See Mark Pinsky, "The Gospel According to Homer" *Orlando Sentinel* (August 15, 1999). *The Simpsons* offers an insightful response to Bush's barb in "Two Bad Neighbors."
10. See Scott Satkin, "*The Simpsons* as a Religious Satire," http://www.snpp.com/other/papers/ss.paper.html.
11. Scott M. Gimple, *The Simpsons Guide to Springfield* (New York: Harper-Perennial, 1998), 8.

12. See John Sohn, "Simpson Ethics," http://www.snpp.com/other/papers/ js.paper.html. In a similar vein as Pinsky, Sohn concludes that religion is present and part of the show's broader satirical angle. However, the critique is far more substantial than the topical examples that Sohn cites.

13. William Irwin and J. R. Lombardo, "*The Simpsons* and Allusion: 'Worst Essay Ever,'" The Simpsons *and Philosophy: The D'oh! of Homer,* ed. William Irwin et al. (Chicago: Open Court, 2001), 91.

14. Pinsky offers several voices that identify that an intellectual rigor defines much of what *The Simpsons* has to say about religion in general. See especially Pinsky, *The Gospel According to* The Simpsons, 143–52. That the discussion unfolds in such general terms misses what seems to be an intentional and pointed theological argument underneath the show's sociological analysis of American culture.

15. Paul Cantor, "*The Simpsons*: Atomistic Politics and the Nuclear Family," Political Theory 27, No. 6 (Decembar 1999): 742.

16. Ibid.

17. See "Krusty Gets Busted," "Black Widower," and "Cape Feare" for the early episodes that established Sideshow Bob's character.

18. Leo Tolstoy recognizes this pattern in *Resurrection,* the novel that ultimately led to his excommunication from the Russian Orthodox Church. As Nekhlyudov sits on a jury, he notices an icon of "Christ crowned with thorns; a lectern stood beneath the icon and to the right of the lectern was the public prosecutor's desk" (46). With the same subtlety, Tolstoy realizes that Christianity's role in the court system is no longer salvific. Rather, Christianity yields to secular interests, as embodied by the lectern, or worse, to the specific interests of those with power. In this scene, the public prosecutor holds the position of honor. Christ's role as savior is merely decorative. For Tolstoy, society's distinctly secular interests have commandeered Christian influence. As in Springfield's penitentiary, Christianity's presence does not lead to the conclusion that its moral and theological beliefs demand for believers.

19. When Sideshow Bob is talking to his brother, Cecil, about his past, he asserts: "I am all murdered out." Reverend Lovejoy, who is watching the entire conversation with the same contented smile as he had in the chapel, responds, "Praise the Lord!"

20. Cantor, 175.

21. See Molly Snodgrass and Irene Vlachos-Weber, "'Which One of Us Is Truly Crazy?'" *The Psychology of The Simpsons: D'oh!* (Dallas: Benbella Books, 2005), 42.

22. McGrath, 64.

23. Ibid.

24. Ibid., 65.

Chapter One

1. "Weekend at Burnsie's."
2. Kevin J. H. Dettmar, "Countercultural Literacy: Learning Irony with *The Simpsons*," *Leaving Springfield:* The Simpsons *and the Possibility of Oppositional Culture,* ed. John Alberti (Detroit: Wayne State University Press, 2004), 88.
3. My concerns in the following project are distinctly Christian. Thus, I will rarely mention other religious traditions in Springfield, despite their obvious presence. For more religious traditions other than Christianity, see Mark I. Pinsky, *The Gospel According to* The Simpsons: *The Spiritual Life of the World's Most Animated Family* (Louisville, KY: Westminster John Knox Press, 2001), 108–130.
4. For more on this point, see John Alberti, "Introduction," *Leaving Springfield:* The Simpsons *and the Possibility of Oppositional* Culture, ed. John Alberti (Detroit: Wayne State University Press, 2004), xi–xxxii.
5. In *The Simpsons Movie*, this point appears almost immediately. The first item on Homer's list of chores is "Go to church."
6. Brian L. Ott, "'I'm Bart Simpson, Who the Hell Are You?' A Study in Postmodern Identity (Re)Construction," *Journal of Popular Culture* 37, no. 1 (2003); 58.
7. Ibid., 62.
8. William Irwin and J. R. Lombardo, "*The Simpsons* and Allusion: 'Worst Essay Ever,'" The Simpsons *and Philosophy: The D'oh! of Homer,* ed. William Irwin et al. (Chicago: Open Court, 2001), 85.
9. Kurt M. Koenigsberger, "Commodity Culture and Its Discontents: Mr. Bennett, Bart Simpson, and the Rhetoric of Modernism," *Leaving Springfield:* The Simpsons *and the Possibility of Oppositional Culture,* ed. John Alberti (Detroit: Wayne State University Press, 2004), 29–62
10. Arnold Bennett, quoted in Koenigsberger, 37.
11. Koenigsberger, 37.
12. Ibid., 41.
13. In his essay, "'And the Rest Writes Itself:' Roland Barthes Watches *The Simpsons*," David L. G. Arnold makes the point well: "The bottom line of this method of analysis is its suggestion that meaning is not inherent in objects themselves, but resides outside, in their relationships to other structures" (254). See The Simpsons *and Philosophy: The D'oh! of Homer,* ed. William Irwin et al. (Chicago: Open Court, 2001), 252–68.
14. Jennifer L. McMahon, "The Function of Fiction: The Heuristic Value of Homer," The Simpsons *and Philosophy: The D'oh! of Homer,* ed. William Irwin et al. (Chicago: Open Court, 2001), 217.
15. A particularly good example of this self-awareness comes in "Boy Scoutz 'N the Hood." While watching *Itchy & Scratchy*, Lisa explains, "Oh, Bart, cartoons don't have to be one hundred percent realistic." Homer is sitting on the couch with Bart and Lisa, but just as Lisa finishes her logical argument, a second Homer passes by the window that is visible from the couch where Homer is already sitting.

16. See McMahon, 220–21.

17. Ibid.

18. Ibid., 218.

19. 1 Corinthians 13:9–12.

20. See Romans 6:1–15 for a more extensive argument from Paul on this point. For a helpful discussion on how Christianity recasts a person's life, see Diogenes Allen, *Christian Belief in a Postmodern World: The Full Wealth of Conviction* (Louisville, KY: Westminster John Knox Press, 1989), 142ff.

21. Wendy Wick Reeves, "The Art in Humor, the Humor in Art," *American Art* 15, no. 2 (Summer 2001): 2.

22. Ibid.

23. Steven Johnson provides an excellent discussion of this point in his book, *Everything Bad Is Good for You: How Today's Popular Culture Is Actually Making Us Smarter* (New York: Riverhead Books, 2005). *The Simpsons* notoriously causes its fans to obsess over details. My colleagues and I often joke that if we knew as much about our fields as we do about *The Simpsons*, we would have been considered experts long ago.

24. Wick Reeves states, "The initial impression is so strong that we often absorb—without observing—underlying messages" (2).

25. Ibid.

26. See Pinsky, *The Gospel According to* The Simpsons, 25–26. See also Karin H. Bruckner's essay, "Hope Springs Parental: *The Simpsons* and Hopefulness," *The Psychology of The Simpsons: D'oh!* (Dallas: Benbella Books, 2005),166; and Elton Trueblood, *The Humor Christ* (San Francisco: Harper & Row, 1975). Pinsky supports Trueblood's claim that Jesus used humor, but Pinsky also sees *The Simpsons* as adopting only a mild form of such humor.

27. Pinsky, *The Gospel According to* The Simpsons, 26.

28. See Alister McGrath, *Christian Theology: An Introduction* (Oxford: Blackwell Publishers, 1997), 386–422.

29. Ted Cohen, *Jokes: Philosophical Thoughts on Joking Matters* (Chicago: University of Chicago Press, 1999), 29.

30. Donald Capps, *A Time to Laugh: The Religion of Humor* (New York: Continuum, 2005), 49.

31. Quoted in Capps, 68.

32. See Capps, 48ff.

33. James M. Wallace, "A (Karl, not Groucho) Marxist in Springfield," The Simpsons *and Philosophy: The D'oh! of Homer*, ed. William Irwin et al. (Chicago: Open Court, 2001), 238.

34. Robert Sloane presents a particularly helpful portrait of the extent to which viewers are aware of Springfield's cultural identity. The willingness of fans (and perhaps detractors) to pore over the show in search of evidence that supports their claims shows that the writers of *The Simpsons* are conscious of how many viewers react to the show. See Robert Sloane, "Who Wants Candy? Disenchantment in *The Simpsons*," *Leaving Springfield*: The Simpsons *and the Possibility of Oppositional Culture*, ed. John Alberti (Detroit: Wayne State University Press, 2004), 137–71.

35. Such hypocrisy is rampant in Christian congregations. *The Simpsons* is aware of this, which largely explains why the show is willing to make a joke at Jesus's expense. The supposed paragon of the Christian lifestyle, the Flanders family, exhibits this tendency consistently.

36. Enforcing distinctions upon members of a group, as often happens in *The Simpsons*, provides in many ways the basis for the show's postmodern critique of Christianity. Margaret Betz Hull offers an insightful reading of *The Simpsons* through the lens of Michel Foucault. See Margaret Betz Hull, "Postmodern Philosophy Meets Pop Cartoon: Michel Foucault and Matt Groening," *Journal of Popular Culture* 34, no. 2 (Fall 2000): 57–67.

37. To support my argument, I turn to the episodes that capture a specific point most clearly. Certain episodes offer more substantive examples, but this does not mean that the same critical concerns are not present in other episodes. *The Simpsons* presents a remarkably consistent spiritual climate in Springfield, and offers fertile opportunities for further critical analysis.

Chapter Two

1. "Hungry Hungry Homer."

2. In "Duffless," Homer participates in the church-run support group for alcoholics. When Homer confesses that his struggle to remain sober has lapsed ("The other day I was so desperate for a beer I snuck into the football stadium and ate the dirt under the bleachers"), Reverend Lovejoy shows his cards. Rather than support Homer, Reverend Lovejoy expels him from the group. "I cast thee out!" He uses words that recall Jesus's exorcisms of demons—a reference that applies a distinctly dismissive layer to how he responds to Homer's problem (see Mark 1:34).

3. Just as Reverend Lovejoy leads the rush to the bar, Moe leads the rush to the church. Throughout *The Simpsons*, Moe comes across as fatally flawed morally, interested in any number of spiritual practices (such as snake handling; see "Homer the Heretic"), and almost summarily dismissed by Christians. In the episode "In Marge We Trust," for example, Moe calls the church to talk about his sense that his life is useless. Marge, who is filling in for Reverend Lovejoy, encourages Moe by telling him, "You have lots to live for." Moe responds with a measure of shock; he is used to hearing quite the opposite: "Gee, really? That's not what Reverend Lovejoy's been telling me." If anyone in Springfield should understand Christianity as irrelevant in a time of need, it would be Moe. His general character on the show only amplifies his rush to church as he faces disaster.

4. "Homer's Triple Bypass."

5. "'Tis the Fifteenth Season."

6. "Fraudcast News."

7. This rhetorical strategy would seem to violate the commandment not to make false idols (see Exodus 20:4–6), but Mr. Burns's assistant, Waylon Smithers, does not react to the description. Thus, Smithers provides tacit approval of Mr. Burns's use of messianic terms as self-descriptive.

8. Jim Guida. "The Ten Commandments vs. The Simpsons," http://www.snpp.com/other/papers/jg.paper.html.

9. See Exodus 19, 32–24.

10. For an excellent discussion on all seven sins as they appear on *The Simpsons*, see Lisa Frank, "The Evolution of the Seven Deadly Sins: From God to the Simpsons," *Journal of Popular Culture* 35, no. 1 (2001).

11. Diogenes Allen, *Spiritual Theology: The Theology of Yesterday for Spiritual Help Today* (Cambridge, MA: Cowley Publications, 1997), 68.

12. Ibid.

13. Another example of Homer's gluttony comes when he visits the Sea Captain's all-you-can-eat seafood buffet ("New Kid on the Block"). Homer proves to be the first person who can push the limits of such promotions. After several hours of watching Homer gorge himself, the Sea Captain cuts him off from eating any more food. Here, what runs counter to Homer's appetite does not even include resisting completely the thought of eating something. Rather, Homer fails in a simpler task. He lacks the ability to recognize that just because the promotion offers him unlimited seafood, he does not and should not eat to the point when someone must forcibly stop him from eating more.

14. Allen, 77.

15. See Genesis 3.

16. Homer's self-absorbed approach to life is hard to miss, but in "Co-Dependent's Day," the extent to which Homer will sacrifice Marge's interests to protect himself manifests itself forcefully. After a night of drinking together, Homer drives home. Not surprisingly, he crashes the car. Marge has passed out, so Homer decides to move Marge to the driver's seat so that she will have to take the blame for driving under the influence.

17. The promotion also underscores the way in which spirituality intersects with economics. More specifically, Homer understands his divine authority in a specifically business context. For more on the relationship between Christianity and economics, see chapter eight.

18. For another clear example of this dynamic, see "A Star Is Burns." In this episode, Mr. Burns hires a director to create a biographical movie that will win the Springfield Film Festival. The director, Senor Speilbergo, refuses to produce an outright lie about Mr. Burns's character, so Mr. Burns does the job himself. The result is a film that shamelessly attempts to portray Mr. Burns as a kind, generous soul. Everyone in the audience recognizes what Mr. Burns is doing and greets the movie with a chorus of boos.

19. See Gerald J. Erion and Joseph A. Zeccardi, "Marge's Moral Motivation," The Simpsons *and Philosophy: The D'oh! of Homer*, ed. William Irwin et al. (Chicago: Open Court, 2001), 46–58.

20. Ibid., 46.

21. "Homer vs. Lisa and the Eighth Commandment."

22. "Homer the Heretic."

23. "The Old Man and the Lisa." Marge consistently rejects easy money from ill-gotten sources. See also "Bart Gets Hit by a Car." When Mr. Burns hits Bart with his car, Homer wants to sue. With the help of Lionel Hutz and

the testimony of the quack, Dr. Nick Riviera, Homer reaches a moment when Mr. Burns is willing to offer a huge cash settlement. Marge, however, feels uncomfortable with the idea and she tells Homer as much. Mr. Burns hears that Homer is trying to take him for a ride and thus withdraws his settlement offer. Standing up to Homer's scheme takes moral fortitude, which Marge rarely lacks.

24. See Erion and Zeccardi, 46–58.

25. *The Simpsons* echoes this link between menial tasks and Marge's identity in "You Only Move Twice." When the family moves to a new town and into an ultra-modernized home, all the chores are automated. Marge thus has nothing to do, a void she fills by beginning to drink wine.

26. Another example of Marge's willingness to compromise her moral beliefs occurs in "Scenes from the Class Struggle in Springfield." As with "The Last of the Red Hat Mamas," Marge desires so strongly to participate in a social group that she alienates her family and sacrifices most of her fiscal and moral principles. So strong is the pull to fit in that she asks her family not to be themselves. Only Homer's response to his kids, that "you kids should thank your mother. Now that she's a better person, we can see how awful we really are," causes Marge to realize her moral lapse. The strong risk in this moral weakness, as identified clearly in Homer's words, is that the family relies on Marge for guidance. If she ultimately proves to be unreliable as a moral guide, then one can safely say that all of Springfield sins in one way or another.

27. "A Star Is Burns." See also Exodus 2:1–3.

28. Jesus establishes sincerity, along with humility, as the criteria for proper prayer. See Matthew 6:5.

29. "Team Homer."

30. See "Dead Putting Society."

31. An exception to this general pattern comes when, surprisingly, Bart offers a sincere prayer in "Bart Sells His Soul."

Chapter Three

1. "Bart Gets an F."

2. "Pray Anything."

3. See Luke 22:14–23. Jesus's place at God's right hand signals the foundational role Jesus plays in God's redemptive plan for the fallen world. As God incarnate and the atoning sacrifice for human sin, Jesus Christ is the most important component of God's plan, and thus in heaven, Jesus Christ is the only person who deserves the most honorable seat at God's right hand. Homer conflates God and fast-food consumption in "I'm Spelling as Fast as I Can." After sampling Krusty Burger's new sandwich, the Ribwich, Homer exclaims, "I have eaten the ribs of God!" Homer's frame of reference is both biblical and the product of his own experience. He clearly inverts the relationship between God and humanity in the biblical account of humanity's creation (see Genesis 2). In Krusty Burger, Homer

is the one who exerts control over God, as he quite literally consumes a body part that biblically is the basis for existence. That Homer can buy this experience furthers the notion that God can be passed around in human experience. Such a conception undermines any notion of God as sacred or wholly other. Moreover, as a Christian, Homer presumably has eaten God before, insofar as Homer likely has received Communion. To equate a central component of Christian practice with eating fast food captures a tendency in American culture. The sacred significance that one ought to be aware of with respect to the Christian tradition has been subsumed in America's secularized, convenience-driven lifestyle. God's holiness and how God injected that holiness into humanity via the person of Jesus Christ lies at the heart of Christianity, but in Homer's world, such theological points and spiritual significance are reducible to a fast-food sandwich.

4. Michael Glodo, quoted in Mark Pinsky, "The Gospel According to Homer," *Orlando Sentinel* (August 15, 1999).

5. For a helpful survey of God's presence in Springfield and the lives of its residents, see Mark Pinsky, *The Gospel According to* The Simpsons*: The Spiritual Life of the World's Most Animated Family* (Louisville, KY: Westminster John Knox Press, 2001), 13–26.

6. Daniel Migliore, *Faith Seeking Understanding: An Introduction to Christian Theology*, 2nd ed. (Grand Rapids, MI: William B. Eerdmans Publishing Company, 2004), 64.

7. Migliore, 5.

8. Exodus 33:20.

9. "Pray Anything."

10. See Genesis 7.

11. George Lakoff and Mark Johnson, *Metaphors We Live By* (Chicago: University of Chicago Press, 1980), 5.

12. Ibid.

13. Ibid., 12.

14. This quality in Homer reflects perhaps the most common metaphor for God in the Christian tradition. In describing God as "Father," Christians import certain qualities that they desire in a God to whom they devote themselves. Jesus uses the metaphor to describe how God cares for each person as one of God's own children (see Luke 12:22–31). People can relate to the notion of a caring father either because they had such a father growing up and appreciate what such a parent brings to a child's life, or because they did not have a father and desire someone to fill that role. Moreover, this gentle, caring character provides the basis for the idea that God forgives. In the story of the prodigal son, God is a father figure whose love for his son transcends all possible misdeeds on the son's part (see Luke 15:11–32). For a particularly good analysis of how the story characterizes God in the person of the older son's father, see Henri Nouwen, *The Return of the Prodigal Son: A Story of Homecoming* (New York: Image Books, 1992).

15. Grandpa Simpson clearly and consistently proves to be a bad father in Homer's flashbacks. Even when Abe and Homer get along, such as in

"Grandpa vs. Sexual Inadequacy," by the end a certain distance is unmistakable in their relationship.

16. This dynamic extends to Homer's relationship with Bart. In *The Simpsons Movie*, such tension receives particular attention, as Bart temporarily rejects Homer as a father in favor of Flanders. The choice parallels Homer's choice of metaphor to describe God. In place of a dysfunctional father, Bart seeks someone who embodies a love that is itself characterized in Christian terms. Not surprisingly, Bart seeks out Flanders to serve as a salve for his own psychological pain. Flanders is obviously not God, though in Springfield he is certainly the most loving person. In fact, in "Simpsons Bible Stories," Flanders provides the metaphor for God in Marge's daydream. That Flanders offers a ready image to describe important qualities either to be desired or perceived in God underscores the extent to which the systemic metaphor of God as father figure grows out of particular experiences.

17. According to Lakoff and Johnson, the corollary to a particularly clarifying metaphor is that what makes the metaphor beneficial is to ignore certain aspects of the broader topic. As a result, "a metaphorical concept can keep us from focusing on other aspects of the concept that are inconsistent with that metaphor" (10). For example, feminist theologians recognize this risk with respect to the metaphor of God as the caring old father. In using this kind of metaphor, one can lose sight of other possible qualities in God. For feminist theologians, the result can be a conception of God that reinforces a patriarchal theology by ignoring feminine qualities as a way to characterize God.

18. Sallie McFague, *Metaphorical Theology: Models of God in Religious Language* (Philadelphia: Fortress Press, 1982), 1.

19. Lakoff and Johnson, 13.

20. Ibid.

21. The way in which the *The Simpsons* characterizes heaven reiterates the same points about metaphor. The notion of heaven as a paradise gains traction through the notion of a vacation locale wherein all needs are addressed. The metaphor also limits certain ideas that might otherwise be part of the broader concept of heaven. For example, Homer must experience heaven bodily, but this quality hides the fact that heaven is often understood as something that exists outside of space and time.

22. Lakoff and Johnson, 13.

23. Ibid., 16.

24. For an excellent article that discusses the patriarchal texture of Springfield's culture, see Dale E. Snow and James J. Snow, "Simpsonian Sexual Politics," The Simpsons *and Philosophy: The D'oh! of Homer*, ed. William Irwin et al. (Chicago: Open Court, 2001), 126–44.

25. Lakoff and Johnson, 22–24.

26. For an instructive survey of the extent to which race has shaped American history and culture, see Joe Feagin, *Racist America: Roots, Current Realities, and Future Reparations* (New York: Routledge, 2000).

27. Within the black population, one cannot help but notice a lack of frequent women characters, as Dr. Hibbert's wife certainly does not appear regularly. The same dynamic holds for other minority groups. Dr. Nick and Bumblebee Man are the only prominent Hispanics. Asian characters play an even smaller role on the show.

28. Benjamin E. Mays, *The Negro's God: As Reflected in His Literature* (New York: Atheneum, 1969), 18.

29. Cornel West, *Race Matters* (New York: Vintage, 1993), 98.

30. *The Simpsons* reiterates the vibrancy that defines black Christianity in "Faith Off." A faith healer, Brother Faith, inspires Bart to nurture his spirituality. Bart responds to the call and at least for the rest of the episode embraces the spiritual vibrancy that he learns from a black Christian leader.

31. It is beyond the scope of this particular point to elaborate on the Christian doctrine of the Holy Trinity. A quick clarification here will suffice. Christian theology holds that God the creator is of the same substance as Jesus Christ. The two persons of God take different forms, but in the complete nature of God, no substantive distinction exists between God and Jesus Christ. For more on the doctrine of the Trinity, see Alister McGrath, *Christian Theology: An Introduction* (Oxford: Blackwell Publishers, 1997), 292–318.

32. "A Star Is Born Again."

33. Ned also turns to Homer in a crisis moment during "Viva Ned Flanders" and "Alone Again, Natura-Diddly." Both examples cement further the point that Christians do not always perceive God to have authority over life in their contemporary culture.

34. A similar metaphysical struggle occurs in "Pray Anything" when Springfield experiences a potentially devastating flood after Homer's housewarming party desecrates the church. Here, God spares the town through God's representative in Springfield, Reverend Lovejoy, but this example's tenor resonates clearly with the ending of "Mr. Plow."

35. Ironically, characters on *The Simpsons* tend to understand their Christian faith in terms that are very much aware of God's potential wrath. I will discuss this point in more depth in chapter four. Here, however, I merely wish to point out that the threat of God's punishment never fully appears in the metaphors used to understand God.

Chapter Four

1. "Faith Off."

2. *The Simpsons Movie.*

3. Alister McGrath, *Christian Theology: An Introduction* (Oxford: Blackwell Publishers, 1997), 52.

4. Daniel Migliore, *Faith Seeking Understanding: An Introduction to Christian Theology*, 2nd ed. (Grand Rapids, MI: William B. Eerdmans Publishing Company, 2004), 44.

5. Ibid.

6. Ibid., 45.
7. Ibid.
8. Ibid., 50.
9. The question of infallibility goes hand in hand with this point. Some Christians believe in literalism, i.e., the notion that every word in the Bible is true. Thus, no real question of interpretation exists, as the Bible says what it says. Several problems arise with this kind of approach. First, the Bible requires interpretation with respect to human language. Original texts were written in Greek and Hebrew, so to translate the Bible into English requires humans to interpret these classic languages. To ensure the literalist claims, one would then have to argue that God works through every interpreter. This claim cannot logically be true, as different people translate different words in different ways. A second problem with the notion of literalism is that certain parts of the Bible prove to contradict one another. One only need open the Bible and read the first two chapters of Genesis to see narrative inconsistencies. Ned Flanders recognizes this problem in "Hurricane Neddy." He says, "I've done everything the Bible says, even the stuff that contradicts the other stuff! What more could I do?" Ned does not seem to be aware of the tension between the notion that the Bible is a literal doctrine and the practical reality that the Bible cannot all be taken literally, because God would then be contradicting God's self. Other, more subtle issues such as cadence, vocabulary, and cultural context seem to make clear that literalism is not an intellectually sound approach to interpreting the Bible as a story about God told in human language to specific human contexts. For more on problems with understanding the Bible in a particular way, see Migliore, 47–50.
10. Exodus 20:15.
11. Migliore, 8.
12. Gerry Bowler, "God and *The Simpsons*: The Religious Life of an Animated Sitcom," http://www.snpp.com/other/papers/gb.paper.html.
13. It is important to note that Homer responds to Reverend Lovejoy in a manner similar to his response to Marge. Homer tells Reverend Lovejoy to remember "Matthew 21:17," which Reverend Lovejoy also knows by heart: "And he left them and went out of the city into Bethany and he lodged there." Homer repeats the same strategy and appeals to the notion of moral authority that the Bible represents, not to any actual content. His random selections reveal both his strategy and his general ignorance about the Bible's specifics.
14. "Whacking Day."
15. See Matthew 5:14.
16. See John Winthrop's sermon, "A Model of Christian Charity," http://religiousfreedom.lib.virginia.edu/sacred/charity.html.
17. As the intellectual voice on *The Simpsons*, Lisa is often portrayed as the lone source of reason when others on the show set out on journeys, errands, or in pursuit of ideas that are clearly wrong. Often, the tension between Lisa's intellect and the town's general course of action revolve around a question framed by Christianity.

18. Jesus says, "Do not think that I have come to abolish the law or the prophets; I have come not to abolish but to fulfill the law. For truly I tell you, until heaven and earth pass away, not one letter, not one stroke of a letter, will pass from the law until all is accomplished. Therefore, whoever breaks one of the least of these commandments, and teaches others to do the same, will be called least in the kingdom of heaven; but whoever does them and teaches them will be called great in the kingdom of heaven" (Matthew 5:17–19). In Galatians 5:1–6, Paul echoes this point. Whereas the Old Testament provides a framework of laws for a fallen people, Jesus overrides the reality that all people will fail to uphold the law. God is no longer interested in punishing people. Rather, God forgives out of God's love.

19. For more on this point, see Mark Pinsky, *The Gospel According to* The Simpsons: *The Spiritual Life of the World's Most Animated Family* (Louisville, KY: Westminster John Knox Press, 2001), 24ff.

20. The way in which Christianity and Judaism interact is a complex story, which lies outside this current book's scope. However, the relationship is a rich source of reflection, and *The Simpsons* represents the shared past between the two major religions. "Like Father Like Clown" offers a helpful, specific look at Judaism in contemporary American culture. More broadly, Krusty the Clown's role in Springfield weaves in and out of the town's general Christian climate. For a helpful discussion on the Jewish question in *The Simpsons*, see Pinsky, 109–22.

21. This detail is significant, as it frames the larger approach to the Bible, that secularized interests or ways of interpreting the Bible take precedent over what the Bible actually says. I discuss the way in which this tendency rests on a collapse of economics and faith in chapter eight, as well as what the bunny says in general about the character of Springfield's Christianity.

22. See Genesis 3.

23. See Isaiah 11:1–6.

24. See Alison Jaggar, "Feminist Ethics," *The Blackwell Guide to Ethical Theory* (Oxford: Blackwell Publishing, 2000), 348–74.

25. When I discuss this passage in my courses, I always ask students whose fault the Fall is. Inevitably, those who are paying attention respond immediately that the Fall is Eve's fault. They insist she was the one who could not resist temptation. However, when we read the actual text, they realize that Adam is beside Eve as the moment of temptation unfolds. Adam is thus complicit in the Fall, which helps my students realize the extent to which a masculine bias underscores how American culture routinely understands this text.

26. Ironically, Homer/Adam is the one who invokes a Christian understanding of God, but God does not acknowledge the theologically consistent point.

27. See Exodus 1–15.

28. See Exodus 3:1–3.

29. See "Bart Sells His Soul." In this episode, Milhouse earns the same punishment as Bart does for playing a prank in church when Milhouse turns Bart in to the teacher.

30. See Genesis 7.

31. Dale E. Snow and James J. Snow, "Simpsonian Sexual Politics," The Simpsons *and Philosophy: The D'oh! of Homer*, ed. William Irwin et al. (Chicago: Open Court, 2001), 133.

32. Yet again, the show presents the Bible in terms that emphasize punitive characteristics in God.

33. "The Simpsons Spin-off Showcase."

34. Robert Sloane, "Who Wants Candy? Disenchantment in *The Simpsons*," *Leaving Springfield:* The Simpsons *and the Possibility of Oppositional Culture*, ed John Alberti (Detroit: Wayne State University Press, 2004), 159.

Chapter Five

1. "Lisa's Wedding."

2. "In Marge We Trust."

3. This complaint lies at the heart of Homer's resistance to church.

4. "In Marge We Trust."

5. Quoted in Mark Pinsky, *The Gospel According to* The Simpsons*: The Spiritual Life of the World's Most Animated Family* (Louisville, KY: Westminster John Knox Press, 2001), 61.

6. Quoted in Pinsky, 60.

7. "In Marge We Trust."

8. Pinsky, 65.

9. "Bart Sells His Soul."

10. "Homer vs. Lisa and the Eighth Commandment."

11. "Take My Wife, Sleaze."

12. See Pinsky, 61–62.

13. "Krusty Gets Busted."

14. Reverend Lovejoy exhibits a similar overzealousness in "Treehouse of Horror V." In this particular episode, once again Reverend Lovejoy recalls Christian leaders in times when violence was used to enforce a particular set of beliefs. He lights the fire that will burn Patty and Selma at the stake for being witches. As he does in "Krusty Gets Busted," Reverend Lovejoy does not wait to establish the truth before lighting fires. Rather, he rushes to judge in order to satiate the mob. Moreover, in "They Saved Lisa's Brain," Reverend Lovejoy drives a book-burning mobile. Yet again, Reverend Lovejoy acts in a way that echoes the willingness of Christian leaders to dispense judgment without any rational basis.

15. "Homer Loves Flanders."

16. "Bart Sells His Soul."

17. See Dale E. Snow and James J. Snow, "Simpsonian Sexual Politics," The Simpsons *and Philosophy: The D'oh! of Homer*, ed. William Irwin et al. (Chicago: Open Court, 2001), 133.

18. See, for example, John Dart, "Simpsons Have Soul," *The Christian Century* (January 31, 2001), 12–14.

19. Paul Cantor, "At Home with *The Simpsons*," *Prospect Magazine* 53 (June 2000).

20. "In Marge We Trust."
21. Ibid.
22. See Matthew 5:5.
23. It is worth noting that, later in this episode, Marge encounters similarly non-church-related concerns when she begins work as the Listen Lady. In one telephone call, she counsels the Sea Captain that his Game Boy probably sank to the bottom of the ocean, hardly a concern for the church. Given that Marge encounters questions from Springfield residents that are similar to the ones Ned poses to Reverend Lovejoy, one can see more clearly that Reverend Lovejoy's apathy might stem more from whom he must deal with than from his own personal commitment to his job.
24. Another common point that calls attention to Reverend Lovejoy's status as a normal resident in Springfield is his hobby: he loves model trains. See "Home Sweet Homediddily-Dum-Doodily."
25. It is important to note that the First Church of Springfield seems to be an independent, nondenominational church. Reverend Lovejoy does claim that the church is part of "the Western Branch of American Reform Presbylutheranism" ("Father, Son, and Holy Guest-Star"), but it seems clear that the church does not belong to a mainline denomination. Thus, one can assume that Reverend Lovejoy lacks financial support from a national church body, which in turn aggravates his financial concerns vis-à-vis the church's life.
26. Scott M. Gimple, *The Simpsons Guide to Springfield* (New York: Harper-Perennial, 1998), 46. The notion of having credit card kiosks in the church to accept donations may seem to be an extreme form of chasing financial support, but the practice is very much in evidence in contemporary American churches. A recent *Time* article, "The ATM in the Church Lobby" (July 30, 2007), by Rita Healy/Denver, discusses this new phenomenon. Moreover, the Web site http://www.mychurchdonations.com allows people to donate money electronically, either through credit, debit, or electronic check. Reverend Lovejoy, then, seems to be a bit of a pioneer with respect to fundraising. The important point to remember is that the congregation's unwillingness to pay generated the need for the electronic option at the First Church of Springfield.
27. Tellingly, Reverend Lovejoy describes the need to pacify God in words that recall financial planning. One must plan ahead to buy a house, send one's kids to college, and, apparently, to contribute sufficiently to the local church. I discuss the collapse of economics and faith in more detail in chapter eight.
28. "When you give alms, do not let your left hand know what your right hand is doing, so that your alms may be done in secret; and your Father who sees in secret will reward you" (Matthew 6:3–4).
29. "Screaming Yellow Honkers."
30. "In Marge We Trust."
31. See Luke 15:3–7.

Chapter Six

1. "Homer Loves Flanders."
2. According to the Baylor Religion Survey, 33.6 percent of American Christians consider themselves to be Evangelicals.
3. Gerry Bowler, quoted in Les Sillars, "The Last Christian TV Family in America," *Alberta Report* (October 21, 1996).
4. Michael Glodo, a professor of Old Testament and Preaching at Reformed Theological Seminary, states that the Flanders family is "fallibly but sympathetically" understood on the show. "They are simple, sincere, earnest —a good package of virtue, especially in a post-modern culture where cynicism and irony and satire are the prevailing elements." Quoted in Mark Pinsky, "The Gospel According to Homer," *Orlando Sentinel* (August 15, 1999).
5. For an excellent discussion of Ned Flanders's Christian ethic, see David Vessey, "Hey Diddily-ho, Neighboreenos: Ned Flanders and Neighborly Love," The Simpsons *and Philosophy: The D'oh! of Homer*, ed. William Irwin et al. (Chicago: Open Court, 2001), 202–14.
6. "In Marge We Trust."
7. The notion that church is a once-a-week activity appears consistently throughout *The Simpsons*. For example, in "Lisa the Greek," Homer talks about getting rid of "the unpleasant aftertaste of church."
8. An interesting side point to consider here is the question of whether Ned might be violating a common understanding of the Second Commandment: "You shall not make for yourself an idol, whether in the form of anything that is in heaven above, or that is on the earth beneath, or that is in the water under the earth. You shall not bow down to them or worship them" (Exodus 20:4–5a). Ned's actions introduce the possibility that acting out one's faith rashly may, in fact, violate an important component of that faith.
9. Pinsky, 42–43.
10. See James L. Hall, "Religious Dialogues in Prime Time," http://www.snpp.com/other/papers/jlh.paper.html.
11. See Genesis 4:1–16.
12. Ned explains that he has blocked out "over 230 channels" that come with his satellite dish. "Homer Loves Flanders."
13. See "Itchy & Scratchy & Marge."
14. Frank G. Sterle, Jr., "*The Simpsons*: Morality from the 'Immoral,'" http://www.snpp.com/other/papers/fs.paper.html.
15. Another strong example of this willingness to condemn solely based on its relationship to an unquestioning allegiance to the biblical tradition comes in "Trilogy of Error" when Ned Flanders is discussing the Harry Potter books with his kids. He tells his sons: "Harry Potter, and all his wizard friends, went straight to hell for practicing witchcraft." This echoes a naïve critique of J. K Rowling's novels that comes from many corners of the Evangelical community. Such condemnations seemingly ignore the actual content of the books, which uphold values that are very much biblical: love,

compassion, sacrifice, etc. For an excellent argument on this hypocrisy, see Tom Morris, "The Courageous Harry Potter," *Harry Potter and Philosophy: If Aristotle Ran Hogwarts* (Chicago: Open Court, 2004), 9–21.

16. Granted, Ned Flanders may be the most morally upstanding resident in Springfield. However, his inability to recognize that he often exhibits moral hypocrisy in his attitudes toward social issues invites a deserved criticism. The point remains that even the benchmark for Christianity in Springfield is deeply flawed.

17. It is worth noting that the only tape to make it into the "Nice" pile is a copy of the 700 Club, a move that reinforcesNed's sympathies with Evangelical culture in America.

18. This move is theologically inconsistent insofar as it understands God's character is purely human terms. Homer makes a similar theological mistake when he removes a crayon from his brain in "HOMR" and proves that God does not exist. In this episode, Ned takes the bait and quickly burns Homer's calculations. The theological point here is that God cannot be wholly contained within the limits of science, must less in what is appropriate human language.

19. The fact that Ned does not acknowledge Homer's role in the situation shows how far he'll go to apply the morally "Naughty" label to anyone who does not meet the standards he derives from a convenient but theologically unsound standard concerning what God thinks about swear words.

20. Matthew 7:1.

21. Matthew 7:3–5.

22. That is not to say, however, that Reverend Lovejoy is not overly cynical in his response.

23. A more troubling possibility depends on which denominational affiliation Ned Flanders belongs to. In most major denominations, only ordained ministers can perform baptisms insofar as it is a sacrament. Ned, then, is overstepping several sets of boundaries in breaking open his emergency baptism kit.

24. John Calvin, *Institutes of the Christian Religion,* ed. John T. McNeill, trans. Ford Lewis Battles (The Library of Christian Classics: Louisville, KY: Westminster John Knox Press, 1960) IV., xv., 13.

25. Calvin echoes this point later on when he discusses Paul's words in I Corinthians 1:13. Calvin states, "[It is] implied that, in being baptized in his name, they had devoted themselves to him, sworn allegiance to his name, and pledged their faith to him before men" (*Institutes* IV.,xv.,13).

26. Again, Calvin offers a clear rebuke to the type of action Ned wants to perform: "It is wrong for private individuals to assume the administration of baptism; for this as well is a function of the ecclesiastical ministry" (*Institutes* IV.,xv.,13). By attempting to baptize the Simpson children without consent, Ned sacrifices the theological significance of the act itself in order to fulfill his self-appointed agenda.

27. The critique of Evangelicals as forcing their faith upon others appears elsewhere in popular culture's criticism of the Evangelical community. In the 2004 film *Saved!,* Hilary Faye orchestrates a similarly forceful (and illegal)

plan to kidnap Mary in order to force her into complying with a particular Evangelical understanding of an appropriate Christian faith.

28. The political implications of Ned's words are clear. If he is going engage in ecumenical dialogue, the result will have to produce a crusade against social issues that the Evangelical community stereotypically supports.

29. Hall understands Ned to be an extreme of denying all desires. See James L. Hall, "Religious Dialogues in Prime Time," http://www.snpp.com/other/papers/jlh.paper.html.

30. "Jesus said to his disciples, 'Therefore I tell you, do not worry about your life, what you will eat, or about your body, what you will wear. For life is more than food, and the body more than clothing . . . Do not be afraid, little flock, for it is your Father's good pleasure to give you the kingdom'" (Luke 12:22–23, 32).

Chapter Seven

1. "She of Little Faith."

2. "Bart's Inner Child."

3. Bart and Lisa experience the suffocating emphasis on Christianity in all parts of life when the Flanderses become their temporary parents. Perhaps more tellingly, Christianity saturates Rod's and Todd's perspective of the world so thoroughly that depriving them of a bedtime Bible story constitutes punishment. See "Home Sweet Homediddly-Dum-Doodily" and "Bart the Lover."

4. When Bart and Lisa visit Professor Frink in "Future-Drama," Bart's high school girlfriend tries her hardest to convince Bart to have sex with her. His constant distractions cause her to exclaim, "I never had this problem with Todd Flanders." Ned Flanders fears that his boys will stray from their moral ways appear to come true. See "A Star Is Born Again."

5. Robert Wuthnow, *After Heaven: Spirituality in America Since the 1950s* (Berkeley: University of California Press, 1998), viii.

6. One can see in Rod's reaction the way in which American Christianity focuses on God's judgment, which constitutes a problematic point of emphasis within Christianity's larger belief system.

7. Wuthnow, 2.

8. Ibid.

9. Ibid., 3.

10. Jesus states clearly, "Again, truly I tell you, if two of you agree on earth about anything you ask, it will be done for you by my Father in heaven. For where two or three are gathered in my name, I am there among them" (Matthew 18:19–20).

11. John Calvin, *Institutes of the Christian Religion,* ed. John T. McNeill, trans. Ford Lewis Battles (The Library of Christian Classics, Louisville, KY: Westminster John Knox Press, 1960), IV.iii.1.

12. Ibid. See also Ephesians 4:8, 10–16.

13. *Institutes* IV.,iii.,2.

14. "By the term 'church' [Scripture] means that which is actually in God's presence" (*Institutes* IV.,i.,7).
15. Wuthnow, 4.
16. Ibid.
17. When Homer arrives, it becomes clear just how important the once-a-year cook-off really is to him. Chief Wiggum, who has the hottest chili around, cannot help but comment on the way Homer carries himself: "That Simpson, he thinks he's the pope of chili town." On the surface, Wiggum's words appear to be a throwaway line. However, Homer's title could not be more distinctly religious. The suggestion is clear. For Homer, there is nothing more important than proving himself capable of eating any chili, hardly the substance of a sincere spirituality.
18. For an excellent discussion on the desert's role in Christian spirituality, see David Jasper, *The Sacred Desert: Religion, Literature, Art, and Culture* (Oxford: Blackwell Publishing, 2004), 42–108.
19. Wuthnow, 168.
20. Ibid.
21. Ibid., 5.
22. *The Simpsons Movie* reiterates this tendency in Homer's character. When Marge leaves Homer in Alaska, Homer must figure out how to put his life back together. As he does in "El Viaje Misterioso de Nuestro Jomer," Homer initially looks for the easiest possible solution. He runs after Marge. Making little progress, Homer tries a different route. He agrees to drink a bubbling elixir from a local Inuit medicine woman, which induces a hallucination that recalls his experience with the coyote. This altered state allows Homer to explore the events that caused the initial problem, a journey that concludes when he realizes that he needs to care about other people, not just himself.
23. Wuthnow, 8.
24. Ibid., 168.
25. Ibid., 2.
26. See Wuthnow, 138ff. The basis for negotiating one's own spiritual growth relies in part on the cultural resources that have influenced one's spiritual development As with Rod and Todd, defining the world in an individual's own terms will oftentimes require one to rebel against one's upbringing.
27. Wuthnow, 15.
28. Ibid., 131.
29. The ultimate cause for the problem with the pants lies more with Homer's gluttony than with anything the church did. Homer blames the church for his own condition, which, had he paid attention, he might have been able to prevent.
30. Wuthnow, 17.
31. Lisa provides a nice contrast to Homer's journey in "She of Little Faith." In contrast to Homer's experience with the insanity peppers, which leads to a kind of spiritual enlightenment (to the extent that Homer is capable of having such an experience), Lisa finds herself exploring new spiritual avenues based on her negative experiences at an actual church service.

Thus, she has a legitimate reason to be skeptical of the church's role in nurturing spirituality. Lisa eventually decides to accept Buddhism, though the locale for so doing resembles a house of worship that has fallen victim to social influences. Much like Homer, Lisa lacks a definitive spiritual guru. Rather, she plants her own meditation tree and seeks out positive religious influences. She finds Richard Gere, who as a religious guide embodies everything Reverend Lovejoy is not, at least on the surface.

32. Eric Michael Mazur, and Monica Siems, "Homer the Heretic and Charlie Church," in *God in the Details: American Religion in Popular Culture*, ed. Eric Michael Mazur and Kate McMarthy, (New York: Routledge, 2000), 245.
33. Wuthnow, 115.
34. Ibid., 116.
35. Ibid., 123.
36. Ibid.
37. Ibid., 124.
38. Ibid., 130.
39. See Ibid., 127.
40. The episode's conclusion reveals just how fleeting the spiritual embrace of the skeleton really is.
41. See Wuthnow, 17.

Chapter Eight

1. "Homer the Heretic."
2. "Hurricane Neddy."
3. See Mark I. Pinsky, *The Gospel According to* The Simpsons: *The Spiritual Life of the World's Most Animated Family* (Louisville, KY: Westminster John Knox Press, 2001), 26ff. for a helpful discussion on the topic in general.
4. Robert Wuthnow, *After Heaven: Spirituality in America Since the 1950s* (Berkeley: University of California Press, 1998), 15.
5. Ibid., 130.
6. Ibid., 132.
7. The scene successfully recalls the Garden of Eden story in Genesis 3. Homer disobeys a direct order, which produces a consequence that excludes humanity from a paradisiacal life.
8. My focus here is an economic model that describes the tendency in American Christianity to jettison one's church for another religious opportunity.
9. Wuthnow, 131.
10. Brian L. Ott, "'I'm Bart Simpson, Who the Hell Are You?' A Study in Postmodern Identity (Re)Construction," *Journal of Popular Culture* 37, no. 1 (2003): 65.
11. Ibid., 66.
12. See Luke 15:3–7.
13. "Simpsons Bible Stories."

14. See Christopher Hibbert, *The House of Medici: Its Rise and Fall* (New York: HarperPerennial, 1999).

15. See Alister McGrath, *Christian Theology: An Introduction* (Oxford: Blackwell Publishers, 1997), 64.

16. Max Weber, *The Protestant Ethic and the Spirit of Capitalism,* trans. Talcott Parsons (New York: Routledge, 2006; originally published 1904).

17. Weber, 40.

18. For example, Calvin's famous doctrine of Predestination collapsed the notion of doing one's job to the best of one's ability with the theological belief that God directed all such action. When the goal in life is to provide and succeed in a worldly context, and if the results are valuable in religious terms, then the jump to describing economics in the same terms is easy to make. God permits and even encourages acquisition if that is the plan God has predetermined for that individual. Increasing one's net worth can thus constitute a spiritual journey of sorts. See Weber, 56–80.

19. "Jesus, looking at him, loved him and said, 'You lack one thing; go, sell what you own, and give the money to the poor, and you will have treasure in heaven; then come, follow me.' When he heard this, he was shocked and went away grieving, for he had many possessions" (Mark 10:21–22). The implication is clear: material possessions pose a serious threat to success on the spiritual journey that Jesus outlines. While not necessarily prohibitive, materialism will, practically speaking, prevent one from journeying successfully in terms traditionally associated with Jesus's ministry.

20. Weber, 19.

21. The idea that one can transfer one's soul merely by writing on a piece of paper is not metaphysically sound. Such easy transitivity diverges from the idea that the soul is a spiritual component that is distinct from the physical body. In this episode, the emphasis on the soul unfolds in symbolic and economic terms.

22. This moment captures the brilliance of *The Simpsons*. Bart cannot fog up the ice cream counter because he somehow lacks breath. In Judaism, the Hebrew word *ruach*, which translates as "breath," is understood as that which gives life to humans. God breathes into humans (see Genesis 2:7). Likewise, in Christianity Jesus breathes the Holy Spirit into his disciples, an act that gives them new life (John 20:21). Thus, a quick visual gag underscores the theological astuteness that the show's writers so often exhibit.

23. Given the problems with prayer on *The Simpsons*, Bart's prayer in this episode is noteworthy. Both what motivates him to pray and the actual prayer itself seem to be sincere. This contrasts sharply with the quality of other prayers on the show.

24. See Robert Sloane, "Who Wants Candy? Disenchantment in *The Simpsons*," *Leaving Springfield:* The Simpsons *and the Possibility of Oppositional Culture,* ed. John Alberti (Detroit: Wayne State University Press, 2004). Specifically, Sloane discusses the episode "Homer's Enemy." Bart provides the subplot's narrative focus when he accidentally walks in on a foreclosure auction and buys himself a factory. Sloane takes the ease with which Bart acquires the property to "suggest that the workings of capitalism are so

ingrained in the American people that, even as children, we enact the corporate structure" (151).

25. Kurt M. Koenigsberger, "Commodity Culture and Its Discontents: Mr. Bennett, Bart Simpson, and the Rhetoric of Modernism," *Leaving Springfield: The Simpsons and the Possibility of Oppositional Culture*, ed. John Alberti (Detroit; Wayne state University Press, 2004).

26. Vincent Brook, "Myth or Consequences: Ideological Fault Lines in *The Simpsons*," *Leaving Springfield:* The Simpsons *and the Possibility of Oppositional Culture*, ed. John Alberti (Detroit: Wayne State University Press, 2004), 177.

27. See Koenigsberger, 56, for more on this scene. Tellingly, he connects Bart's actions to a biblical example, which seems to underscore the constant but difficult relationship between economics and religion.

28. For another helpful discussion of the "finance of salvation" in this episode, see Koenigsberger, 29–62.

29. Weber, 20.

30. Ibid., 21.

31. Ibid., 31.

32. Ibid.

33. Ibid., 32.

34. "Insane Clown Poppy."

35. Even though each of the above people has clear flaws in his or her Christianity, one cannot ignore the common denominator: each consistently commits a measure of time and resources to Christianity's presence in the town's day-to-day life.

36. Mr. Burns's influence can be seen perhaps most strongly in the number of people who work at the power plant. Despite a spotty safety and environmental record, the power plant does not seem to dissuade people from seeking employment. For an excellent essay on the social implications of the power plant as Springfield's primary employer, see Mick Broderick, "Releasing the Hounds: *The Simpsons* as Anti-Nuclear Satire," *Leaving Springfield:* The Simpsons *and the Possibility of Oppositional Culture*, ed. John Alberti (Detroit: Wayne State University Press, 2004), 244–72.

37. Weber, 9.

38. Ibid., 17.

39. Luke 19:12–27.

40. Luke 19:13.

41. Weber, 19.

42. Proverbs 22:29 quoted in Weber, 19.

43. See Daniel Barwick, "Enjoying the So-called 'Iced Cream': Mr. Burns, Satan, and Happiness," The Simpsons *and Philosophy: The D'oh! of Homer*, ed. William Irwin et al. (Chicago: Open Court, 2001), 191–201.

44. This is clearly something that Mr. Burns thinks about. See "Fraudcast News."

45. The skewed reference to Jesus's disciple obscures what may actually be an apt comparison. Thomas doubted Jesus's bodily resurrection and refused to believe that Jesus had actually risen from the dead until he could touch

Jesus's physical wounds. His disbelief is understandable; he was not in the room when the rest of the disciples claim to have seen Jesus. See John 20:24–31.

46. See Matthew 21:12–13.

Chapter Nine

1. "They Saved Lisa's Brain."
2. In "Sideshow Bob's Last Gleaming," one finds a clear indictment of television's role in contemporary American society. Citing the way that television has rotted Springfield's minds, Sideshow Bob threatens to blow up the town with a stolen nuclear bomb if its citizens do not shut off their televisions for good.
3. See "Homer Goes to College."
4. While *The Simpsons* does not show the actual proof, the fact that Homer was doing his taxes suggests that his arithmetic led to his discovery. Moreover, the point underscores yet again the connection between economics and Christianity, especially the ways in which the economic structure of American culture undermines Christianity's beliefs.
5. Diogenes Allen, *Christian Belief in a Postmodern World: The Full Wealth of Conviction* (Louisville, KY: Westminster John Knox Press, 1989), 45.
6. See Alister McGrath, *Christian Theology: An Introduction* (Oxford: Blackwell Publishers, 1997), 239–79.
7. Christianity would also likely reject the possibility that Kang and Kodos actually exist. They usually appear only in the "Treehouse of Horror" episodes, which are understood to be fantasies, not part of Springfield's actual "reality." However, they do surface in a handful of "real" episodes. The most important example comes during "Gump Roast" when Kang and Kodos crash a party in Homer's honor. They tell the crowd that they have been observing the earth since God created it five thousand years ago. They then reveal that they are "Quantum Presbyterians," a confession that they punctuate by performing the sign of the cross. This suggests that Kang and Kodos are not only real, but that they, too, affirm some kind of Christian faith.
8. How God relates to the universe will, of course, resist definitive answers. However, issues of how God relates to the universe vis-à-vis time offers a point of entry for those who feel God must somehow be contained within the universe. For two helpful discussions of this point, see Dean Zimmerman, "God Inside Time and Before Creation," *God and Time: Essays on the Divine Nature* (New York: Oxford University Press, 2002); and Alan Padgett, *God, Eternity and the Nature of Time* (New York: St. Martin's Press, 1992).
9. For more on Galileo and his role in the tension between science and religion, see Allen, *Christian Belief in a Postmodern World*, 26ff.
10. Ibid., 27.
11. Ibid., 24.

12. Ibid.
13. Ibid.
14. See Frank C. Keil, Kristi L. Lockhart, Derek C. Keil, Dylan R. Keil, and Martin F. Keil, "Looking for Mr. Smarty Pants: Intelligence and Expertise in *The Simpsons*" *The Psychology of The Simpsons: D'oh!* (Dallas: Benbella Books, Inc. 2005): "Scientists are also frequently portrayed as having baser motives than the pure pursuit of knowledge" (179). Apparently the professionals also fail to act appropriately within their intellectual sphere of inquiry.
15. "Treehouse of Horror XIV."
16. "Simpsons Bible Stories."
17. Lisa consistently holds out when other religious swells arrive in Springfield. This hesitancy to immediately embrace the presence of something that appears to be sacred ostracizes her elsewhere.
18. See Paul Halpern, *What's Science Ever Done for Us? What* The Simpsons *Can Teach Us about Physics, Robots, Life, and the Universe* (Hoboken, NJ: John Wiley & Sons, 2007), 61–68.
19. It is worth noting how the conversation ends. Lisa tells Gould that she cannot afford to pay for Gould's service. Gould responds that he did not go into science for the money, so "whatever little money" Lisa has "will be fine." Despite their different approaches to the world, science and religion apparently share the same economic motivations and concerns.
20. Too often, extreme Christian viewpoints rest on completely untenable propositions. For example, in order to uphold the earth's age as six thousand years and thus understand the creation myth as literal, some Christians will explain that God, or even Jesus, buried dinosaur bones. Such examples do not explain carbon dating, but the extreme explanations that extreme positions produce illustrate the intellectual inabilities that warrant the scientific dismissal that they often receive. Understanding the creation story as a myth that tries to understand the universe in terms that reflect our own sense of time is one thing, but rejecting science on the basis of the most fantastic assumptions is quite another.
21. Within the context of *The Simpsons*, Lisa's examples of "fantasy" all appear at some point. In "Simpsons Bible Stories," Homer kills a unicorn in the Garden of Eden. In "Treehouse of Horror XII," Homer and Moe have a discussion about the leprechauns' origins. Finally, in "Montie Can't Buy Me Love," Mr. Burns and Homer travel to Scotland, capture Nessie, and return to Springfield.
22. See Robert Wuthnow, *After Heaven: Spirituality in America Since the 1950s* (Berkeley: University of California Press, 1998), 132.
23. Ibid., 134.
24. Ibid.
25. Allen, 128.

Conclusion

1. "You Kent Always Say What You Want."
2. See "The Monkey Suit."
3. Quoted in Mark Pinsky, "The Gospel According to Homer," *Orlando Sentinel* (August 15, 1999).
4. Quoted in Mark Pinsky, *The Gospel According to* The Simpsons: *The Spiritual Life of the World's Most Animated Family* (Louisville, KY: Westminster John Knox Press, 2001), 151.
5. Ibid.
6. At times, *The Simpsons* is not subtle. This episode responds clearly to the jab that former President Bush, Sr., took at *The Simpsons* when he said American needed more families like the Waltons and fewer families like the Simpsons.
7. See Exodus 10:1–16.
8. Paul Cantor, "At Home with *The Simpsons*," *Prospect Magazine* 53 (June 2000).
9. Robert Wuthnow, *After Heaven: Spirituality in America Since the 1950s* (Berkeley: University of California Press, 1998), 11.
10. M. S. Mason, quoted in John Dart, "Simpsons Have Soul," *The Christian Century* (January 31, 2001): 14.
11. Steve Tompkins, quoted in John Dart, "Simpsons Have Soul," 14.
12. Cantor,
13. James L. Hall, "Religious Dialogues in Prime Time," http://www.snpp.com/other/papers/jlh.paper.html

Selected Bibliography

Printed Sources

Alberti, John, ed. *Leaving Springfield:* The Simpsons *and the Possibility of Oppositional Culture*. Detroit: Wayne State University Press, 2004.

Allen, Diogenes. *Christian Belief in a Postmodern World: The Full Wealth of Conviction*. Louisville, KY: Westminster John Knox Press, 1989.

———. *Spiritual Theology: The Theology of Yesterday for Spiritual Help Today*. Cambridge, MA: Cowley Publications, 1997.

Baggett, David, and Shawn E. Klein. *Harry Potter and Philosophy: If Aristotle Ran Hogwarts*. Chicago: Open Court, 2004.

Book of Catechisms: Reference Edition. Louisville, KY: Geneva Press, 2001.

Brown, Alan, and Chris Logan. *The Psychology of The Simpsons: D'oh!* Dallas: Benbella Books, 2005.

Calvin, John. *Institutes of the Christian Religion*. Edited by John T. McNeill. Translated by Ford Lewis Battles. The Library of Christian Classics. Louisville, KY: Westminster John Knox Press, 1960.

———. "*The Simpsons*: Atomistic Politics and the Nuclear Family." *Political Theory* 27, no. 6 (December 1999).

Capps, Donald. *A Time to Laugh: The Religion of Humor*. Continuum, 2005.

Cohen, Ted. *Jokes: Philosophical Thoughts on Joking Matters*. Chicago: University of Chicago Press, 1999.

Dart, John. "Simpsons Have Soul." *The Christian Century,* January 31, 2001.

Feagin, Joe. *Racist America: Roots, Current Realities and Future Reparations*. New York: Routledge, 2001.

Frank, Lisa. "The Evolution of the Seven Deadly Sins: From God to the Simpsons." *Journal of Popular Culture* 35, no. 1 (2001) 195–105.

Ganssle, Gregory E. and David M. Woodruff. *God and Time: Essay on the Divine Nature*. New York: Oxford University Press, 2002.

Gimple, Scott M. *The Simpsons Beyond Forever! A Complete Guide to Our Favorite Family . . . Still Continued*. New York: Perennial, 2002.

_____. *The Simpsons Forever! A Complete Guide to Our Favorite Family . . . Continued*. New York: HarperPerennial, 1999.

_____. *The Simpsons Guide to Springfield*. New York: HarperPerennial, 1998.

_____. *The Simpsons One Step Beyond Forever! A Complete Guide to our Favorite Family . . . Continued Yet Again*. New York: Harper, 2005.

Halpern, Paul. *What's Science Ever Done For Us? What* The Simpsons *Can Teach Us about Physics, Robots, Life, and the Universe*. Hoboken, NJ: John Wiley & Sons, 2007.

HarperCollins Study Bible, new ev. standard version. Edited by Wayne A. Meeks. New York: HarperCollins Publishers, 1993.

Hibbert, Christopher. *The House of Medici: Its Rise and Fall*. New York: HarperPerennial, 1999.

Hobbs, Renée. "The Simpsons Meet Mark Twain: Analyzing Popular Media Texts in the Classroom." *English Journal* 87, no. 1, Media Literacy (January 1998) 49–53.

Hull, Margaret Betz. "Postmodern Philosophy Meets Pop Cartoon: Michel Foucault and Matt Groening." *Journal of Popular Culture* 34, no. 2 (2000): 57–67.

Irwin, William, Mark T. Conard, and Aeon J. Skoble, eds. The Simpsons *and Philosophy: The D'oh! of Homer*. Chicago: Open Court, 2001.

Jasper, David. *The Sacred Desert: Religion, Literature, and Culture*. Oxford: Blackwell Publishing, 2004.

Johnson, Steven. *Everything Bad Is Good For You: How Today's Popular Culture Is Actually Making Us Smarter*. New York: Riverhead Books, 2005.

Kelsowitz, Steven. *The World According to* The Simpsons: *What Our Favorite TV Family Says About Life, Love and the Pursuit of the Perfect Donut*. Naperville, IL: Sourcebooks, 2006.

Kisken, Tom. "The Gospel of Homer." *Ventura Country Star*, September 4, 1999.

Lafollete, Hugh. *The Blackwell Guide to Ethical Theory*. Oxford: Blackwell Publishing, 2000.

Lakoff, George, and Mark Johnson. *Metaphors We Live By*. Chicago: University of Chicago Press, 1980.

Lobdell, William. "D'oh God! 'The Simpsons' and Spirituality." *Los Angeles Times*, September 1, 2001.

Mays, Benjamin E. *The Negro's God: As Reflected In His Literature*. New York: Atheneum, 1969.

Mazur, Eric Michael, and Kate McCarthy, eds. *God in the Details: American Religion in Popular Culture*. New York: Routledge, 2000.

McFague, Sallie. *Metaphorical Theology: Models of God in Religious Language*. Philadelphia: Fortress Press, 1982.

McGrath, Alister. *Christian Theology: An Introduction*, 2nd ed. Oxford: Blackwell Publishers, 1997.

Migliore, Daniel L. *Faith Seeking Understanding: An Introduction to Christian Theology*, 2nd ed. Grand Rapids: William B. Eerdmans Publishing Company, 2004.

Nouwen, Henri. *The Return of the Prodigal Son: A Story of Homecoming*. New York: Image Books, 1992.

Ott, Brian L. "'I'm Bart Simpson, Who the Hell Are You?' A Study in Postmodern Identity (Re)Construction." *Journal of Popular Culture* 37, no. 1 (2003) 56–82.

Padgett, Alan. *God, Eternity and the Nature of Time*. New York: St. Martin's Press, 1992.

Pinsky, Mark I. "The Gospel According to Homer." *Orlando Sentinel*, August 15, 1999.

_____. *The Gospel According to* The Simpsons: *The Spiritual Life of the World's Most Animated Family*. Louisville, KY: Westminster John Knox Press, 2001.

Reeves, Wendy Wick. "The Art in Humor, the Humor in Art." *American Art* 15, no. 2 (Summer, 2001).

Richmond, Ray. The Simpsons: *A Complete Guide to Our Favorite Family*. New York: HarperPerennial, 1997.

Saved! Dir. Brian Dannelly. United Artists. 2004.

Scanlon, Stephen J., and Seth L. Feinberg. "The Cartoon Society: Using 'The Simpsons' to Teach and Learn Sociology. *Teaching Sociology* 28, no. 2 (April 2000): 127–39.

Sillars, Les. "The Last Christian TV Family in America." *Alberta Report*, October 21, 1996.

The Simpsons Movie. Matt Groening. Dir. David Silverman. Twentieth Century Fox Film Corp. 2007.

Tolstoy, Leo. *Resurrection*. Translated by Rosemary Edmonds. London: Penguin Books, 1966.

Trueblood, Elton, *The Humor of Christ*. San Francisco: Harper & Row, 1975.

Turner, Chris. *Planet Simpson*. London: Ebury Press, 2005.

Weber, Max. *The Protestant Ethic and the Spirit of Capitalism*. Translated by Talcott Parsons. New York: Routledge Classics, 2001.

West, Cornell. *Race Matters*. New York: Vintage, 1993.

Wuthnow, Robert. *After Heaven: Spirituality in America Since the 1950s*. Berkeley: University of California Press, 1998.

Online Sources

Baylor Religion Survey. http://www.baylor.edu/isreligion/index.php?id=40634.

Bowler, Gerry. "God and *The Simpsons*: The Religious Life of an Animated Sitcom." http://www.snpp.com/other/papers/gb.aper.html.

Cantor, Paul. "At Home with The Simpsons." *Prospect Magazine* 53, (June 2000).

Guida, Jim. "The Ten Commandments vs. The Simpsons." December 9, 2004. http://www.snpp.com/other/papers/jg.paper.html.

Hall, James L. "Religious Dialogues in Prime Time." http://www.snpp.com/other/papers/jlh.paper.html.

Healy/Denver, Rita. "The ATM in the Church Lobby." June 30, 2007. http://www.time.com.

Http://www.mychurchdonations.com.

Http://www.snpp.com.

Mullin, Brett. "*The Simpsons*, American Satire." http://www.snpp.com/other/papers/bm.paper.html.

Satkin, Scott. "*The Simpsons* as a Religious Satire." http://www.snpp.com/other/papers/ss.paper.html.

Shalda, Jeff. "Religion in *The Simpsons*." http://www.snpp.com/other/papers/jsh.paper.html.

Sohn, John. "Simpson Ethics." http://www.snpp.com/other/papers/js.paper.html.

Steiger, Gerd. "*The Simpsons*—Just Funny or More?" http://www.snpp.com/other/papers/gs.paper.html.

Sterle, Frank G., Jr. "*The Simpsons*: Morality from the 'Immoral.'" http://www.snpp.com/other/papers/fs.paper.html.

Winthrop, John. "A Model of Christian Charity." http://religiousfreedom.lib.virginia.edu/sacred/charity.html.

Episode Guide
(through Season 18)

Season 1

1) "Simpsons Roasting on an Open Fire," 7G08, December 17, 1989.
2) "Bart the Genius," 7G02, January 14, 1990.
3) "Homer's Odyssey," 7G03, January 21, 1990.
4) "There's No Disgrace Like Home," 7G04, January 28, 1990.
5) "Bart the General," 7G05, February 4, 1990.
6) "Moaning Lisa," 7G06, February 11, 1990.
7) "The Call of the Simpsons," 7G09, February 18, 1990.
8) The Telltale Head," 7G07, February 25, 1990.
9) "Life in the Fast Lane," 7G11, March 18, 1990.
10) "Homer's Night Out," 7G10, March 25, 1990.
11) "The Crepes of Wrath," 7G13, April 15, 1990.
12) "Krusty Gets Busted," 7G12, April 29, 1990.
13) "Some Enchanted Evening," 7G01, May 13, 1990.

Season 2

14) "Bart Gets an F," 7F03, October 11, 1990.
15) "Simpson and Delilah," 7F02, October 18, 1990.
16) "Treehouse of Horror," 7F04, October 25, 1990.
17) "Two Cars in Every Garage and Three Eyes on Every Fish," 7F01, November 1, 1990.
18) "Dancin' Homer," 7F05, November 8, 1990.
19) "Dead Putting Society," 7F08, November 15, 1990.
20) "Bart vs. Thanksgiving," 7F07, November 22, 1990.
21) "Bart the Daredevil," 7F06, December 6, 1990.
22) "Itchy & Scratchy & Marge," 7F09, December 20, 1990.
23) "Bart Gets Hit by a Car," 7F10, January 10, 1991.
24) "One Fish, Two Fish, Blowfish, Blue Fish," 7F11, January 24, 1991.
25) "The Way We Was," 7F12, January 31, 1991.
26) "Homer vs. Lisa and the Eighth Commandment," 7F13, February 7, 1991.

27) "Principal Charming," 7F15, February 14, 1991.
28) "O Brother, Where Art Thou?" 7F 16, February 21, 1991.
29) "Bart's Dog Gets an F," 7F14, March 7, 1991.
30) "Old Money," 7F17, March 28, 1991.
31) "Brush with Greatness," 7F18, April 11, 1991.
32) "Lisa's Substitute," 7F19, April 25, 1991.
33) "The War of the Simpsons," 7F20, May 2, 1991.
34) "Three Men and a Comic Book," 7F21, May 9, 1991.
35) "Blood Feud," 7F22, July 11, 1991.

Season 3

36) "Stark Raving Dad," 7F24, September 19, 1991.
37) "Mr. Lisa Goes to Washington," 8F01, September 26, 1991.
38) "When Flanders Failed," 7F23, October 3, 1991.
39) "Bart the Murderer," 8F03, October 10, 1991.
40) "Homer Defined," 8F04, October 17, 1991.
41) "Like Father Like Clown," 8F05, October 24, 1991.
42) "Treehouse of Horror II," 8F02, October 31, 1991.
43) "Lisa's Pony," 8F06, November 7, 1991.
44) "Saturdays of Thunder," 8F07, November 14, 1991.
45) "Flaming Moe's," 8F08, November 21, 1991.
46) "Burns Verkaufen Der Kraftwerk," 8F09, December 5, 1991.
47) "I Married Marge," 8F10, December 26, 1991.
48) "Radio Bart," 8F11, January 9, 1992.
49) "Lisa the Greek," 8F12, January 23, 1992.
50) "Homer Alone," 8F14, February 6, 1992.
51) "Bart the Lover," 8F16, February 13, 1992.
52) "Homer at the Bat," 8F13, February 20, 1992.
53) "Separate Vocations," 8F15, February 27, 1992.
54) "Dog of Death," 8F17, March 12, 1992.
55) "Colonel Homer," 8F19, March 26, 1992.
56) "Black Widower," 8F20, April 9, 1992.
57) "The Otto Show," 8F21, April 23, 1992.
58) "Bart's Friend Falls in Love," 8F22, May 7, 1992.
59) "Brother, Can You Spare Two Dimes?" 8F23, August 27, 1992.

Season 4

60) "Kamp Krusty," 8F24, September 24, 1992.
61) "A Streetcar Named Marge," 8F18, October 1, 1992.
62) "Homer the Heretic," 9F01, October 8, 1992.
63) "Lisa the Beauty Queen," 9F02, October 15, 1992.
64) "Treehouse of Horror III," 9F04, October 29, 1992.

65) "Itchy & Scratchy: The Movie," 9F03, November 3, 1992.
66) "Marge Gets a Job," 9F05, November 5, 1992.
67) "New Kid on the Block," 9F06, November 12, 1992.
68) "Mr. Plow," 9F07, November 19, 1992.
69) "Lisa's First Word," 9F08, December 3, 1992.
70) "Homer's Triple Bypass," 9F09, December 17, 1992.
71) "Marge vs. the Monorail," 9F10, January 14, 1993.
72) "Selma's Choice," 9F11, January 21, 1993.
73) "Brother from the Same Planet," 9F12, February 4, 1993.
74) "I Love Lisa," 9F13, February 11, 1993.
75) "Duffless," 9F14, February 18, 1993.
76) "Last Exit to Springfield," 9F15, March 11, 1993.
77) "So It's Come to This: A Simpsons Clip Show," 9F17, April 1, 1993.
78) "The Front," 9F16, April 15, 1993.
79) "Whacking Day," 9F18, April 29, 1993.
80) "Marge in Chains," 9F20, May 6, 1993.
81) "Krusty Gets Kancelled," 9F19, May 13, 1993.

Season 5

82) "Homer's Barbershop Quartet," 9F21, September 30, 1993.
83) "Cape Feare," 9F22, October 7, 1993.
84) "Homer Goes to College" 1F02, October 14, 1993.
85) "Rosebud," 1F01, October 21, 1993.
86) "Treehouse of Horror IV," 1F04, October 28, 1993.
87) "Marge on the Lam," 1F03, November 4, 1993.
88) "Bart's Inner Child," 1F05, November 11, 1993.
89) "Boy-Scoutz 'N The Hood," 1F06, November 18, 1993.
90) "The Last Temptation of Homer," 1F07, December 19, 1993.
91) "$pringfield (Or, How I Learned to Stop Worrying and Love Legalized Gambling)," 1F08, December 16, 1993.
92) "Homer the Vigilante," 1F09, January 6, 1994.
93) "Bart Gets Famous," 1F11, February 3, 1994.
94) "Homer and Apu," 1F10, February 10, 1994.
95) "Lisa vs. Malibu Stacy," 1F12, February 17, 1994.
96) "Deep Space Homer," 1F13, February 24, 1994.
97) "Homer Loves Flanders," 1F14, March 17, 1994.
98) "Bart Gets an Elephant," 1F15, March 31, 1994.
99) "Burns' Heir," 1F16, April 14, 1994.
100) "Sweet Seymour Skinner's Baadasssss Song," 1F18, April 28, 1994.
101) "The Boy Who Knew Too Much," 1F19, May 5, 1994.
102) "Lady Bouvier's Lover," 1F21, May 12, 1994.
103) "Secrets of a Successful Marriage," 1F20, May 19, 1994.

Season 6

104) "Bart of Darkness," 1F22, September 4, 1994.
105) "Lisa's Rival," 1F17, September 11, 1994.
106) "Another Simpsons Clip Show," 2F33, September 25, 1994.
107) "Itchy & Scratchy Land," 2F01, October 2, 1994.
108) "Sideshow Bob Roberts," 2F02, October 9, 1994.
109) "Treehouse of Horror V," 2F03, October 30, 1994.
110) "Bart's Girlfriend," 2F04, November 6, 1994.
111) "Lisa on Ice," 2F05, November 13, 1994.
112) "Homer Badman," 2F06, November 27, 1994.
113) "Grandpa vs. Sexual Inadequacy," 2F07, December 4, 1994.
114) "Fear of Flying," 2F08, December 18, 1994.
115) "Homer the Great," 2F09, January 8, 1995.
116) "And Maggie Makes Three," 2F10, January 22, 1995.
117) "Bart's Comet," 2F11, February 5, 1995.
118) "Homie the Clown," 2F12, February 12, 1995.
119) "Bart vs. Australia," 2F13, February 19, 1995.
120) "Homer vs. Patty and Selma," 2F14, February 26, 1995.
121) "A Star Is Burns," 2F31, March 5, 1995.
122) "Lisa's Wedding," 2F15, March 19, 1995.
123) "Two Dozen and One Greyhounds," 2F18, April 9, 1995.
124) "The PTA Disbands," 2F19, April 16, 1995.
125) "Round Springfield," 2F32, April 30, 1995.
126) "The Springfield Connection," 2F21, May 7, 1995.
127) "Lemon of Troy," 2F22, May 14, 1995.
128) "Who Shot Mr. Burns (Part One)," 2F16, May 21, 1995.

Season 7

129) "Who Shot Mr. Burns (Part Two)," 2F20, September 17, 1995.
130) "Radioactive Man," 2F17, September 24, 1995.
131) "Home Sweet Homediddly-Dum-Doodily," 3F01, October 1, 1995.
132) "Bart Sells His Soul," 3F02, October 8, 1995.
133) "Lisa the Vegetarian," 3F03, October 15, 1995.
134) "Treehouse of Horror VI," 3F04, October 29, 1995.
135) "King-Size Homer," 3F05, November 5, 1995.
136) "Mother Simpson," 3F06, November 19, 1995.
137) "Sideshow Bob's Last Gleaming," 3F08, November 26, 1995.
138) "The Simpsons 138th Episode Spectacular," 3F31, December 3, 1995.
139) "Marge Be Not Proud," 3F07, December 17, 1995.
140) "Team Homer," 3F10, January 7, 1996.
141) "Two Bad Neighbors," 3F09, January 14, 1996.
142) "Scenes from the Class Struggle in Springfield," 3F11, February 4, 1996.

143) "Bart the Fink," 3F12, February 11, 1996.
144) "Lisa the Iconoclast," 3F13, February 18, 1996.
145) "Homer the Smithers," 3F14, February 25, 1996.
146) "The Day the Violence Died," 3F16, March 17, 1996.
147) "A Fish Called Selma," 3F15, March 24, 1996.
148) "Bart on the Road," 3F17, March 31, 1996.
149) "22 Short Films about Springfield," 3F18, April 14, 1996.
150) "Raging Abe Simpson and His Grumbling Grandson in 'The Curse of the Flying Hellfish,'" 3F19, April 28, 1996.
151) "Much Apu About Nothing," 3F20, May 5, 1996.
152) "Homerpalooza," 3F21, May 19, 1996.
153) "Summer of 4 Ft. 2," 3F22, May 19, 1996.

Season 8

154) "Treehouse of Horror VII," 4F02, October 27, 1996.
155) "You Only Move Twice," 3F23, November 3, 1996.
156) "The Homer They Fall,"" 4F03, November 10, 1996.
157) "Burns, Baby, Burns," 4F05, November 17, 1996.
158) "Bart after Dark," 4F06, November 24, 1996.
159) "A Milhouse Divided," 4F04, December 1, 1996.
160) "Lisa's Date with Density," 4F01, December 15, 1996.
161) "Hurricane Neddy," 4F07, December 29, 1996.
162) "El Viaje Misterioso de Nuestro Jomer (The Mysterious Voyage of Homer)," 3F24, January 5, 1997.
163) "The Springfield Files," 3G01, January 12, 1997.
164) "The Twisted World of Marge Simpson," 4F08, January 19, 1997.
165) "Mountain of Madness," 4F10, February 2, 1997.
166) "Simpsoncalifragilisticexpiala(Annoyed Grunt)cious," 3G03, February 7, 1997.
167) "The Itchy & Scratchy & Poochie Show," 4F12, February 9, 1997.
168) "Homer's Phobia," 4F11, February 16, 1997.
169) "Brother from Another Series," 4F14, February 14, 1997.
170) "My Sister, My Sitter," 4F13, March 2, 1997.
171) "Homer vs. the Eighteenth Amendment," 4F15, March 16, 1997.
172) "Grade School Confidential," 4F09, April 6, 1997.
173) "The Canine Mutiny," 4F16, April 13, 1997.
174) "The Old Man and the Lisa," 4F17, April 20, 1997.
175) "In Marge We Trust," 4F18, April 27, 1997.
176) "Homer's Enemy," 4F19, May 4, 1997.
177) "The Simpsons Spin-Off Showcase," 4F20, May 11, 1997.
178) "The Secret War of Lisa Simpson," 4F21, May 18, 1997.

Season 9

179) "The City of New York vs. Homer Simpson," 4F22, September 21, 1997.
180) "The Principal and the Pauper," 4F23, September 28, 1997.
181) "Lisa's Sax," 3G02, October 19, 1997.
182) "Treehouse of Horror VIII," 5F02, October 26, 1997.
183) "The Cartridge Family," 5F01, November 2, 1997.
184) "Bart Star," 5F03, November 9, 1997.
185) "The Two Mrs. Nahasapeemapetilons," 5F04, November 16, 1997.
186) "Lisa the Skeptic," 5F05, November 23, 1997.
187) "Reality Bites," 5F06, December 7, 1997.
188) "Miracle on Evergreen Terrace," 5F07, December 21, 1997.
189) "All Singing, All Dancing," 5F24, January 4, 1998.
190) "Bart Carny," 5F08, January 11, 1998.
191) "The Joy of Sect," 5F23, February 8, 1998.
192) "Das Bus," 5F11, February 15, 1998.
193) "The Last Temptation of Krust," 5F10, February 22, 1998.
194) "Dumbbell Indemnity," 5F12, March 1, 1998.
195) "Lisa the Simpson," 4F24, March 8, 1998.
196) "This Little Wiggy," 5F13, March 22, 1998.
197) "Simpson Tide," 3G04, March 29, 1998.
198) "The Trouble with Trillions," 5F14, April 5, 1998.
199) "Girly Edition," 5F15, April 19, 1998.
200) "Trash of the Titans," 5F09, April 26, 1998.
201) "King of the Hill," 5F16, May 3, 1998.
202) "Lost Our Lisa," 5F17, May 10, 1998.
203) "Natural Born Kissers," 5F18, May 17, 1998.

Season 10

204) "Lard of the Dance," 5F20, August 23, 1998.
205) "The Wizard of Evergreen Terrace," 5F21, September 20, 1998.
206) "Bart the Mother," 5F22, September 27, 1998.
207) "Treehouse of Horror IX," AABF01, October 25, 1998.
208) "When You Dish upon a Star," 5F19, November 8, 1998.
209) "D'oh-in in the Wind," AABF02, November 15, 1998.
210) "Lisa Gets an 'A,'" AABF03, November 22, 1998.
211) "Homer Simpson in: 'Kidney Trouble,'" AABF04, December 6, 1998.
212) "Mayored to the Mob," AABF05, December 20, 1998.
213) "Viva Ned Flanders," AABF06, January 10, 1999.
214) "Wild Barts Can't Be Broken," AABF07, January 17, 1999.
215) "Sunday, Cruddy Sunday," AABF08, January 31, 1999.
216) "Homer to the Max," AABF09, February 9, 1999.
217) "I'm with Cupid," AABF11, February 14, 1999.

218) "Marge Simpson in: 'Screaming Yellow Honkers,'" AABF10, February 21, 1999.
219) "Make Room for Lisa," AABF12, February 28, 1999.
220) "Maximum Homerdrive," AABF13, March 28, 1999.
221) "Simpsons Bible Stories," AABF14, April 4, 1999.
222) "Mom and Pop Art," AABF15, April 11, 1999.
223) "The Old Man and the 'C' Student," AABF16, April 25, 1999.
224) "Monty Can't Buy Me Love," AABF17, May 2, 1999.
225) "They Saved Lisa's Brain," AABF18, May 9, 1999.
226) "30 Minutes Over Tokyo," AABF20, May 16, 1999.

Season 11

227) "Beyond Blunderdome," AABF23, September 26, 1999.
228) "Brother's Little Helper," AABF22, October 3, 1999.
229) "Guess Who's Coming to Criticize Dinner?" AABF21, October 24, 1999.
230) "Treehouse of Horror X," BABF01, October 31, 1999.
231) "E-I-E-I-(Annoyed Grunt)," AABF19, November 7, 1999.
232) "Hello Gutter, Hello Fadder," BABF02, November 14, 1999.
233) "Eight Misbehavin," BABF03, November 21, 1999.
234) "Take My Wife, Sleaze," BABF05, November 28, 1999.
235) "Grift of the Magi," BABF07, December 19, 1999.
236) "Little Big Mom," BABF04, January 9, 2000.
237) "Faith Off," BABF06, January 16, 2000.
238) "The Mansion Family," BABF08, January 23, 2000.
239) "Saddlesore Galactica," BABF09, February 6, 2000.
240) "Alone Again Natura-Diddily," BABF10, February 13, 2000.
241) "Missionary Impossible," BABF11, February 20, 2000.
242) "Pygmoelian," BABF12, February 27, 2000.
243) "Bart to the Future," BABF13, March 19, 2000.
244) "Days of Wine and D'oh'ses," BABF14, April 9, 2000.
245) "Kill the Alligator and Run," BABF16, April 30, 2000.
246) "Last Tap Dance in Springfield," BABF15, May 7, 2000.
247) "It's a Mad, Mad, Mad, Mad Marge," BABF18, May 14, 2000.
248) "Behind the Laughter," BABF19, May 21, 2000.

Season 12

249) "Treehouse of Horror XI," BABF21, November 1, 2000.
250) "A Tale of Two Springfields," BABF20, November 5, 2000.
251) "Insane Clown Poppy," BABF17, November 12, 2000.
252) "Lisa the Tree Hugger," CABF01, November 19, 2000.
253) "Homer vs. Dignity," CABF04, November 26, 2000.
254) "The Computer Wore Menace Shoes," CABF02, December 3, 2000.

255) "The Great Monkey Caper," CABF03, December 10, 2000.
256) "Skinner's Sense of Show," CABF06, December 17, 2000.
257) "HOMR," BABF22, January 7, 2001.
258) "Pokeymom," CABF05, January 14, 2001.
259) "Worst Episode Ever," CABF08, February 4, 2001.
260) "Tennis the Menace," CABF07, February 11, 2001.
261) "Day of the Jackanapes," CABF10, February 18, 2001.
262) "New Kids on the Blecch," CABF12, February 25, 2001.
263) "Hungry Hungry Homer," CABF09, March 4, 2001.
264) "Bye Bye Nerdy," CABF11, March 11, 2001.
265) "Simpsons Safari," CABF13, April 1, 2001.
266) "Trilogy of Error," CABF14, April 29, 2001.
267) "I'm Goin' to Praiseland," CABF15, May 6, 2001.
268) "Children of a Lesser Clod," CABF16, May 13, 2001.
269) "Simpsons Tall Tales," CABF17, May 20, 2001.

Season 13

270) "Treehouse of Horror XII," CABF19, November 6, 2001.
271) "The Parent Rap," CABF22, November 11, 2001.
272) "Homer the Moe," CABF20, November 18, 2001.
273) "Hunka Hunka Burns in Love," CABF18, December 2, 2001.
274) "The Blunder Years," CABF21, December 9, 2001.
275) "She of Little Faith," DABF02, December 16, 2001.
276) "Brawl in the Family," DABF01, January 2, 2002.
277) "Sweets and Sour Marge," DABF03, January 20, 2002.
278) "Jaws Wired Shut," DABF05, January 27, 2002.
279) "Half-Decent Proposal," DABF04, February 10, 2002.
280) "The Bart Wants What It Wants," DABF06, February 17, 2002.
281) "The Latest Gun in the West," DABF07, February 24, 2002.
282) "The Old Man and the Key," DABF09, March 10, 2002.
283) "Tales from the Public Domain," DABF08, March 17, 2002.
284) "Blame It on Lisa," DABF10, March 31, 2002.
285) "Weekend at Burnsie's," DABF11, April 7, 2002.
286) "Gump Roast," DABF12, April 21, 2002.
287) "I Am Furious at Yellow," DABF13, April 28, 2002.
288) "The Sweetest Apu," DABF14, May 5, 2002.
289) "Little Girl in the Big Ten," DABF15, May 12, 2002.
290) "The Frying Game," DABF16, May 19, 2002.
291) "Papa's Got a Brand New Badge," DABF17, May 22, 2002.

Season 14

292) "Treehouse of Horror XIII," DABF19, November 3, 2002.

293) "How I Spent My Strummer Vacation," DABF22, November 10, 2002.
294) "Bart vs. Lisa vs. 3rd Grade," DABF20, November 17, 2002.
295) "Large Marge," DABF18, November 24, 2002.
296) "Helter Shelter," DABF21, December 1, 2002.
297) "The Great Louse Detective," EABF01, December 15, 2002.
298) "Special Edna," EABF02, January 5, 2003.
299) "The Dad Who Knew Too Little," EABF03, January 12, 2003.
300) "Strong Arms of The Ma," EABF04, February 2, 2003.
301) "Pray Anything," EABF06, February 9, 2003.
302) "Barting Over," EABF05, February 16, 2003.
303) "I'm Spelling as Fast as I Can," EABF07, February 16, 2003.
304) "A Star Is Born Again," EABF08, March 2, 2003.
305) "Mr. Spitz Goes to Washington," EABF09, March 9, 2003.
306) "C.E. D'oh," EABF10, March 16, 2003.
307) "'Scuse Me While I Miss the Sky," EABF11, March 30, 2003.
308) "Three Gays of the Condo," EABF12, April 13, 2003.
309) "Dude, Where's My Ranch?" EABF13, April 27, 2003.
310) "Old Yeller Belly," EABF14, May 4, 2003.
311) "Brake My Wife, Please," EABF15, May 11, 2003.
312) "Bart of War," EABF16, May 18, 2003.
313) "Moe Baby Blues," EABF17, May 18, 2003.

Season 15

314) "Treehouse of Horror XIV," EABF21, November 2, 2003.
315) "My Mother the Carjacker," EABF18, November 9, 2003.
316) "The President Wore Pearls," EABF20, November 16, 2003.
317) "The Regina Monologues," EABF22, November 23, 2003.
318) "The Fat and the Furriest," EABF19, November 30, 2003.
319) "Today I Am a Clown," FABF01, December 7, 2003.
320) "'Tis the Fifteenth Season," FABF02, December 14, 2003.
321) "Marge vs. Singles, Seniors, Childless Couples and Teens, and Gays," FABF03, January 4, 2004.
322) "I (Annoyed Grunt)-Bot," FABF04, January 11, 2004.
323) "Diatribe of a Mad Housewife," FABF05, January 25, 2004.
324) "Margical History Tour," FABF06, February 8, 2004.
325) "Milhouse Doesn't Live Here Anymore," FABF07, February 15, 2004.
326) "Smart and Smarter," FABF09, February 22, 2004.
327) "The Ziff Who Came to Dinner," FABF08, March 14, 2004.
328) "Co-Dependent's Day," FABF10, March 21, 2004.
329) "Wandering Juvie," FABF11, March 28, 2004.
330) "My Big Fat Geek Wedding," FABF12, April 18, 2004.
331) "Catch 'Em If You Can," FABF14, April 25, 2004.

332) "Simple Simpson," FABF15, May 2, 2004.
333) "The Way We Weren't," FABF13, May 9, 2004.
334) "Bart-Mangled Banner," FABF17, May 16, 2004.
335) "Fraudcast News," FABF18, May 23, 2004.

Season 16

336) "Treehouse of Horror XV," FABF23, November 7, 2004.
337) "All's Fair in Oven War," FABF20, November 14, 2004.
338) "Sleeping with the Enemy," FABF19, November 21, 2004.
339) "She Used to Be My Girl," FABF22, December 5, 2004.
340) "Fat Man and Little Boy," FABF21, December 12, 2004.
341) "Midnight Rx," FABF16, January 16, 2005.
342) "Mommie Beerest," GABF01, January 30, 2006.
343) "Homer and Ned's Hail Mary Pass," GABF02, February 6, 2005.
344) "Pranksta Rap," GABF03, February 13, 2005.
345) "There's Something about Marrying," GABF04, February 20, 2005.
346) "On a Clear Day I Can't See My Sister," GABF05, March 6, 2005.
347) "Goo Goo Gai Pan," GABF06, March 13, 2005.
348) "Mobile Homer," GABF07, March 20, 2005.
349) "The Seven-Beer Snitch," GABF08, April 3, 2005.
350) "Future-Drama," GABF12, April 17, 2005.
351) "Don't Fear the Roofer," GABF10, May 1, 2005.
352) "The Heartbroke Kid," GABF11, May 1, 2005.
353) "A Star Is Torn," GABF13, May 8, 2005.
354) "Thank God It's Doomsday," GABF14, May 8, 2005.
355) "Home Away from Homer," GABF15, May 15, 2005.
356) "Father, Son, and Holy Guest-Star," GABF09, May 15, 2005.

Season 17

357) "Bonfire of the Manatees," GABF18, September 11, 2005.
358) "The Girl Who Slept Too Little," GABF16, September 18, 2005.
359) "Milhouse of Sand and Fog," GABF19, September 25, 2005.
360) "Treehouse of Horror XVI," GABF17, November 6, 2005.
361) "Marge's Son Poisoning," GABF20, November 13, 2005.
362) "See Homer Run," GABF21, November 20, 2005.
363) "The Last of the Red Hat Mamas," GABF22, November 27, 2005.
364) "The Italian Bob," HABF02, December 11, 2005.
365) "Simpsons Christmas Stories," HABF01, December 8, 2005.
366) "Homer's Paternity Coot," HABF03, January 8, 2006.
367) "We're on the Road to D'oh-where," HABF04, January 29, 2006.
368) "My Fair Laddy," HABF05, February 26, 2006.
369) "The Seemingly Never-ending Story," HABF06, March 12, 2006.

370) "Bart Has Two Mommies," HABF07, March 19, 2006.
371) "Homer Simpson, This Is Your Wife," HABF08, March 26, 2006.
372) "Million Dollar Abie," HABF09, April 2, 2006.
373) "Kiss Kiss Bang Bangalore," HABF10, April 9, 2006.
374) "The Wettest Stories Ever Told," HABF11, April 23, 2006.
375) "Girls Just Want to Have Sums," HABF12, April 30, 2006.
376) "Regarding Margie," HABF13, May 7, 2006.
377) "The Monkey Suit," HABF14, May 14, 2006.
378) "Marge and Homer Turn a Couple Play," HABF16, May 21, 2006.

Season 18

379) "The Mook, the Chef, the Wife and Her Homer," HABF15, September 10, 2006.
380) "Jazzy and the Pussycats," HABF18, September 17, 2006.
381) "Please Homer, Don't Hammer 'Em," HABF20, September 24, 2006.
382) "Treehouse of Horror XVII," HABF17, November 5, 2006.
383) "G.I (Annoyed Grunt)," HABF21, November 12, 2006.
384) "Moe 'N' A Lisa," HABF19, November 19, 2006.
385) "Ice Cream of Margie (With the Light Blue Hair)," HABF22, November 26, 2006.
386) "The Haw-Hawed Couple," JABF02, December 10, 2006.
387) "Kill Gil: Volumes I & II," JABF01, December 17, 2006.
388) "The Wife Aquatic," JABF03, January 7, 2007.
389) "Revenge Is a Dish Best Served Three Times," JABF05, January 28, 2007.
390) "Little Big Girl," JABF04, February 11, 2007.
391) "Springfield Up," JABF07, February 18, 2007.
392) "Yokel Chords," JABF09, March 4, 2007.
393) "Rome-old and Juli-eh," JABF08, March 11, 2007.
394) "Homerazzi," JABF06, March 25, 2007.
395) "Marge Gamer," JABF10, April 22, 2007.
396) "The Boys of Bummer," JABF11, April 29, 2007.
397) "Crook and Ladder," JABF13, May 6, 2007.
398) "Stop or My Dog Will Shoot!" JABF12, May 13, 2007.
399) "24 Minutes," JABF14, May 20, 2007.
400) "You Kent Always Say What You Want," JABF15, May 20, 2007.

Index

Abe Simpson (fictional character), 160n15
Adam, 58–60, 163n25
Advertising, 115, 126–27
After Heaven: Spirituality in America Since the 1950s (Wuthnow), 97–98
Afterlife, 33
Alberti, John, 171–72n24
Alcohol, 23, 63–64, 93, 101, 156n2
Allen, Diogenes
    on gluttony, 26
    on pride, 27
    on rational inquiry, 141
    on reason, 133
    on science, 130
American Christianity, 14–15
    Bible in, 63
    black church and, 46
    characterization of, 7
    conceptualization of God by, 44
    economics in, 114
    failings of, 149–51
    membership in, 106
    Reverend Lovejoy and, 67
    spiritual anxiety in, 111
    in Springfield, 97
    state of, 68
    texture of, 111
American culture
    blacks in, 46
    criticism of, 10
    metaphors in, 41–42
    moral policing of, 88–89
American dream, failure of, 9–10
Angels, 110–11, 136–42
Apocalypse, 23–24, 29
Attention deficit disorder, 99
Audience
    jokes and, 19–20
    value of, 12–13

Baptism, 90–91, 167n23
"Bart Gets Hit by a Car," 158n23
"Bart Sells His Soul," 120–24
Bart Simpson (fictional character)

alcohol and, 93
Christmas and, 127
conversion to Catholicism of, 91
economic assumptions of, 114
Ned Flanders' judgment of, 149
relationship to Homer Simpson of, 160n16
shunning of Homer Simpson by, 93–94
soul of, 121–24
stealing and, 75
"Bart, the Mother," 76
"Bart's Comet," 33–34, 70–71
"Bart's Girlfriend," 75
Belief systems, 36
Bennett, Arnold, 13
Bible
    in American Christianity, 63
    approach to, 51
    authority of, 148–49
    Christianity and, 51–52
    distortion of, 55–56, 58–60, 63–64
    enlightenment and, 51
    impending disaster and, 50
    interpretation of, 52–54, 162n9
    judgment in, 57
    moral authority of, 53–54
    as privilege, 56
    relevance of, 65
    Reverend Lovejoy and, 55–56
Biblical narratives, 64
Birch Barlow (fictional character), 145
Black(s), 45–46, 161n30
Blame, deflecting, 98
Blisstonia, 78
Book of Proverbs, 126
Bowler, Gerry, 54, 83–84
Bowling, 47
"Boy Scoutz 'N the Hood," 154n15
Breath, 171n22
Brook, Vincent, 122
"Brother from Another Series," 4–5
"Brother's Little Helper," 99
Buddhism, 170n31
Burning bush, 61
Bush, George H.W., 3, 148–49